PAINTBALL LOVE
CIERRA BLUU

7 Butterflies Publishing Group
2017

To James, for all of my firsts.

Contents

Introduction

Who is responsible for modeling how to love and give love to others? Is it a child's parents, church family, or their school? I say it is all of them. All are responsible for the upbringing of this precious soul. A child could thrive most when exposed to diverse examples of love from those around them. The sad truth is many children experience more examples of selfish love than they do of unconditional love. Is there any way to stop this path of destruction from damaging an innocent soul?

The voice of Candee Black matured over the course of this story as she struggles to find unconditional love because her family barely expresses love to one another. Her parents go through the motions, not displaying true love to each other. Her relationship with her sisters is distant. Although, she does have a close relationship with her Grandmother and it grows deeper as she finds herself going through motherhood alone. Growing up in her small circle, Candee learned early on she must fight to stay above the high tides or be swallowed up by the tumultuous waves. Instead of processing her inner fears, disappointments, and anger, she holds in the pain which ignites the agony. She does not validate her pain, and as a result, she suppresses them.

Since she was young, Candee was taught to not dream outside the bubble. In time, she grew accustomed to it. In her neighborhood, people knew each other and looked out for one another. If you got in trouble at a neighbor's house, the adult there would not hesitate to scold you. People did not worry about locking doors or windows because trust came easy in those days. Eggs, milk, and flour, borrowed with the knowledge your day would come to do the same.

Instead of leaving when she got older, Candee daydreamed her life away. She imagined a handsome boy settling into the neighborhood and choosing her as his girlfriend. They would fall crazy in love, get married, and have a slew of beautiful and smart kids (at least four). Their house would have a white picket fence. They would live on a vast farm like her grandparents and go to church each Sunday. Life would be grand, and her world would be perfect!

Speaking of love...who makes up the rules? Is there a pattern to follow? Many ask questions about the 4-letter word takes on diverse meanings for the individual experiencing it. Is there a right or wrong way to love someone? Some may recognize their self-awareness about love changes with age, circumstances, and wisdom. Others want to believe experiences teaches how to love. As humans, we all habitually expect compensation in return when we confess our love. As soon as a person does not conform to our rules, we dismiss them as though they are not worthy of receiving love. In a relationship, one must be willing to build the relationship. If one person gives more than the other does, the relationship discombobulates and the weight becomes burdensome. Giving simply means spending time getting to know the person. It requires exchanging information about yourself and listening to what the other person has to say. A give and take situation moves a relationship forward. If the two have enough in common to keep the relationship going, it will come together. If the two are not balanced, both must agree to move on. Occasionally, a painful moment shakes one from the slumber it held them captive for too long.

If a young child grows up around negative examples of how to treat others, they will use those examples as a way to express themselves. Candee watched how her father, Joseph, treated her mother, Charlene. Although he was a good provider, he was habitually unfaithful. He made no excuses for his wayward ways. Charlene, a patient and balanced soul, worked hard inside and outside the home. She focused her attention on ensuring her four girls had enough food, clean iron pressed clothes, and neatly combed hair. Since Candee was the oldest, her mother overlooked her. This dictated Candee's individuality, and her decisions would have been easier if she'd been given a heads up.

With four baby girls, Joseph struggled to find ways to show each one individual attention. It was a result of how he learned to cope with forming attachments. At two years old, Joseph was adopted into a foster family along with two other children. He grew up in Greensboro, NC with one older brother and one younger sister. He mentioned to Charlene how they treated him differently.

Not in a mean way, but with enough difference for him to perceive he did not fit in. The foster family was a middle-class white family while Joseph was mixed race. His adopted brother picked on him until the age of ten years old. One day, he wrote a letter to his adoptive parents telling them he wanted another family. He left the letter under their bedroom door and waited until the next morning hoping they would agree to move him. To his surprise, his adoptive parents had a family meeting, apologized to him, and made the children write him apologetic letters. After the incident, Joseph learned to blend in. If his siblings got tough, he ignored the issue and did not tattle again. Dealing with family issues was not his thing. As a result, Charlene dealt with the hardships.

Charlene Peoples was the youngest of three brothers and one sister and lived with her family in Troutman, NC where they produced tobacco and cotton for many years. When Charlene turned seventeen, the family relocated to Siler City to be closer to her maternal grandparents. In the fall season in 1962, during a school basketball game, she met Joseph. Even though he came with another girl, he could not take his eyes off Charlene. She had a Coke bottle-shaped body and walked like a runway model. Her hair was long with thick black bouncy curls on her neck. Her petite statue stood out as her blue jeans snuggle her curves. When intermission came, Joseph leaped at the chance to speak to her. He made it known he wanted to get to know her better. Charlene, with her spunkiness and even-temperament, smiled at him but walked away without a word. This response made Joseph more eager to investigate the mystery girl with peanut butter skin and tawny colored eyes.

After the game, it was several months until their paths crossed again. This time, they ran into each other at a funeral. Joseph's adoptive grandmother had passed away unexpectedly at the age of 72. Mr. Peoples had worked with the woman for over 30 years and wanted to pay his condolences. The woman had also been Charlene's elementary school Principal. After the funeral, Charlene had seen

Joseph standing alone at the gravesite. She remembered his good-looking features. He was tall and skinny, with wavy sandy blonde hair, and bronze skin. As soon as she spoke to him, his eyes lit up like a full moon, and they were inseparable.

They dated for several months before Joseph proposed on Valentine's Day. Being young adults, both of their parents frowned on the idea of them getting married. Since Joseph was three years older than Charlene was, they both agreed to wait until she graduated from high school. It was one month before graduation when Charlene announced she was two months pregnant. Of course, this was not the greatest news, but it did push the marriage date up. Joseph attended technical school to get his certification in plumbing and worked third shift at the cotton mill. They agreed to keep the pregnancy a secret until after their marriage. Charlene did her best to cover the growing bump. One of her sisters teased about her butt was getting wide, but Charlene ignored the teasing. Even though Joseph loved her and wanted to marry her, he wanted to have his beautiful bride to himself, he was not thrilled about the pregnancy.

The stress of the pregnancy created tension during their short courtship. Joseph was soft-spoken and not easily rattled, but his demeanor gradually changed and his motives became selfish. Two weeks after Charlene's graduation, they were married at the Greensboro courthouse. Charlene was dressed in a yellow chiffon sundress, and Joseph wore his best black suit without a necktie. Their families prepared a modest reception in the People's' beautiful flower garden. During the champagne toast, Joseph's father announced he was not joyful about the marriage. It had been his hope for Joseph to finish school and make a decent living before considering marriage.

Surprisingly, Mr. Peoples also stood up, adding some mercy to the speech. He and the family welcomed Joseph and were willing to help them with their new life together.

Mr. Peoples allowed them to move into one of his rental properties on the south side of town. The rent and utilities were free, and Joseph was able to take care of the food, gas, and medical visits for Charlene. Joseph had a closer relationship with his mother than his father, and she worked hard to make sure Joseph was treated fairly. She encouraged her husband to make sure Joseph had a decent vehicle to drive after he finished school. Time passed, and Joseph relocated his ready-made family to Jamestown, where he found a good paying job as a plumber. After Candee was born, Charlene found a job cleaning houses and the family grew every two years. Joseph was disappointed not to have at least one baby boy. There were arguments on top of arguments about nothing. Joseph used this as a reason to stay out most nights chilling, and the cheating reared its ugly head. As the babies grew older, each one demanded more time from their parents. Joseph began drinking alcohol, gambling after work, and hanging with the fellas late into the night. Sadly, Charlene ended up doing most of the duties as mother and father, and Candee abandoned her toys and tackled chores at an early age.

When Candee entered kindergarten, she made friends easily and blossomed without any academic problems. In fact, being at school was her sanctuary. The teacher doted on her because she worked hard to get along with others and frequently volunteered to help others. At school, Candee met her best friend Vaughn Richardson during outdoor playtime when they were both avoiding touching the toys for fear of getting dirty. It was picture day, and Vaughn told Candee she liked her red plaid skirt outfit. Likewise, Candee commented she liked Vaughn's bright hair bows which matched her colorful pantsuit. From day one, their friendship intertwined like a sisterhood.

Chapter One: Practice Makes Perfect

The summer of 1977 in Jamestown, NC was freaking hot causing our box fan to blow dusty warm air. We lived in a two-bedroom and one-bathroom wood framed ranch-style house. Our neighborhood was a decent place. Kids ran up and down the street, keeping the place active. Playing outside was a luxury; we rode on bicycles, skateboards, roller-skates, and play hopscotch to pass the time. I was a true tomboy. I loved to swing in trees, fish, walk on railroad tracks, and run with the boys. We called our neighborhood Backtracks because the train tracks ran behind our houses.

There was one traffic light in the middle of town. This was where the heaviest traffic ran. Several train tracks cut through the back of town. And to see a train was the thrill of the day. Now and then, we played on the tracks until we heard the horn blowing and the train came barreling on the tracks. It was a rush to watch the tons of steel rolling by. We watched the black smoke get closer and our hearts race from fear and excitement. The balmy air slapped me across my face making it difficult to keep my eyes open as it flew by.

At fourteen, I secretly had a baby doll to dress-up like an actual baby. I called her baby Sophia. She was a cute white baby doll with blue eyes. School was out for summer break. Growing up in a small house, my three younger sisters and I realized space was a luxury. Along with our unique personalities sharing, a bedroom was a bit challenging. For me, bedtime was a nightmare. We had two sets of bunk beds. I slept on the top and my middle sister, Cara slept on the bottom. She passed gas while sleeping stinking up the enclosed room. My next oldest sister; Crystal slept on the bottom bunk because she was a sleepwalker. Thank goodness, our baby sister Christian was calm as an angel. To make our situation worse, I used to wet the bed as well, up until ten years old. I dreamed I was peeing in the toilet, but nope – I wasn't even close.

As girls, we had colorful posters covering the walls with music stars such as; Jackson Five, Bee Gees, Al Green, and The Sylvers. Our house was filled with music it seemed 24/7; radio or LP playing any time of the day. I had a bedtime ritual to listen to the radio while I slept. It disturbed my sister Crystal the most because she had a fear of noises during the night. Being the oldest, I got some perks!

I opened the dull white freezer door to get my frozen Snicker's bar, and I muttered, *I might as well go outside, and sit under a shade tree.* "Ma!" I shrilled. I bit hard into the candy bar. I savored the taste of the peanuts, caramel, and chocolate coating. "I'm going in the backyard to cool off. It's too hot in here," I complained with a mouth full of candy.

"Candee, don't go any further; dinner's almost ready," she commanded.

"I won't," I mumbled back. This was a good day to lie out in the sun and get a suntan on my pale skin. I evaluated my body while stretching out on my towel. My boney legs, flat chested, and body shaped like a coke bottle. And all depending on my long giraffe neck. Mallory Miller, with her loud mouth, came bouncing towards me, interrupting my Zen.

Mallory was the first girl I knew did not wear the same outfit twice. Her mother worked at the JCPenney store, and her dad worked at the city water department. Mallory had long thick black hair pulled back in a ponytail. She wore eyeglasses I hoped would kill her ego. Not a chance, they made her treat us like little peons. She and her family left New York City when she was a toddler. They were the first solitary white family to live in our hood for many years. She had one older sister who was in college. Mallory talked to you as if you were deaf. I stopped her plenty of times to correct how she is talking. She detested it.

"Whatcha up to, Candee!" she blasts. I looked sideways to warn about her loud mouth. She covers her mouth with her left hand and apologizes. "I'm sorry."

Now I can answer her. "Mallory, I want to find some shade under the tree. I was baking in my house. It's ridiculous today!"

"Girl, I know what you mean. I'm going to the swimming pool. You want to come?"

"Dinner's almost ready. You know how Momma Charlene is about her cooking." We both laughed. At least this time I didn't have to lie to her.

"Sure, another time." She swung her long horsetail to the right side. "Oops, I meant to mention this the other day, the talent show is going to be in two weeks. You know we had it right before school break is over." Her neck moves from side to side, her hands in rhythm with each word. "Not this time, my mom, and the other judges have changed it this year."

I crossed my eyes after hearing this.

"Girl you scare me when you do that. They might get stuck." She giggles and continues talking. "It's best to get it out of the way now while school is out," she says smiling.

"I guess," I replied.

"Yeah, I know two weeks doesn't give much time to practice if one needs to," she boasted, looking at me with one eyebrow up. "You plan to sing *Blessed Assurance*, right? It's such a hard song to sing," shaking her head left to right as she cautions me.

"Yeah, I've been practicing in the shower each chance I get," I answered proudly. *I trust God will let me win with this song.*

"I know you will breeze on through the challenging notes," she encouraged sounding like a country girl. She clearly expressed I wasn't good enough to beat her. I would show her. I held a fake smile.

My time under the tree cut short because I need to find Vaughn and tell her about the talent contest. I ran as fast as I could to her house, which was five houses from mine. I ran up to the front porch and knocked on the door. I could see through the green wooden screen door the TV was on, but nobody was in the living room. I knocked harder with panic in my knuckles. Vaughn's dad came to the door and informed me Vaughn had gone to the store with her mom.

"Can you tell her to come and see me as soon as she gets back please?" I asked, smacking on the bazooka chewing gum.

Mr. Don who wore his ball cap and sunglasses inside the home. For him, it was a hip thing to do at his Neanderthal age. Vaughn's mom got pregnant when she was going through it's called

16

'the change.' I had no clue what it entailed. Her mom had two miscarriages before Vaughn. All I knew for sure was when Vaughn graduated from high school her parents were both going to be close to dying.

"Sure, I'll tell her to come see you. May take her a few minutes because she has to help unload the groceries," he announced dryly.

"Thanks," I replied.

I blew bubbles, as I trekked back up the street. As I got close to my house, I saw Jemma, a close friend of my sister, Crystal. Jemma was about two years younger than I was. Her birth name is Jamaica Cantu. I heard her mother got pregnant while on vacation in Jamaica. Her father was a native of Jamaica. It was how she got a ridiculous name. She claimed her father spoke Creole dialect to the family and she could speak it too. For as long as I knew her, I had yet to hear her jibber jabber. She sounded like the rest of us… nothing special about it. Jemma had hickory colored, naturally curly hair she wore as an Afro. I envied her flawless bronze skin and long legs; she was taller than all my friends were. She had her right eyebrow pierced as well. In my opinion, she acted too grown-up for her age.

"Candee, is Crystal home?" she asked, sucking up the purple ice from the freeze pop in her hand.

"She was before I left the house. Do you need her?" I asked.

"Kind-of-sort-of. I want to see if she is going to enter the talent show in two weeks," Jemma said.

"I bet she's chickened out, as usual." I grinned. "Hold on, I'll get her for you."

As I entered the house, I smelled the roast beef, the cream

potatoes, and the biscuits. Everyone was already at the table. I washed up before joining them. Eyes roll when I make it to the table. Dad was absent of course, somewhere getting busy with who knew whom and God knew where. Momma said grace. The foods smelled mouthwateringly good. I knew Momma was the best cook in the world, I'd bet my allowance money on it. We understood to be well-mannered at the table eating in silence. It dawned on me Jemma was waiting outside in the hot sun for Crystal to come out. I whispered to Crystal, "Jemma wants to see you hurry up and eat."

Crystal said nothing, but mouthed, "Okay."

After dinner, I was bloated, and all I could do was lay on my bed. I heard Christian say, "She in the bedroom lying on her bed." I heard shoes scuffing across the vinyl kitchen floor coming towards my room. I gazed up at the ceiling hoping it was Vaughn. I treasured my friendship with Vaughn because she had not done me wrong. From day one when we were five years old, we had been thick as trees. Vaughn liked to wear stilettos no matter what the weather. She also loved to wear bright colored skirts and dresses. She shaved her head on her thirteenth birthday to honor her grandmother who died from brain cancer and at 14 years old, she got a nose ring. From time to time, she threw on a white girl wig to accent her mood. Vaughn had milk chocolate skin like a baby's bottom. She told me her secret was baby oil. It was no secret now because I used it daily too.

"Candee, Dad said you need me. Wassup?"

"Yeah, did you know the talent show is in two weeks?" I blurted out.

"Where did you hear that from?" she asks.

"From the horse's mouth. Mallory told me today," I hissed.

"I'm not ready to perform, are you?" she asked, looking doubtful.

"Girl, I hope to God it sounds like angels from heaven. I mean we have to do our best to make sure she doesn't win again," I declared with confidence.

"Yep, you are right. My dance routine needs a little more practice, though," Vaughn confessed.

"Let's make plans to practice this Saturday for at least two hours. Are you available to come over?" I asked.

"Yeah, I'll come right over after I finish my chores."

"All right, girl. I will see you soon." Vaughn and I did two finger-snaps before saying goodbye. *Snap, snap.*

Saturday was chore day in my house. I did the bathroom and my side of the bedroom. Lastly, I dusted the living room wooden entertainment center. I sang "Kung Fu Fighting" by Carl Douglas as I finished dusting and I heard momma shouting for me.

"Candee, did you wash your dirty clothes on your wash day?"

I retrace my chores for the week and ending up in front of my white large plastic clothes basket. "No, I forgot," I sulked regretfully, rolling my eyes.

"Come here now!"

I cringed when she shouted. I found momma in her bedroom ironing my dad's work uniforms. She flipped the white-collar shirt around to iron the sleeves. Steam spouted towards the ceiling. "Girl, you know you ain't going outside until your chores are done," she shouted at me. Little beads of sweat had formed on her forehead. Her shoulder length hair was wet at the ends. Momma seemed exhausted. Seeing her this way, she appeared shorter.

"I know… I know…," I mumbled. Mom's eyes blackened as though they were burning a hole through my soul.

"You better not be talking back!"

I waltzed back toward my room. Well, not in reality. My feet dragged as if covered in thick molasses, and my head hung. I was ready to go practice with Vaughn. Time was ticking by, and Vaughn would arrive soon. I was nowhere near ready. I see Cara sitting on her bed looking at magazines. She peeped up and revealed, "What time you going to practice with Vaughn? I want to practice too."

I loved my sister, but to compete against her was a whole another story. I wish she could stay motivated enough to take part in an activity. It would be good for her. One thing for sure, Cara loved to eat junk food. She had been overweight since the day she was born. She weighed the most of Mom's four babies, close to 10 pounds. She would prefer to sit in the house all day, eat a whole bag of Lay's potatoes chips, a half-gallon of Vanilla ice cream, and flush it all with a couple glasses of Kool-Aid. Her cheeks puffed out like a cute blowfish when she was gobbling. My parents tried to encourage her to eat healthy by telling her to save food for the rest of her sisters. Unmoved by this sweet idea; which seldom worked and she seemed to get bigger with each birthday. Overall, she was a sweet person who I was proud to say was my favorite sister. She was the smartest kid in her class and the teacher's pet.

I glared and raised one eyebrow at her. "What are you going to do?"

"Me, Tiny, and Lil FIFI talking about doing Double Dutch to the song, 'Dancing Machine' by the Jackson 5. At the end, we drop our ropes and do the robot dance, like Michael did on the Soul Train show." I could see my little sis was serious about the talent show. I was too jealous to admit it was a good gig. My sister and her goofy friends; twins sisters Tiny (aka Talisha) and Lil FIFI (aka Felisha) are too flaky to do the talent show. Each year, they boast about their act and each year, they backed out.

"Girlfriend, you should go for it." I coaxed, pretending to care. Their gig might be good enough to win the show. Her desire to be in the talent show might help her lose weight. The jump rope alone helps burn fat away. "Practice makes perfect" I continued. "I have to practice later today, but I need to finish washing my dirty clothes first," I mentioned, leaving her in the room. I went to our tin can kept on the top kitchen shelf to get $2.00 in quarters to wash and dry my clothes. I sang *Blessed Assurance* as I grabbed the dirty clothes, detergent, and headed to the laundromat in our neighborhood.

The laundromat was rolling over as if everybody and they momma was there. I spotted a washer not occupied and hurried to sit my clothes in front of it. This would stake my claim on it, and nobody would touch it. I loaded the washer and sat in a chair close by, already bored. I scanned the laundromat to see if any of my peers were there. And there he was Brandon Cummings, taking out clothes from the dryer. I had to admit, I had a serious crush on him. He was extremely handsome. He was fifteen years old, with dark brown eyes, a front gap tooth, tall, skinny body, caramel skin, and long braided hair. I was itching to go talk to him. I stood up and approached him. He stepped backward and our paths collided.

"Oops, I'm ssorry," he apologized, looking right into my dreamy hazel eyes. Even though he had a lisp in his speech, it never mattered to me. When he was taunted in grade school, I defended him, as a good friend should. Seeing him today, was not how I imagined we would engage in conversation. However, we were nose to nose. I smelled the Root Beer from his breath. I did not step back, and neither did he. *Now what do I say?* I reacted as if I was going to turn around and run back to the chair. All of a sudden, two rambunctious kids came running towards us chasing each other. The girl stepped on my foot, and the boy fell into Brandon. Within seconds, the spell broke. I snapped back to the present and asked Brandon how he was doing. He rambled on about how bored he had been since summer break. I could relate to his boredom.

Later that same day, Vaughn, and I practiced in her backyard until the streetlights came on. Our alarm clock to let us know it was time to go inside the house. "Candee, you sound amazing! I bet you will do well at the talent show," Vaughn boasted.

"And you, my friend, can dance circles around James Brown. I guess we are as good as we are going to be. We need to do our thing in two weeks," I encouraged smiling at her. Changing the subject, I told Vaughn about seeing Brandon at the laundromat.

"What did y'all talk about?" she asked curiously, rolling her eyes at me.

"We talked small talk. You know, about school, the talent show, and school again. I asked him if he liked my sister Cara's friend, Gina. He claimed they hang out from time to time but nothing else. He told me we should pick up where we left off in 4th grade and hang out sometime," I blushed looking at the ground.

"Girl, you know Brandon is no good! He wants to get in between ya legs and leave you looking stupid! Don't listen to see him!" Vaughn responded with an attitude, rolling her eyes and shaking her head at me. In unison before parting, we snapped our fingers twice, even though we did not agree about Brandon.

Chapter Two: The Talent Show

My heart raced like a freight train. The ceiling stage lights blinded my eyes. I tightened both eyes as I stepped closer to the opening curtain. I saw Vaughn finishing her dance act. She was dancing to 'Walk This Way' by Aerosmith. We both loved all kinds of music. At a little over 4 feet tall, Vaughn was shorter than me. But today, on stage, she looked like a giant stepping high in those glittery high heels. I heard the MC announce my full name, "Candee Black." My boney legs would not move. All of sudden, my right earlobe throbbed with the painful reminder I got a second homemade ear piercing yesterday. I heard my name again. However, this time the MC also looked over at me and motioned for me to come out on the stage. My mother and sisters were there to support me. I saw them from where I was frozen. They frowned when I didn't come out.

When Vaughn waltzed off stage, she whispered in my ear, "Don't be afraid, you can do it."

I worked up the nerve and tottered on stage. I picked up the microphone and opened my mouth to sing. As my voice flowed into the microphone, my heart pulsated normally again. I could not see anyone in the audience because the glow was sunlight bright. I was mesmerized. It was as if I was at the beach watching the waves go in and out. I swayed side to side trying not to lose the beat. I had planned to tap my free hand on my leg, but it didn't happen. Before I knew it, it was over, and I heard the applause. I stood motionless as the MC came out, thanked me, and motioned for me to get off the stage. As I scurried behind the curtain, I realized I had forgotten to take a bow. The MC came out to announce the last act while I stood beside Vaughn and we joined hands hoping for the best. The last act was a tap dance act by none other than Mallory, whose momma was also a judge. She was a good tap dancer and a flashy dresser. She had vanilla cream skin and a pear-shaped body. I knew she was going to win based on her pretty looks.

Vaughn whispered to me, "She isn't a great tap dancer."

I whisper back, "She hasn't missed a beat yet."

The audience mesmerized by her moves and how lucid she appeared on the stage. Her ponytail bounced around as her feet clicked heel, toe, tap, and tap. The music was the Ohio Players song, "Fire." Who knew you could tap dance to an R&B song? I declared in my heart God in the heavens heard my beautiful voice singing to him and his angels. It should account for some favoritism; I hoped. Mallory has won more than most of us. We were sick and tired of it! It was time for someone else to win, like Vaughn or me. The tapping was over, and Mallory took a bow and exited the stage.

Now it was time for the judges to tally up the points. The stage went shadow dark, and the house lights came on. I scanned across the audience to find my family. I saw the back of my momma's head as she talked to somone behind her. Close by were my sisters. It was intermission time. Vaughn and I went to get a cold drink. We smiled at our friends in the talent contest. We laughed and mumbled to each other about how bad their acts was compared to ours. As we approached the concession stand, my eyes locked on Brandon holding hands with Gina. Brandon and I used to be close in elementary school, but the world had changed for us in middle school. I had not figured out why.

"Candee, you see lover-boy is on his game?" Vaughn cooed. I pretended not to see him, but it was too late. He was looking right at us. I stared into his eyes and smiled.

"Hi, Brandon. Did you like the show?" He froze like a squirrel in the middle of the road. Gina, however, threw up her hand. I played it off and waved back. Vaughn ignored them both.

I hear the announcer say, "Intermission will end in five minutes. Contestants, please return to the staging area on time."

I broke gazes with Brandon as he blurted, "Candee, great show. You too, Vaughn."

I thanked him and ordered two cups of free ice water. We moseyed back toward the staging area to take our places to hear the results. My sisters had left their seats and were coming towards Vaughn and me. "You guys were great up there," Christian beamed.

"Our nerves got the best of us at the last minute, and we chickened out," Crystal admitted with her head bowed.

"Not a big thang you can try again next year," I said courteously.

"These talent shows are not easy. It takes a lot of practice to get the nerves under control," Vaughn added.

"So true, we wanted to participate too, but our nerves took over. I hope one of you win this year," declared Cara.

Vaughn and I thanked my sisters and went backstage.

"Y'all, I'm shaking. I am ready to get this over with," whispered Mallory. My fake smile said, *I hope you do not win this time.*

Mrs. Penny Miller, Mallory's mom, took the stage to thank the audience for supporting the talent show and making donations by selling Girl Scout cookies. She was a heavyset woman with black bifocal glasses. She had pale sun deprived skin and a bun on top of her head. She seldom wore it loose. She cleared her throat and tapped the microphone to make sure it was on.

"Thank you all for coming out tonight." Her voice was low but got stronger as she continued. "The Jamestown community and the New River Baptist Church are pleased to report we sold over 1,105 boxes of cookies, which made a profit of $1,657.50. The first, second, and third place contestants will get a cash award; all contestants will receive a trophy for participating. Now, to announce our winners, I welcome the Reverend Percy Williams," she finished.

The reverend was wearing a dark suit with a light blue-collared shirt. He was a nice-looking man for his age; which I'd heard was about 80 years old. Close to death. "Let all the people say, Amen and Amen!" he shouted.

The audience repeated, "Amen, Amen."

He held three envelopes in his hands, marked first, second, and third place. I held the air in my lungs and squeezed Vaughn's hand tightly. She bowed her head as though she was praying. "Third place goes to Darwin Steel with a prize of $25.00."

Darwin nerdy and introverted, but was a good trumpet player for the church. He sauntered out, shook the Reverend's hand, and took a bow. "Second place goes to Mallory Miller with a prize of $50.00."

I was in shock. Did my ears hear, right? Mallory was in second place. My heart was beating out of my chest. Mallory strolled on the stage like a seasoned model; lose or win she was smiling, and she took a bow.

"And the first-place winner of this year's talent show of 1977 goes to Vaughn Richardson with a prize of $100.00. Congratulations!"

Vaughn squeezed my hand. I popped her on the back, and rooted, "You won!"

She looked at me with tears streaming. She seemed thrilled hopping in a circle like a rabbit on steroids. "I won! I won!"

As we left the talent contest, Vaughn was shocked she had won. "I cannot believe this. Pinch me please," she giggled. My alter ego told me to pinch her until she bled. All the same, the best friend in me hinted to remind her she deserves to be the first-place winner. "Vaughn, you worked hard to earn the prize! But most of all, you broke Mallory's winning streak." We both laughed and met up with our families. We headed home from the church, reliving the talent show. Gossip was thick in the air about who did what and how they should have done it better.

Chapter Three: Summertime Blues

The next day I planned to meet my friends at the swimming pool around 12:30 p.m. I arrived early to save us a spot at the tables. To no surprise, it was already swarming with little kids and their parents. There were no empty tables in sight. I took out my towel and sat near the entrance to spot my friends. I shrink from the heat. It made me sticky from sweating. In addition, my skin burned because I put on butter before leaving the house hoping to get a suntan. I was utterly annoyed as I waited. Gnats were flying around me as if I was a piece of food. I covered myself up with my huge yellow beach towel to try to avoid them.

I see Vaughn, Mallory, Jemma, and Crystal coming through the entrance. "Y'all, we have nowhere to sit," I huffed with disgust.

"Cool, no problem. We came here to get wet. Let's go in the pool now," instructed Mallory. Without any hesitation, they all scattered into the pool. Even though I was hot, I was not too quick on jumping in the pool because I could not swim. I also did not like how I looked in my tiny bikini. Momma bought it at the Roses Department store because it was on sale. When she guessed my size, she did not factor in my boy chest and bubble butt. "Come on, Candee. Whatcha waiting for?" Vaughn hissed.

"I'm coming," I replied.

As soon as I got up, I heard someone say, "Candee, you was

under the towel?"

I turned around. The voice belonged to Boombox, aka Jermaine McDoogle. He got the nickname while singing in the church choir. He was seventeen years old and notably mature. He had dark chocolate skin. His arms showed he lifted weights. He had muscles all over his body. Above all, he had a handsome smile.

"Hi, Boombox. How you doing?" I asked.

"I am good. I have been to my grandparents' house since school's been out. I came back yesterday. Are you going in the pool now?" he asked.

"Yep, I am. In the three feet, though. I can't swim," I admitted.

"Ah, it is easy. I can teach ya if you want me to?" he graciously offered. "I taught myself and a few cousins. The trick is to not fear the water," he explained.

"I don't know. I don't want to drown," I whined like a little kid.

Boombox swam to the other side of the pool where the three feet drop was and motioned for me to come too. His eyes followed me as I swayed toward him. He could see in my body language I was terrified. When I am nervous, I rub my hands together. "Come on, Candee girl, I am going to be right here. I'm serious I will not let you go under", he reassured me. I could tell in his voice he was serious and I could trust him. I paced towards him and extended my right hand as he led me into the cool, crisp water. I cautiously examined the water for dead bugs. I did not see any.

My body tensed up, and my eyes grew wide as I took the scene in. "All right, keep coming and allow your body to get wet up to your waist," he whispered. His voice put me a short trance as I made my way into the deeper end. I smelled the chlorine and my eyes burned.

"Whoa, the smell is too strong," I gasped, coughing.

"Yeah, it's a good thang. It kills germs. You know people take a piss in here all the time," he chuckles. He jokes for a few minutes to keep my mind distracted. It worked, though, because when I gazed to the right side of the pool, I could see we were standing in four feet of water.

My heart raced faster. I squeezed Boombox's hands tight. He whispered, "Stay calm, I am going to put you on my back."

I giggled and hopped on his back.

"Now I am going to dip under the water. You need to hold your breath and close your eyes. I did as he instructed, but I panicked when the water rushed into my ears. I do not like the water. My eyes closed for a few seconds and when I tried to open them out of fear, they burned. I was drowning. I kicked as if I was in a fight to the death.

My nose burned and Boombox's hands reached to get a hold of me. He yanked me up and pulled me to the edge of the pool. I was choking and sobbing like a baby. Snot was pouring out of my nose. I was rattled. My close to drowning caused concern because when I opened my eyes, my friends were screaming my name. "Candee, Candee are you alright?" I was freaked out, but I pulled it together and climbed out. I see Boombox staring at me from the other side of the pool. I did not know what to say. I stared back. I should make up an excuse about reacting like a baby. However, when I search for him again, he is gone.

31

The following day, momma announced she would take us school shopping when we finished raking the yard from the fresh cut grass. I loved the smell of cut grass. It did not like me, though, because I itched and sneezed afterward, but it was a good way for us to burn some energy. I couldn't work, study, or sleep without listening to music. Therefore, I brought out the portable electric radio and cranked it up loud. I listened to all types of music. My favorites were Pop and R&B. I heard "You Make Me Feel Like Dancing," by a white man with an Afro named Leo Sayer. Crystal and I worked together better with music. We bobbed our heads to the beat as I held the plastic garbage bag and she scooped up the grass with the iron rake. Brandon rode past the street, and I waved at him. He was wearing a baseball outfit and sunglasses. He hit his bike horn but did not stop. I guessed Brandon did not like me as much as I liked him. A painful rejection I need to stop chasing him.

"Sis, why do you like him? You know he is a two-timer and is after one thing. Even I know he a dog!" She blasted. *How she knows so much at 12 years old?* Crystal was the introverted sister. At times, I was convinced our parents might have adopted her because she was an oddball. She was the one who normally got sick first. The flu, cold, chicken pox, diarrhea, you name it – it would hit her before getting to any of us. She had dad's features with thick, reddish-blonde wavy hair. She did not have to sit half the day getting her hair hot pressed. Her skin tone was the darkest, and she was the tallest resembling daddy. One thing was for sure, Crystal did not have any close friends. She rarely dealt with people on a social level. She seemed content to play with Ken, Barbie dolls and jack rocks all by herself. Such a weird bird. I could not help but agree with her.

"I guess you're right. He is not what I need to be messing with," I replied, deciding it was time to move on.

Besides, at fourteen years old I was closed-mouthed as a virgin. Half of the girls I hung out with were not virgins. I did not consider playing with myself as having sex, which was normal girl stuff.

My menstrual cycle came at twelve years old, an embarrassing moment I would not forget. I was at school in gym class sitting with legs crossed on the shiny polished basketball court. We were getting ready to choose teams to play dodgeball. My stomach was cramping, but I did not know why. I became warm between my legs. It tickled, but I was not amused. *Did I pee on myself?* The blue team picked me, and when I got up from the floor, one of my classmates whispered, "Candee, there's blood on the back of your pants." I could not see it. I told the teacher I needed to go to the restroom. I was flustered for bleeding at the worst time. My new colorful striped Capri pants ruined with blood. I balled up a handful of tissue and stuffed it between my legs. Before leaving the restroom, I sobbed profusely because I was deathly afraid of the unknown. I had not even had the birds, and the bees talk with my mom. I left the bathroom and tied my pale-yellow sweater around my waist. I was asked several times throughout the day, "Why your sweater around your waist?"

I replied, "I don't want to forget it." When I got home, I went to the bathroom to scan under the sink cabinet to find a sanitary pad. I found a few in a large white box. They looked like a bulky napkin. I took a quick birdbath, changed underwear, and placed the napkin in the middle of my panties.

It reminded me of a diaper. I was too bashful to tell momma, I told Vaughn instead. She had her menses at eleven years old. She nurtured me and told me about the dos and don'ts and to expect it 'to come one time a month'. "Girl we got to deal with this curse until we are about 50 years old. Next, our bodies go through the 'change'." My eyes crossed hearing this drastic news. Vaughn went on to say, "You know I am a miracle baby when my mom was going through the change and miraculously got pregnant with me. Girlfriend, I have no idea what this all means. I guess we'll find out when we old and gray!" She snickered, and we looked at each other and rolled over laughing.

During my normal menses, I cramped for the first two days; a dreadful death sentence. Cramps, pain, bleeding, and it repeated month after month. My mom, however, learned I had my period and showed me how to use the pads with belt straps. On that day, I acted as though I was clueless about what to do. I wanted to share the moment with my mom. I knew it was time to grow up. I was ready to pass baby Sophia to Christian. She was elated to get the white baby doll with outfits galore and bags full of baby items. All she had to do was fit the part as the new mommy.

My tits were in the brewing stage. They were flat like pancakes. Crystal's boobs popped up before mine; I was jealous. The other day I asked her how she got boobs before me. She winked with a smirk, "I've been putting butter on them for a long time."

I am a copycat so likewise; I smeared my boobs with cold butter. It turned soft after covering my tits. The sick part was I put the used butter back in the fridge. *Nasty!* Momma figured out we had been using all the butter on our bodies. She grounded Crystal and me and threatened to break our arms if we tried it again. Momma put an end of us trying to perform homemade treatments to jump-start our anatomical growth.

We finished the yard and took a quick wash to remove the fresh grass scent. Momma had a black 1975 Mercury Grand Marquis car she'd bought with the income tax money. It was clean inside, with a radio and black shiny plastic seats which got extremely hot in the summer. We all piled in the car ready to go uptown to the Roses Department Store for school shopping. Since I was the oldest, I sat in the front seat unless another adult was riding with us. I was excited about shopping for new clothes. Seems as though, I would most likely not find what I wanted to wear. Momma did not buy name brand clothes, shoes, or house stuff. She had four girls to dress, and she was a thrifty shopper. It was no surprise; she had no shame in shopping at the Goodwill stores. I could not fib, a few of my best pairs of patent leather shoes were from the Goodwill. The rich white folks get rid of their clothes after wearing them one time. Dad would give mom extra money if he had not already spent it, momma was the one who budgeted. I knew if she had $200.00 to spend, my stuff would be less than $50.00 bucks.

Momma was strict about us staying together while shopping. She knew her pretty girls were targets for nasty old men and fast ass little boys. Therefore, while in the girl's sections, she allowed us to spread out a little to see what was there. I loved to wear jeans, capris, and cotton button shirts. Momma picked out dull dresses and baggy jumpsuits. I was skinny for my body frame and avoided wearing dresses to school. I begged momma not to buy a dress and instead get me jeans and capris. Christian chimed in she didn't want to wear dresses this school year either, momma miraculously agreed with us. She even told us to pick out two outfits instead of one. I could shop like a full-fledged teenager. I even picked out a stylish navy flared skirt for church. We all left the store satisfied.

Chapter Four: Hide & Seek

It was a tradition for my family to visit the Johnson Camp Grounds before summer break was over. The drive to the Campgrounds was about three and half hours away. We stopped at the local Hardees to get lunch to eat on the way. I loved their hamburgers with pickles, mustard, onions, and lots of ketchup. Momma ordered us each a hamburger, and we got a large drink to share in the car as we continued to our destination. The Camp Grounds established in 1874, by five partnering churches for a revival meeting. There was a lot of preaching, gospel singing, and bible studies held there for about four weeks while the people stayed in wooden cabins. I had stayed in them with my grandparents and my cousins previously, which frightened me because I could see through the holes of the cabin. During the night, I heard noises from bugs and small animals crawling around. I break out in a sweat from trying to fall asleep in those raggedy wooden cabins.

At the Camp Grounds, you saw dozens of folks you hadn't seen since you were a baby or since school was out. I enjoyed going there because it gave me a chance to gossip with the other girls who had left the neighborhood. It was a great place to hang out with the boys. Most of the kids made up games to play to keep themselves entertained. This game meant the fast boys chased the hot girls. I loved to play hide and seek go get it. I wanted to get my first kiss soon. I was hopeful today was my chance. What I also loved about the Camp Grounds was the food. There were red caramel candy apples, snow cones, fried fish sandwiches, hot dogs, cotton candy, pickled pig feet, and homemade vanilla ice cream. To me, Momma made the best homemade vanilla ice cream in the world. Licking on a cone of ice cream helps cool us from the muggy heat. The drive to the Camp Grounds was extremely boring too. Naturally, we took a nap on the way. On that day, my dad was with us, and while I was in and out of consciousness, I overheard him and mom fussing.

"Joseph, I am getting exhausted from ya cheating ass. This coming in whenever you please has got to stop!" I could tell momma was clenching her teeth hard to keep from cussing.

"Look here, Charlene. I take good care of you and the girls don't I? You know I work hard. I want to hang out with the menfolk. Baby, stop this damn nagging!" I heard my father scolding.

Momma mumbled words back at him. She slammed the brakes hard at the red light. I hoped we would make it to the Camp Grounds without any accidents. It irritates me when they fight. My dad had been a heavy liquor drinker for as long as I could remember. After work, all he did was drink with his drunken buddies. Lately, I had seen him coming in hours late and arguing with mom about the details. A couple weeks ago, he went to the church alone and came back with a plan to quit drinking. He attended church with us if he was not on the road driving. The marriage seemed to be going smoothly up until the last few months when he visibly acts cold towards momma. Now, instead of drinking alcohol, he smoked the killer sticks – Camel cigarettes. I had been holding onto the gossip I overheard while visiting Vaughn. Her dad was talking openly to someone on the telephone he had seen my dad coming out of the Budget Inn Motel with a young, dark-skinned petite woman the other day. I pretended to use the restroom to hear the conversation, but as soon as Mr. Don saw me, he derailed from the subject. I refused to speak a word about it to anyone – not even Vaughn. I was too ashamed.

As soon as the car came to a stop; I opened the car door and hopped out on the straw-covered ground. I sniffed the hot, sticky air lingered over the holy ground. The smell of sweet candy apples and cotton candy filled the air.

"Candee, I didn't tell you to open the door. Get ya hips back in here!" Momma demanded.

"Shit Charlene, let the girls go and play, they been cooped up in this car for hours," my dad pleaded, smoothing things over as he often did. He had a sweet, charming voice momma could not resist. Momma and daddy gave us the *'stay with your younger sisters and do not leave them speech',* and off we dashed on the wide dirt roads.

As we strolled through the wooden tents, we passed by the wooden arbor, the place where all the preaching, singing and praising was held. We saw a crowd of adults and kids standing at the snow cone machine. My mouth watered remembering the sweetness of a red and blue snow cone, but I forgot to ask for the money. I held tight to Christian's left hand and turned around to ask Crystal to go back and find momma and daddy to get the money.

However, out of nowhere, my Uncle Paul, mom's oldest

39

brother came up to us. "Why hello… little ladies where's your mom and dad at?"

"They were back near the arbors. Uncle Paul, you got $2.00 to get us a snow cone?" I boldly asked.

"I guess I can let go of two green ones for you pretty girls," he chuckled as he pulled out his worn-out brown wallet and handed me the money. We thanked him as he turned and strolled back toward the arbors.

We file in the long line to get a snow cone. As we stand there waiting patiently, I looked around to see who else was there. Boombox standing over at the hotdog stand with a tall white girl who had her hands on her hips. She was not cute, at least not to me.

Her face distorted into a frown and her make-up made her look like a clown. She had short dark hair. She wore an excessively short white and black polka dotted dress. They faced each other closely and seemed to be arguing because their gums were flapping like hungry birds. We ordered our snow cones and found a spot to stand and eat. At the campgrounds, there were no public chairs; if you did not bring one, you stood the whole time. My mind was busy trying to figure out who the butt ugly girl was with Boombox. *Why do I care? He isn't my boyfriend.* I concentrated on eating the snow cone because it melted like it was 1,000 degrees.

I heard Christian whimpering. When I looked, her freaking snow cone was upside down in the dirt. "How did you drop it? Dang it!" I asked in frustration.

Crystal heard me fussing. "Christian, stop dropping your food!"

Christian was shedding tears harder, this time screaming, "Ma, momma!" Her screams made me curse from the high-pitch. I took one last suck of grape juice (which was blue and red mixed juices) and gave her my snow cone.

"Here! Now shut the hell up!" I handed it to her, and she stopped instantly. "Sit on the ground and finish it!" I demanded sounding like a distraught parent. Her mouth poked out frowning at my demands.

Christian favored mom with her walnut colored eyes and curled bottom lip. Her hair was the best grade too. It was silky, long brown and flowed like a white girl's hair in the wind. Momma used water and pomade grease to style her hair. Not with the rest of us. We needed to get our hair hot pressed. I was already planning to put a perm in mine as soon as I turned sixteen. I was losing my patience because I wanted to go and find my friends to hang out with instead of babysitting.

"I gotta pee," Cara, pleaded holding her legs closed.

I took a deep sigh and rolled my eyes at her. "Come on let's go to the outhouse."

We trotted to the front of the campground and along the way; we spotted our Auntie Belinda. She is mom's sister. "Hey, girls. Y'all, growing up fast. Where ya, dad and mom at?"

"We left them at the arbors," I said.

"Alright. Where y'all headed to in such a hurry?" she asked. Cara was in tears from standing too long.

"Cara has to pee, we gotta run. See you later, Auntie Belinda."

We made it in time and thank God, there was no line waiting

at the outhouse. I would pee in the woods before I used the disgusting wooden toilet, though. It smelled like dirty diapers and one time I got a splinter in my butt.

"There ain't no mo toilet paper!" Cara spat out.

"Shake it off," I chimed back at her.

We strode the dirt road to the main entrance. This was where we ran into a few of our cousins. We all played a game of hopscotch. We found a clean spot on the ground to draw out the hopscotch and collect rocks to throw in the squares. I was a champion at the game and confident I was going to win. "The loser has to do 50 jumping jacks!" I shouted out. We all agreed. This game could go on forever with too many players.

The game included nine of us, it dropped to five, and lastly, it was my cousin Sylvia and me. She threw her rock into box number nine, and it landed effortlessly inside the box. She hopped through the empty squares with ease, bent over to get her rock, and hopped back up.

I needed to throw my rock into box ten and have no wobbles coming back. The rock landed in box ten. I hopped to retrieve it. I should not have any slip-ups. From out of nowhere, a sneeze crawled into my nose like a spider. My nose was itching badly; I needed to rub it, but I knew it would knock my balance off. I looked at the ground. I was standing with one foot in box seven. If I bend down, I could grab the rock. The itch was agonizing causing my nose to run with clear mucus. I have allergies. "Ah-Choo!" I squealed. My entire body wobbled like Humpty Dumpty, and now both feet were in box seven. Sylvia smirked and reminded me, "Loser has to do 50 jumping jacks."

I disliked jumping jacks, but most of all I hated to lose. I jumped and counted with *'sore loser'* written on my face.

The sun was setting, and the heat had cooled off when I looked around to see where my sisters were. I saw Crystal and Christian standing near the popcorn stand with dad. I didn't see Cara right away. Therefore, I promenaded over to where dad was. "Where is Cara, daddy?"

"She and your mom went to see Mrs. Duncan. She been deathly ill; they went over to her tent to check on her."

Mrs. Duncan was about 73 years old. She was our babysitter when my mom went to get her high school diploma a few years ago. Mrs. Duncan lived alone, and I did not know her first name. What I did remember was she was a tough babysitter and holy religious. We could not go outside and play; we sat in her dark house and read books. She had a swing set she would let us play on if we were good. Of course, it did not happen a lot.

I was bored waiting with dad and getting ready to leave when Brandon shuffled toward me. I knew my dad would flip out if he saw him with me because he was silly protective of his little girls. Therefore, I sauntered in front of Brandon and whispered, "Follow me." To my surprise, Brandon did what I asked, and we ended up in front of the hotdog stand.

"What you up to Candee?" he asked looking serious.

"Nothing right now. We finished playing hopscotch. I lost to my cousin," I giggled.

"We gonna play hide and sseek. You want to play?" he asked, kicking at the dry rocks on the ground.

"Sure, I guess. Who all is playing?" I wanted to know before going.

"Sshante, Ssylvia, Tiny, Jemma, Boombox, Donovan, and Tim," he responded.

"Ok, sounds like fun. Let me tell my dad where I am going," I said stepping back.

He blurted, "No don't tell your dad what we are playing. He might take out his rusty crusty butter knife on us boys." He laughed. He knew my dad all too well.

"I won't." I smiled back. I found dad and told him I was playing dodgeball at the back of the campgrounds.

"You got a half hour, and we are pulling out!" he shouted back. It was creepy dark, and the night-lights were on the food stands. It was like a ghost town along the dusty road at dusk.

When I joined them, the girls were standing together giggling and talking about how cute, the boys were. I knew if I was going to get Brandon's attention, tonight was going to be the night. Donovan volunteered to be the first counter. We darted off to hide. I found a hiding place behind a white truck. I saw Tiny in front of me near another car. She whispered and motioned. "Here he come, hide." I obeyed and glided back toward the dumpster sitting behind me. I saw a body standing near the tall tree in complete darkness.

"Candee, come over here," I heard a voice say. *Brandon?*

I heard Donovan finding the others and shouting, "I got you!" While the others ran to tap the home spot, I ran over to the tree with Brandon. When I arrived, I could see the whites of his eyes. A hand on my left shoulder, a hand on my face, and lips on my mouth. I tasted sweet bubble gum on his tongue. A boy had not kissed me, and it was awkward. I was rattled and frozen. I could not kiss him back. I stood there with my mouth open. My mind was racing with excitement, and I blushed hard. I grabbed the person's shirt and whispered, "Brandon."

There is silence, and the voice says, "No it's Boombox."

A sense of obliviousness comes over me. "What – Boombox? You, you were with another girl. I saw you earlier with her," I remarked adamantly.

"Candee, girl, I like you more than her. I know you don't like me this way. I'm sorry to have kissed you without asking." He apologized, looking me directly in my face. Butterflies dancing in my stomach. I giggled. He smiled at me and broke out in a low chuckle. It got the attention of Donovan. "Ha, ha, I got you both." Game over. We smiled at each other and went our separate ways. On the way to the car, I saw Brandon leaning against a tree kissing and cuddling with an unknown girl.

Chapter Five: Sprung, Strung, & Stuck

Over the next few days, I played the scene of my first kiss repeatedly. It was not with who I desired to suck face with. It was nothing like I dreamed it would be, but it was surprisingly nice. I daydreamed about Boombox all day and was anxious to see him again, becoming obsessed about kissing him again. I was giddy reminiscing about him around my friends. Vaughn was more experienced than I am and she has had several boyfriends. Vaughn knew me too well and asked me what happened at the campground while playing hide and seek. "You have to cross your heart and hope to die a dozen times over if you tell," I demanded, looking serious.

"Goodie gumdrops, this better be good." she responded, rubbing her hands together.

I spilled my guts to my best friend.

"While at the campgrounds we played hide-and-seek. I heard someone calling me to hide with them behind a tree," I divulged.

"You telling me you listened to a total stranger? Girl, you could have been raped and killed you crazy." Vaughn interrupted.

"No, I knew it had to be someone I knew because I'd heard their voice before. I went over there, and they kissed me – on the lips."

"What!" Vaughn shouted. "Who was it? No – let me guess! Was it slimy head Brandon? I told you he ain't good for you."

"Nope," I attest, laughing hard.

"Was it Jason, Tim, or Martin? heck, I give up."

"Since you can't guess, it was Boombox. He has the softest lips I've ever kissed," I reminisced, staring off into the distance.

"Isn't he the *first* boy you've ever kissed?" Vaughn pointed out, bringing me out of the fantasy.

"Yeah, if you don't count being kissed by puppies," I giggled.

"You and Boombox, huh? Y'all going to be girlfriend and boyfriend now?" she asked, straightforward.

I answered hesitantly, "I don't know. He cute and all, but he into other girls. You know how those football boys are, they with everybody. Anyway, I am not his type of girl. I heard he has sex with the girls he likes."

Vaughn's head did a 180. "That's what I heard too. But he might treat you differently if he knows you're a virgin", Vaughn assured.

"You right, he might wait until I am ready to do it. I do like him, though."

We do two fingers snaps, turn, and go our separate ways.

I arrived at home and needed to quench my thirst. I grabbed a plastic cup and went to the fridge without washing my hands. Tattletale Cara was evil eyeing me while she sat at the table eating a bowl of macaroni and cheese.

"You need to wash yo dirty hands, or Imma tell Momma," she insinuated.

I ignored her and spotted the red strawberry Kool-Aid in the fridge.

"Ma... Candee!"

Before I could even pour the ice-cold drink, there was a hard slap on the back of my neck.

"What are you doing? Go wash your nasty hands before I get my belt!"

I wanted to punch Cara in the face for being such a loud blabbermouth. I washed my hands in the bathroom sink, got my cold drink, and exited outside to drink it. I imagined what I wanted to say to Boombox the next time we met. I heard the phone ring, I leaped like a frog to get it.

"Yes, she is please hold on. Candee, telephone." my momma announced.

I picked up the phone from the kitchen counter. "Hello."

An unknown voice hissed in my ear, "You kissed my boyfriend at the campground! I'm going to beat yo yellow ass the next time I see you!" The dial tone blared in my ears. *Her boyfriend?* The fear of having to fight made my heart race fast into overdrive.

I had not been in a fight since elementary school. Alyssa Griffin bullied me from third to sixth grade. She called me names like high yellow, big nose, and bubblegum lips. Alyssa was shorter than I was, she wore two nappy ponytails too short for her hairstyle. Her skin tone shiny blue-black, she must have used a whole bottle of baby oil or Vaseline – skin greasy to fry chicken on it. The only good thing about her was she dressed nicely wearing name brand clothes. She harassed on the bus, in class, the cafeteria, and wherever she cornered me to do damage.

I was frightened because she told me she was going to whoop my butt. I did my best to avoid the confrontations, but the school was small you could not run and hide. One day after school, while waiting for the bus to come, she came over to pick on me. I got to a point and was not afraid of her taunts anymore. She went to put her hand in my face, and I snapped. I grabbed her neck and squeezed it as hard as I could. "Leave me the alone, you bald head ass eagle!" I snarled.

She got the message and did not bother me again. When we both attended middle school, Alyssa became one of my closest friends. As we grew closer, she told me her parents fought all the time at home. She admitted she did not have any friends because she did not know how to treat them. One day, she ran away from home and ended up going with an older boy into his basement where he later raped her. She confessed to me she was too scared to tell anyone about it. I encouraged her to tell her parents or an adult. She got up the nerve and told her Pastor, and the police got involved.

But long story short, I was not looking forward to getting beat up over a boy. I panicked and called Vaughn. "Vaughn somebody called and threatened to beat me up for kissing Boombox. Who is his girlfriend?"

Vaughn was mute for a few seconds and asked, "Did she sound white?"

I replayed her voice for a few seconds. "She sure did. Does he like white girls too?"

"I bet it's country ass Francine Starnes. She ain't nobody. She fast in the ass! She sleeps with everybody!" She laughed loudly.

"Girl, what grade is she in, high school?" I asked intimidated.

"Yep, she older than you. She's in the 10th grade, and she go to a rich private school in the country. You need to talk to Boombox and find out what is going on," Vaughn demanded.

I bob my head as though she could see me through the phone.

My heart was pounding like Congo drums from fear of dealing with the girl who might be Boombox's girlfriend. I needed to hear what he had to say. I dialed his number. He answered the phone on the second ring.

"Hello."

"Boombox, it's Candee. I need to ask you about a girl." I was nervous but kept talking.

"I want you to call me Jermaine," he insisted. "What's going on?"

"A country ass white girl called me a little while ago and declared she gonna beat me up because you her boyfriend. Is it true?"

"Sort of true, but mostly not true. I mean, we been hanging out and stuff, she comes to the football games, and... shit happens. Besides you a virgin, right?" he asked, getting off track.

I went silent of how to respond. Would he like me if he knew I was a virgin? On the other hand, would he run if I stated no? "I am holding out. I want to be in love with someone before I have sex," I replied.

I bit my bottom lip to numb the rejection. He was speechless and a few seconds went by. He affirmed, "I know you are three years younger than me and I have more experience than you. It's no pressure if you want to wait to have sex. Francine means nothing to me. I will not let her mess with you. I will set her straight." Jermaine vowed to keep me safe.

My parents were not amused when the boys looked at us girls like sweet candy. My daddy especially made sure the boys knew he carried a pocketknife with a 4-inch blade. I knew the blade was rusty and dull. I bet it would not cut butter, but it kept the crazies away from his girls.

When I was fifteen, Jermaine and I planned to have sex for the first time. I invited him to come to my house. My dad was away, and I guess God knew where. Momma was a few houses up getting her hair curled. I called Jermaine to tell him to come to my bedroom window. He had a driver's license and was able to borrow his granddad's truck. I let him in the side window to our bedroom and told my sisters I was taking a nap and not to disturb me. My sisters were in the living room watching TV. I was mute and nervous when Jermaine came through the window.

Impulsively, he undressed me and got under the bunk bed with me. The worn-out mattress squeaked as he lowered his masculine body on it. He caressed my plump, immature tits. I was shocked he even noticed them. Jermaine was 6'2 and weighed a ton. His body covered me as a warm heated blanket. His deep brown eyes looked through me. His body was muscular, and he smelled like Irish Spring soap. His teeth sparkled in the dark. I was in a dream.

"I got a condom," he whispered as I hear him tearing the packet. I did not watch him put on the dull white rubber condom. Out of curiosity, my eyes shifted to his stiff penis. I wanted to change my mind. I was nervy and squinted my eyes. In real-life, I had not seen a boy's privates before. Not a black boy's because in the 7th grade we had a science book displayed body parts about sexual reproduction for the boys and girl's bodies. I remember frowning at the bright pink penis and how nasty it looked and vowed I would never have sex.

Jermaine's eyes locked on mine and he pulled at my shorts. He whispered, "Go ahead and take them off or leave one leg out."

I did as he instructed, my heart pounding loud. I did not want him to see I was scared. I was lying on my back with my legs as tight as a rusty metal toolbox.

"Candee, girl, open up," he whispered.

My body was shaking like a scared puppy. My boney knees were knocking. "I'm scared," I whispered.

"I won't hurt you. If it hurts, I will stop," he assured calmly.

I closed my eyes tighter hoping this would ease the pain. My girlie was on fire. The pressure was indescribable. I let out a soft cry. "It hu-ur-ts, I can't," I stammered.

"I'm in there. Let me keep going," he begged. I winced, closed my eyes, and hugged him tight around his waist. Tight enough to squeeze the air from his lungs.

I opened my eyes and focused on the bottom of the top bunk's wooden frame. I followed each nail tacked into the wood. I counted each piece. I counted to twelve before the pain bum-rushed me. He pushed in gently, and my tears flowed softly. I had confidence this was going to make him love me. His body jerked like a car hard to start and his breathing hot and heavy. I could not see his face because he buried it in my pillow. I heard him say inaudible words his body went limp. He lay on top of me for a few seconds and raised his head with a silly grin.

"Damn girl, it was good."

He got up, pulled the condom off, and zipped his pants. "Can you get rid of this?"

It was the droopy condom. I found a dirty sock and rolled it inside. The after effects were awful my girlie being in pain and burning. He kissed me tenderly and professed he would call me tomorrow. He slipped back out the window like a thief in the night and drove away.

I sprinted to the bathroom to inspect the damaged goods. My mind was all over the place. I was jubilated we had sex. Speechless because it was painful. I was not looking forward to doing it again. I wrapped the condom in tissues and tossed in the wastebasket. I wiped my girlie and on the tissues was a stained strawberry color with a piece of pink meat.

I was petrified. Would I need to go to the hospital? I might need stitches. Should I tell my momma? I put on a feminine pad, took two aspirin, and went to bed early. Tears poured as streams. *Is this how love is supposed to feel?* My body is numb. I was surprised my sisters had not disturbed us in those few minutes of the worst day of my life. I did not want to tell anyone about the experience.

My parents made plans for Crystal and me to attend a summer camp for girls who were interested in going to college. The camp was for one week at Black Mountains. I was not as excited as I was when I was accepted. My brain obsessed on Jermaine. Jermaine, dang...Jermaine. A week went by, and he hadn't called me. We were leaving tomorrow for the camp. I did not tell him about it because I assumed we would have spoken by now. When I did call him, he was not at home or at football practice. I called Vaughn to chitchat, hoping to get up the nerve to tell her what had happened.

However, before I could muster up the words, she spouted how mad she was at Jesse Hudson. He was an Asian boy in the tenth grade who she was obsessed with because he was a department store model. "Here I was standing near the restrooms at the football game, and he sways by me and winks at me. Girl, I wanted to pass out. But I needed to talk to him, I eased closer to catch him coming out." She smacked her chewing gum as if it was trying to get away. "Girl…when he came out, his glanced right at me, pulled out a cigarette, and like slow motion, he talked to me. He made a comment about leaving to get to know each other. I was mesmerized by his pretty ass white teeth. I didn't leave, but he took my number."

When she sucked in air, I blurted, "I did it with Jermaine the other night, and it was terrible."

"Just change positions, were you on top or bottom?" She responds as though I had informed her I'd lost a wrestling match. "You know I lost my virginity to Gerald Muse. He had bad breath, and I knew I was not going to have sex with him again. I thank God, I did not get pregnant by his stankin' ass." She sounded as if she was going to set the phone on fire with her attitude. I sidetracked her conversation.

"I gotta go, momma calling me. I'll talk to you later." I hung up before she said good-bye. Her words did not soothe my scars. I was bugging out about this. I guess it wasn't important. I reflected on my parents' relationship; it gave me the impression what I was going

54

through was close to how dad treated momma. *Perhaps, a boy is supposed to treat you like this after you give in and do it.*

Remarkably, being at the camp took my mind away from Jermaine. Crystal and I met a few nice girls who had their heads lined up for greater things in life. They had goals and dreams to work on after they left high school. From a youthful age, I believed I would go to college to become a nurse. I enjoyed helping people, and I heard nurses make tons of money. With this new experience, my focus was on doing well in school, getting great grades, and not allowing any boy to deter me. Crystal announced to me she was pumped about going to college to become an English teacher. It was no surprise to me. She loved to write poems and stories and held us hostage on Saturday nights reading her new writings. Momma was her huge fan and applauded her after she read for an hour. We had to follow Momma's lead or suffer her wrath afterward.

The next week moved in slow-motion as school was a drag. I had not heard from Jermaine. I must be a fool. I needed to hear from Jermaine and told myself I was going to confront him at the football game tonight. Mrs. Penny, Mallory's mom, would be the chaperone. I paced around my room because normally my parents followed up to check my story. However, it did not happen this time, and I went without a hiccup. I dressed in my favorite Wrangler blue jeans and a white button-shirt with blue and yellow flowers. I went to the front door to check the weather temperature by putting my right hand outside. The night air chilly as the goosebumps danced up my arm. I put on my old faithful wool coat and a black scarf. I reviewed how I looked in the bathroom mirror, waved goodbye to momma, and dashed out the front door before things went wrong.

We piled into Mallory's mom station wagon and headed to the game. When we arrived, the school's parking lot was full of cars. Mrs. Penny parked on the side of the street. The game was at Ragsdale High School. This was where I would attend the 10th grade next school year. Jermaine was graduating from here this year. My stomach turned as my head rehearsed what I was going to say when I met up with him after the game. I had no idea or plan on how to get my answers. I hoped I would not miss my ride home. I needed to see his face again. As we headed through the gate, the scoreboard read the game had begun. Vaughn, Jemma, Mallory, and I climbed to the top of the bleachers in search of four empty seats. As expected, there was none; for this reason, we found separate seats and settled.

The Ragsdale Warriors (8-2) were going against their rivals, Northpoint Ravens (9-1). Jermaine played the linebacker position on the field. I had no idea how the game of football worked. I truthfully went to see the boys and now Jermaine. The brightness illuminating from the huge football field fascinated me.

I saw the back of his green jersey number 57. I tried to follow his movements to see what was going on. I smiled when he grabbed the Ravens quaterback and slammed him to the ground. I heard Mallory screaming in front of me, "Good play, Warriors, go get em' Jermaine!" She looked back at me and winked.

At halftime, I needed to go to the restroom but was afraid my seat might be taken. Therefore, I sat and begged for my bladder to forget it's functioning for a little while. Vaughn strolled from nowhere and asked me if I wanted to go and get popcorn and soda. I told her I did not have any extra money. She offered to pay for it, but I told her I would lose my seat.

"Girl, we can wander around and talk about people," she snickers. We made it through the crowds of people and got in the long line at the concession stand. The smell of popcorn made my mouth water. While standing there, Brandon scurried by with Sylvia close to him. They were holding hands. *Were they dating?* She was my first cousin, I should give her the scoop on him, but not tonight.

Vaughn and I stood around and gossiped until the game ended. The Warriors won the score 30-27. I sprinted toward the locker room to try to catch up with Jermaine, but the home crowds were estatic with chanting and cheers. I gave up when I caught a glimpse of his jersey heading toward the back of the gymnasium. I kept my gaze on him and picked up speed to try to catch him. *Is he leaving? Why would he go the wrong way?* I needed to catch up with him before he was out of sight. My airflow was constricted before I made it to the gymnasium. It was dark; like a black hole. It was as if the temperature had dropped at least 10 degrees. I wanted to call out his name, but instead, I keep stepping with caution. My own shadows frightened me, as I eased along the side of the building.

Right before I was getting to the end of the building, I heard inaudible sounds. The voice was familiar. My heart beat faster because I had to confirm who it was. There was a boy standing against the brick wall moaning with his head looking up towards the sky and his eyes closed. It was Jermaine. There below him, a girl's head was between his legs. I needed to see her face. I tiptoed and sneaked right up to both of them. It was pale-faced Francine. I stood there for what seemed like a lifetime. I stumbled over my right foot, and he heard me. I ran as if a monster was grabbing at my heels.

I heard Jermaine screaming my name, but I ignored the urgency in his voice and kept on running. I ran fast through the parking lot. I saw the headlights to the station wagon and Mrs. Miller standing beside it with her arms folded. I knew I was in trouble. As soon as I got closer, I slowed to a crawl. My lungs were on the verge of wheezing. She wasted no time in telling me I was about to be left behind.

"Candee, do I need to talk to your parents about this?"

"No ma'am, I got turned around in the crowds and had to figure out where you were parked."

Her facial expression relaxed, and she seemed to agree with my excuse. "I am glad you alright. Candee is here." She announced and glanced inside the car to count heads. When she finished, she got in the car and drove away.

Adrenaline ran rampant through my veins, but I remained calm inside the car.

"Girl, where did you go?' Vaughn whispered in my left ear.

I could not look at her, oddly I ignored her. I was humiliated to admit what I had seen. Nevertheless, my world was cracking into pieces. My reality seemed cold, clueless, and defeated. I wanted to jump out of the car and run away. I had no idea what to do about it. I struggled to make sense of what I've seen.

Chapter Six: Music in the Dark

For a couple of days, I was depressed and couldn't eat. I lied to momma when she asked if I was sick. "Yeah, I guess I got a stomach virus," I replied.

"You got germs from school. You know sickness going around. Go get the Pepto Bismol and lay down."

I agreed, but faked taking it. The thick pink milky stuff looked disgusting. I did lie down and stared at the dull white ceiling. I wanted to take my mind off my problems, so I pulled out my box of comic books. I loved the heroes and funny stories. *Let me see what Archie and the Gang and Spiderman are up to today*. I was drawn in the book when I heard Crystal

calling my name.

"Candee, you going to church today for revival? It's gonna start at 6:00 tonight."

"I don't want to. Go on without me," I replied, turning the next page to my book.

"Too bad you gonna miss those cute boys in the Southern Gospel Stars band? "See ya later," Crystal teased, prancing away.

I educed what she mentioned about cute boys. *Is this the answer to my heartbreak?* I tossed the paper book back in the box and leaped off the bed. "Crystal, wait on me!" I shrieked while running to catch up with her.

The first night of revival was flowing over with cars lined up on both sides of the road. Church of God Baptist was small and had been a part of the community for at least 100 years. Maybe, not 100, but too old for me to remember. Crystal and I loved going to church for the wrong reasons. We participated by singing, tapping our feet, and clapping for those who shouted around the church because the 'Holy Ghost' was on them. I guessed it might be true because you did not see nothing on the people who were shouting. I was not sure if I trusted in God. Even though the children's church teacher told us, he had a son named Jesus who died for us to go to heaven. My faith was weak because I had to see to believe in God. Right now, I could not do it. How could I pray to someone I did not see? Yet, many people in my church bowed their heads as though he was standing right there in the flesh.

Crystal and I slogged along the left side aisle to find a seat. The shiny wood stained floors squeaked as we side stepped to the last pew. The music played as I scanned for familiar faces in the pews. Mallory and her oldest sister Elsa sang in the choir and played the tambourines. They sang a song and got the crowd going. They sing all right, I guess, because the congregation was saying, "Sang it, Chile. Amen. Thank you, Jesus." The air is clammy from the congregation. I found a paper fan in the seat with a picture of praying hands on the front. I fanned for the both of us.

I peeked around and saw Tiny and Lil FIFI sitting on the front pew with their mother. After the singing, Reverend Samuel Thomas approached the podium and welcomed the congregation. He was a slender coconut-skinned man with white hair. He read a scripture and prayed for the Holy Ghost to come into the church. The congregation bowed their heads, but I kept my eyes wide open looking for the ghost to come through the ceiling.

"This first group of young men has come from Right Way Pentecostal Church to worship the Lord with us tonight." He picked up a white handkerchief and dabbed it across his forehead and under his nose. "They are brothers and cousins who have been singing and playing for God since they were knee-high." He laughed and placed his right hand to his kneecap. "Please welcome the Sons of Yahweh."

In glided six handsome fellas who took their positions and sang *The Lord's Prayer* in Acapella. I liked their version. I looked at each one from head to toe. They were nicely dressed in black pinstripe suits with cream-collared shirts. I locked eyes on the third one to the right side because he had short curly hair. I was like an eagle watching the prey. After the first song, they exchanged positions to play their instruments.

I could see someone take one member by the arm and lead him to a piano. *He must be blind.* I did not recognize the song, but it had a hallelujah sound, and the congregation got on their feet. Crystal hopped up first and clapped her hands to the beat, I mimicked her. Because my butt was going numb sitting too long on the unpadded ancient maple wood.

Revival captured several souls tonight and made a few people cry, shout, and dance around the church. I was anxious to leave right after the singing was over, but I stayed seated until Reverend Thomas did the ending prayer. I eased past Crystal and dashed through the ancient wooden double doors to get a little fresh air. The night air was thick with humidity; my hair would surely act up. The six band members came outside to mingle with the church folks. I looked for Crystal but did not see her. Mallory and Tiny marched up to me.

I commented to Mallory how well she and her sister sounded. "We sing for the Lord," she replied, smiling.

Afterwards, I hurried over to greet the handsome fellas. They introduced themselves as Arthur, Albert, Alton, and Joseph, Kenneth, and Bernard two groups of brothers. They were first cousins who loved playing Gospel music. Arthur was legally blind and relatively shy, but he was cute. I had my eyes on Joseph, the outspoken one with the darkest skin. I winked at Joseph to let him know I was interested in him. However, as we were getting ready to step away from the crowd to talk, Mallory strutted over towards us looking kind of serious. She cleared her throat and proclaimed, "JoJo, I've been looking everywhere for you. Thanks for holding my boyfriend hostage, Candee."

My facial expression insipid from embarrassment. I knew my motives were not godly, I retreated. "Sure, no problem."

I spotted Crystal flapping her gums with an unknown boy. I treaded over to snatch her because it was time to leave. Unexpectedly, I stopped in my tracks, bumping into Arthur. "Whoa, I am sorry Arthur I didn't see you."

He cracked a handsome smile. "You stole my line."

I giggled childishly.

"Is this Candee?" he asked, smiling.

"Yes, it is. Sorry, I was trying to catch up with my sister before she forgot I was waiting on her."

"I bet you are not one to easily forget," he whispered, smiling again. I imagine how smooth his lips were and how attractive he looked with a thick mustache and goatee. I needed to know how old he was because I found him to be charmingly attractive.

"Arthur, I'm close to sixteen, how old are you?"

"Twenty-one," he responds in a deep voice.

I smiled shyly. "I like older men."

We stood talking about anything to keep each other's company and before leaving, we exchanged phone numbers. "If we continue talking, my friends call me Art," he asserted.

"Art, I have to be honest I pitied you before I met you. But you got it going on," I replied.

Before leaving the church, I looked around for Crystal and didn't see her anywhere, even with the crowd thinning out. I figured she had already left to go home. I ended up walking home alone. When I arrived, I could tell dad was not home from work yet because his truck was not in the driveway. I announced loud enough to let Momma know who came inside. "Ma, I'm back. Is Crystal back yet?" She didn't respond. I got a glass to pour some cold water from the fridge.

I stopped when I heard a faint tap at the back door. Good thing we got windows on the door. I pulled the curtain back to look out and saw it was Crystal. She looked disheveled, and her hair was sweaty looking. "Why you look like you were running from the devil?" I asked, laughing.

She giggled back and boasted, "I was, and I got away."

I shook my head in disbelief, gulped down the ice water, and headed to take a bath in the tub. My parents' bedroom door was ajar. I peeked my head in to tell Momma goodnight. I saw Momma lying in bed, and her nose was bright red. *Is she sick?*

"Ma, Ma, you need anything?" she was silent as she stared at the TV, which was loud for this time of night.

"Candee, come in and close the door. I need to tell you what's going on*." Is this going to be terrible news about dad?* My mind raced with awful visions of a truck accident. "Since you are the oldest I am going to tell you what is going on," she stressed blowing her nose. "Your dad and I need to separate from each other. It has nothing to do with you or your sisters. He has admitted son-of-a-bitch.... is in love with another woman. He has another life when he is on the road." She stopped talking and wiped her eyes, which were full of tears. I sat on the edge of the bed, speechless. "God, please help me take care of my babies," Momma sobbed hard and buried her face in the pillows. I want to punch anything, to let out the fury brewing inside of me.

Within a few days, my momma cleaned the house by getting rid of the reminders dad had left behind. She threw out the rest of my dad's clothes, bowling shoes, colognes, and family portraits. My grandparents dropped by a few times to check on us and made sure we had enough food to eat until momma received her next paycheck. This was hard to deal with, sadly we sucked in our pain and kept going. Momma found a second job to go to on third shift to stay caught up on the bills. The bad part was she wasn't getting much rest

64

and took sleeping pills to fall asleep faster. The first week, she took too many by accident, and when the alarm clock went off, she did not move. I found her in a deep sleep and panicked because she was drowsy and not getting up. My sisters and I were able to get her in the tub and ran the shower on cold water. It worked, thank the moon and stars. Soon after this drama, I see Crystal being reclusive; I take a minute to check on her. Since I was the appointed sitter, I had more time to hang out with my sisters.

I find Crystal sitting on the cemented back patio in a lawn chair reading a book. "Crystal, are you alright? I've been watching you what's wrong?"

She looked up. "I'm depressed. I miss daddy and... I—I had a problem a while back, but it's gone."

I was concerned for her, as in overprotective. "You had a problem? What happened?" I sat down to get on her eye level for this sounds serious.

She was mute for a few seconds. "I met someone at the revival. I-I-I tried to have sex with him."

My mouth dropped open. "No... way!" I exclaimed. "Who is this boy? How old is he?"

"He told me he was 14, but he seemed more mature," she disclosed, looking back at the book.

"What you mean you *tried*? Where did you go, did you get caught?" I asked, giving her the third degree. I slapped my bare legs from the pinches of mosquitoes.

"We went behind the storage building at the church. We kissed, and he touched me everywhere. When he was getting ready to pull my panties off, we heard a shuffling in the woods. It scared us to death." Her face filled with humiliation. My words were inadequate to soothe her pain. "His name is BJ. He goes to Parkwood Middle School. I know nothing else about him. I haven't seen or talked to him." She sounded regretful.

"Sis, I am deeply sorry this happened to you." I wanted to give her a hug, but instead I stood and listened.

"I must be stupid. He told me I was beautiful, proclaimed he had a dream he would meet me at a church." She pouted.

"Wow, the lamest crap I have ever heard to get in a girl' drawers!" I shouted. I covered my mouth. This made her bust out laughing. I joined her. Now we both are better. I was relieved she did not have sex with that sack of dirt. I confessed about my experience with Jermaine in hopes of stopping her from making the same mistake.

"Crystal, I hope what I say to you will help you to wait to have sex until you are ready. You cannot take it back and start over. I am no longer a virgin. I had sex with Jermaine a couple of weeks ago. I regret it like more than you know. I cannot say we are boyfriend and girlfriend because he is avoiding me." Breathing heavy I paused. I am tearful. It made me weak in the knees. "Wait for the right time with someone who at least gets to know you and cares for you."

"Sure, big sistah, I won't do it again." We embraced for the first time. Her skin was warm and foreign, but it was a great moment.

I soon forgot about Jermaine and concentrate on getting to know Art. We talked allot on the phone, and he revealed he had his own place since he was 18 years old. His church paid him to sing and play in the group. They received love offerings when they played at church events. Art also received government assistance to help him live independently. We met up each day after I got home from school. His oldest brother Albert met me at the park and secretly drove me over to Art's apartment. I rushed through any homework I had before leaving home. Art encouraged me to avoid procrastination. He even helped me with my Algebra. One day, after about the 3rd week of hanging out together, I received my first kiss on the lips. At first, he kissed me on the forehead when saying goodbye, but I would complain. "Art, I want a sweet kiss. I like you a lot, and I know you like me."

He paused, and got closer and whispered, "I want our day to be special for us both. I don't want to rush. I hope you get what I'm saying." His voice was smooth and warm. Art had the patience of a mother hen. He did not rush me to do anything. And when the kiss happened, it was amazing! His mustache tickled my nose at first, but I melted in his arms. He cupped my face in his hands as he kissed my nose, lips, and cheeks. I did not want to let him go. I caressed him around his narrow waistline as though I would not see him again. I had a smile on my face for a week.

The other day, while I was washing dishes dad, dropped in to see how we were doing since momma was at work. He asked me about my boyfriend, and I acted as though I did not hear him and kept on washing the plates in the hot sudsy water. I heard him say, "Ms. Marks stated she seen you over on Baker street the other day getting out of a blue Crown Victoria car. Who was driving?"

My heart raced like a wild animal caught in a trap. *How was I going to explain this? I will have to lie to my daddy. I stuttered but collected my words.*

"I-I-I... been studying with a tutor. I am not passing Algebra class. I meet the tutor at their house."

He was digging deeper and asked, "Does the tutor have a name?"

"It's Mrs. Carpenter. She tutors on certain days to be home for her own children when they get off the bus." He seemed to take the lie in stride and grabbed a cold canned soda from the fridge.

"I guess it's okay. Make sure you tell us when you are there because your mom is changing shifts at the sewing mill. I believe she informed me she going to second shift starting in a week. Also, I'm driving out of town for work over the next couple of weeks."

"Sure dad," I replied, my throat dry from the taste of lies.

The next day, I arrived at Art's apartment and told him my dad was questioning me about being there. Art did not use a cane or wear his glasses around his home. He took a few steps towards me, putting out his hands. He was mute, but took his smooth hands and found my arms. His hands went upwards to my chest. He was such a gentleman. "Sorry," he mumbled. He kept going up to my neck and touched my chin. He lifted my chin, closed in, and kissed me tenderly. I was in a dream each time he kissed me. "I don't want to say this but I must." His facial expression stoic. I am nervous but did not know why. "I enjoy your company, Candee. To me, you are a smart, witty, and mature young woman. Your parents should know the truth. I do love you, but..." I knew what was coming next. "However, I know this kind of relationship receives no applause. You are a minor, and I am a

68

grown man." I shifted my weight from left hip to right hip. His eyes shifted side to side while he spoke. "I could go to jail for being alone with you. Being a blind man is not the big issue. My age worries me the most. I know we have spent a lot of time together and I don't regret anything we…"

I cut him off. "Wait a minute. You saying we don't need to be together because you are six years older than me?" I foamed at the mouth like a rabid dog ejecting obscenities. "Art, what the fuck? This is crazy shit!" The tears were close behind. I wiped my face with both hands and stepped back from him. I startled him, I could tell because his composure was rigid and his face looked heartbroken. "You are not the first older man I been with. I like older men. Being with you, nothing else matters to me; this is the high of my day."

I sniffled and excused myself to get a tissue to blow my nose. "I will be right back." I went to the bathroom. Art took a seat in the living room. I found a clean washcloth and wet it with warm water. My eyes filled up with tears. My heart was breaking again. I loved him, and I did not want to end what we had.

When I emerged from the bathroom, I could hear Art playing a tune on his keyboard. He was singing low. The melody was slow as he crooned the lyrics. "You came into my life like a fallen star from heaven. Your love sent from heaven. I have waited for the true love. I adore you." He played the melody over again and ended with, "It is you, I adore." When he stopped, I asked him whom the song was about.

He faced me covering his eyes behind his dark sunglasses and remarked, " It's about you. I wrote this song last night."

69

He sat straight up and admitted, "I want to be friends. It would mean a lot to me if you could try to understand where I am coming from." He swallowed hard but kept speaking. "Your life is beginning. You will have time for a committed relationship later in life. I care for you my feelings will not change. If you ever need anything, let me know."

I was sick to my stomach from the break-up. I said nothing and ran out the front door. I couldn't run far. I counted to one hundred and went back inside. "Art, when I am with you, you treat me like a woman. Our conversations are full of insight, and I hunger for more. I don't want this to end." I apologized for being silly and asked him to call his brother to take me home. He was standing near his bedroom door. He turned around, glided his hands across the doorframe, and entered his room to pick up his phone. He informed me Albert would return to pick me up within ten minutes. He made small talk about an upcoming church event until Albert arrived. The awkwardness was stagnant like an eternity. I gave him a hug around his neck one last time and kissed his neck. He smelled heavenly good. The scent of arid woody aroma from the Armani cologne swooped up my nostrils. I would not forget his smell.

Chapter Seven: Chipping Away the Ice Cubes

I left my broken heart with Arthur and tried to forget about our relationship. Pushing on for me was finding another boy I could learn to trust and forget about my past love. With Jermaine in and out of my life, I did have other so-called boyfriends to entertain me while I was in remission. I could not truly commit to anyone else. Most times, I fibbed my way through the details of the last boyfriend or left out information intentionally. Since I lived in such a small ghetto neighborhood, my business seemed to be front-page news. *Who is Candee with now? Is she doing the nasty? Is he an older man?* The gossip runs rampant.

My cousin Sylvia invited me to my first house party. Sylvia was a laidback person. She and her older sister Eunice were my favorite cousins to hang out with. Sylvia wore a pile of makeup to cover the Vitiligo spots on her face. She was such a pretty girl to me, though. I loved her long-braided tresses. She told me last year she was going to chop it off and donated it to cancer victims. I told her it was a selfless act to do for a stranger.

I have a new curfew allowing me to hang out until 11:00 p.m. on the weekends. I was overjoyed and invited Vaughn and Jemma. They accepted, I asked momma to drop us off there. Momma agreed to take and pick us up. Not what I expected, I had to make sure she saw nothing out of character. The party was in the same neighborhood where Jermaine lived. I was hoping he would drop by. In spite of the heartaches, I loved him. I fought the desire to go running back to him.

When we arrived at the party, the music was bumping off the walls of the small trailer. There were people everywhere, in the front yard, backyard, and inside the hot tin box. I was grooving to the music. It was Earth, Wind, & Fire, *Fantasy*. My body swayed with the melody and the rhythm. I wanted to dance but not alone. I closed my eyes and imagined dancing with Arthur and Jermaine at the same time. I imagined us working the dance floor bumping and grinding on each other. All of a sudden, a nudge on my right arm. I opened my eyes and saw a boy standing in front of me with long braided hair.

"You wanna dance before the song goes off?"

Caught off guard by his forwardness, I took his hand, and we stepped on the dance floor and boogied.

After we danced about four songs; we both had sweat pouring off our faces, and my soft curls were wet and puffy. My denim roll sleeve romper had wet armpits. We exchanged names, and he followed me to my seat at the back wall. Sitting there on the orange fabric couch were my partners in crime, Vaughn and Jemma.

"Girl you were jamming out there. I didn't know you were such a good dancer." Jemma cheered.

Vaughn chimed in, "I know Candee likes to shake her bubble booty."

The boy was homely looking but smiled.

Jemma recognized him right away. "Hi, Terence. How have you been?"

"I've been good. I know your face but not your name."

"I'm Jemma, Donovan's first cousin."

He was polite and shook her hand. He turned to Vaughn and shook her hand too. Terrance and I ended up dating for about two months. I did not have sex with him because he too childish about doing it. One day, I told him I needed to stop seeing him. We stayed friends afterward and later, I heard him dating Alyssa. Life could be such a joke.

During tenth grade, I dated several boys one after the other: Gary, Darnell, and Nicholas. One gave me gifts, the other wrote poems, and the last one gave me great sex. I was wild and having fun exploring. I didn't have any regrets when I got bored and broke up with them over the phone, but not with Nicholas. Nicholas Kincaid came from a family of wealthy influential parents in politics. He drove a new Tan BMW two-door car. He was a white boy, older than me by 2 years. I had to admit the older, the better. He enjoyed smoking cigarettes and pot daily. I did try to smoke cigarettes in the seventh grade, made me nauseous. I did not pick up another one.

The best thing about smoking pot was we were having the best sex ever. Nicholas could last for hours with a brick rod. I was learning much about my body with Nicholas. He taught me how to get an orgasm while on top of him. Before him, I had no idea what an orgasm was or even how to get it. During our first encounter, Nicholas and I did it in his new car. There was an erotic explosion in my body from the smell of a new car while humping on the new leather seats. Nicholas was a clean freak. He got the car five months before we met. He had not removed the plastic covering on the floor mats.

One night, he parked on the dark dirt road near a park. He told me to sit on his lap. I watched him gulp the can of cold beer and covered his mouth to burp. He hastily pulled off my blue cotton summer dress and kissed my nipples. I moaned; the foreplay was strangely good! No male had ever kissed me there. He was a great kisser too. Tongue in, wiggle around, and out. I tried to keep up with this mouth massages. I focused on pulling his white cotton t-shirt over his long dirty blonde hair. I was madly attracted to his tanned bronze skin and coconut brown eyes. I was ecstatic to be in a position with a good-looking man. He pounded my bubble butt on top on his long erection, which fit like a glove.

"I want you to come first," he whispered.

I was mute. Too immature to admit I did not know what I was doing. After another minute of silence, I spoke up. "How do I come?" I whispered shyly.

He rolled me over and put my legs over his shoulders. He kissed me between my legs, which tickled. I giggled at first, but soon my body relaxed. No boyfriend had ever kissed me there before.

At 16 years old, with Nicholas, I was a grown woman treated like a queen. I wanted to cry it was so euphoric. I tried to hold back, but like a flood, hurricane, and tornado I let out a scream sounding like a howl.

"Baby, I love doing this for you," he whispered as he wiped his face off with the tissues he found in the back seat.

I wanted to please him too. I offered to do the same to him.

He chuckled. "Do you know how to give a good blowjob?"

I moved my shoulders and chimed, "I could learn, and you could be my first victim." I giggled.

"Naw, my dick too sensitive. I do not want any teeth marks. Let's pass for now." He told me he was good and drove me home.

After my encounter with Nicholas, I was high on puffy clouds close to heaven, if there was such a thing. As I sat in class and fantasized about the night before, I snapped out of my musings when the teacher tapped chalk on the blackboard to get our attention. Back to my real life.

I was passing most of my classes but not Social Studies. Social Studies was the most boring subject to ever torture students. I was not interested in what happened 300 years ago. We should've been learning interesting stuff to not put us to sleep. I hid behind my worn-out musty book as the black and white films rolled on the white background shade. My eyelids were heavy as I gazed at the alumni names etched in wood. *Jake ♥ Cassie –Billy D. was here.* My mouth was wide open and drooling. The teacher flipped on the lights.

"Class we will have a quiz about the film. I hope you took good notes."

I frowned at the smartest boy in the class, Donald Perry. I whispered, "Psst... Don, I know you took good notes. Can I jot a few? I don't feel well; it's why I had my head on the desk."

He smiled. "Sure, Candee. I put stars beside the information that'll be on the quiz." Even though I lied, he seemed to have no problem sharing, no harm done.

I did ride the bus midway home to meet Jermaine at *Jamestown Drug Store.* The store is famous for their creamy homemade milkshakes and tantalizing hamburgers. He had been calling begging to meet and talk. I missed him, but I wasn't willing to easily allow him into my panties. He needed to accept I wasn't going to wait on him. We agreed to meet at the drugstore to eat ice cream and talk. As soon as I got off the bus, I saw him standing near the front door resembling a god. I can tell his Afro had grown out more and he now had a full mustache. Jermaine had graduated from high school the previous May and had been working at Smith's Furniture store. As soon as our eyes met, he smiled and opened the door for me.

"You look nice today," he said.

My heart dancing like before. *I guess I truly miss him.* Butterflies frolicked in my stomach. We walked to the nearest booth and took a seat. He asked me what kind of ice cream I wanted, and chuckled, "Chocolate Chip, right**?**" I started to opt for the mouthwatering burger as the juicy smell hoovers in the air.

I gave him a huge smile. He returned with two scoops on a generous size vanilla cone. He also had a cup of Vanilla ice cream topped with colorful sprinkles. He made conversation about catching up on what I been doing since the last time we were together. We did not mention about the night I caught him with Francine because we broke up after it happened. I went on to date other boys and forgot about him.

He took a spoonful of ice cream in his mouth. "I miss you, and I want to know if we can get back together? If you turned on about me and you're not with another dude, Nicholas, right?"

I took a lick of the ice cream and gazed past him. "Jermaine, it's been a long time. I don't know how we can squash the past. I-I don't..."

He interrupted me. "Let me say this. I know what I did was wrong. It happened, and I can't change it, but I want to be with you," he pleaded.

I melted inside. He leaned over the table to kiss me on the lips, pulling on my bottom lip. He knew I loved it. "Candee girl, I love you." He licked his bottom lip as he took a seat.

I got wet between the legs and knew it was a sign I wanted him too. *This must be true love.* We spent the next hour telling each other more about ourselves to pass the time. Jermaine has an older sister who attended college in Georgia. He lived with his mother. His father had been in prison since Jermaine was nine. He explained his father had plotted to rob a bank with two of his high school friends. They were caught during the robbery. Even today, an unknown ratted his father out to the police. His father sentenced 20 years in a Virginia state prison. Jermaine had been troubled for many years and wanted to forget his father, but he had recently written back to him to start a relationship with him.

Jermaine had wheels now and gave me a ride home. His granddad fixed up a red rusty bucket truck. Inside, the car smelled like dirt because there were no floor mats. The dusty dry dirt covered the floors. There were two air fresheners hanging from the rear-view mirror, slightly helping the smell. We kissed again before I got out of the car.

"We'll talk tomorrow." He winked.

I was optimistic about our visit. The next day, I called Nicholas on the telephone and broke up with him. I told him a lie about how my parents did not accept him being older. I hoped he would express disappointment, but he did not. Instead, he barked, "All the best with the football player."

I was surprised he knew about Jermaine. "How you know...?" I asked softly.

"Baby girl, this is a small ass town. You know word gets around when rumors jump off here. No harm done. Take care." He hung up.

It was Halloween night, and I was too old to go trick-or-treating. Therefore, I went to the haunted house up the street. Cara went with me. Vaughn came over as we were leaving the house.

"I'm glad the rain stopped," she said.

"Girl, me too. You know my hair will not cooperate." I laughed aloud. We strolled up the street passing zombies, angels, princesses, and other costumed kids along the way. We reminisced about how we used to dress up when we were kids.

"Girl you know we didn't have any money for real costumes. Remember my mom would paint our faces to look like a ghost or a vampire," I recalled.

"I am right there with you, girl. We didn't have the money either. I remember one year momma threatened to whoop my butt if I wore her Afro wig. She knew I did not have a costume. Instead, I wore a pair of baggy pants, painted my face, and put on my dad's oversized shoes. I was going to be a clown. Glad those days is over!" Vaughn blasted with a grin.

When we arrived at the haunted house, there were a few people already going inside. I viewed each car to see if Jermaine was already there, but I didn't see his truck.

"Girl, let's go on in," Vaughn directed. "You got your $2.00 to get in?"

"Yeah, I want to wait on Jermaine first, though," I muttered, clearing my throat.

Vaughn cut her eyes at me but said nothing. "Cara you ready to go in with me?" she asked.

"You gonna hold my hand? I scream loud," Cara, admit in her drama queen voice.

Vaughn hissed, "Girl, come on here, you such a freaking baby. And don't you hold my hand too tight, you might break my nails." I watched them enter the house and turned my attention to the incoming traffic. I counted five vehicles pulling up, but none of them was Jermaine. Within a few seconds, I heard a honk and a car rolled up beside me. It was Jermaine. He was driving his mom's' car. He rolled down the window and told me to get in.

"Let's go somewhere to get busy," he suggested smiling. I was horny too. I hopped in the car. We ended up going up the street near the baseball park where there were no streetlights. It was pitch black outside his teeth glowed. We both stripped naked and made out in the back seat of the car. He pulled the condom out of his pants pocket and asked me to put it on. We kissed as he lowered between my legs. It had been three weeks since I had been with anyone. The excitement of him inside of me made me tremble. It took him about ten minutes, and he was ejaculating inside me.

One thing about Jermaine was he did not care if I had an orgasm or not, he was done with me. I knew I should have told him how empty I was after we had sex, but I did not say anything because I did not want to run him off again. He pulled out of me, looked downward, and his jaw opened wide. "Where the fuck is the condom?"

I used two fingers to touch inside my girlie. The semen smelled like chlorine bleach. I touched the tip of the condom and pulled it out gently. I handed the soaking wet rubber to him. He rolled the back window down and tossed it far away.

"You on birth control, right?" he asked me as he fidgets with his zipper on his pants.

"I recently started the pill," I made it known, sounding confident.

"We should be good. Let's go back to the haunted house." We rode in silence. He concentrated on the road while I stared out the passenger window wishing no egg and sperm had hooked up.

The following week, Jermaine and I got together over the weekend and hung out at his cousin Cedric's house. We watched movies, and today, we drank a few beers. I liked the buzz from the beer, but not the burps. Jermaine offered me a joint to smoke with him. At first, I hesitated, but Jermaine reassured me his cousin could care less. Jermaine intensified my sensitive spot when he whispered how much he loved me during sex. A night filled with ecstasy was a special moment. We had been extra careful not to slip up again with the condom.

My screwing position with him was the missionary style. I got to the peak of an orgasm, but he went limp before the orgasm came. He offered to let me rub up against his penis, but it did not stimulate me enough. My vagina was used and not satisfied. *Should I pretend to be with Nicholas?* I confessed after we finished, "Jermaine...I am not getting an orgasm when we have sex. You need to help me."

His facial expression revealed how he disliked my comments. His eyes became watery and red, and he pushed me hard off him. I landed on the blue shaggy stained carpet floor. My heart raced with fear.

"Say what! Candee girl, are you fucking serious? You saying as much sex we been having you been faking getting a nut! What the fuck is this about?"

"I wanted you to care enough to know I used to..." I blubbered.

He blasted back. "You used to what, get off with white mother-fucker, Nicholas?" He stared at me as if he wanted to slap me. It was the first time I was afraid of Jermaine. I did not have the impression I was safe. It was over, his pants were up, and he expressed he was ready to go. When we came out of the bedroom, his cousin Cedric was playing cards with some other boys.

"Yo... man, we out," Jermaine mumbled walking toward the front door. My head low, but I gave Cedric a quick wave goodbye. I was humiliated.

Another hushed ride home with Jermaine seemed like an endless journey. I knew his proud ass was too arrogant to admit he needed to step it up in bed. Moreover, yes, I was too afraid to ask him to bring the subject back up. Therefore, I stared out the window doubtful if my boyfriend even cared for me. My stomach was burning inside making me nauseated. I wiggled from side-to-side trying to get comfortable, swallowing the spit in my mouth, and struggling not to puke inside his truck. I cracked the window to suck in the fresh air. The weather was refreshing it pampered my face. He turned the radio on and turned up the volume. My favorite song was on by Al Green, "Look What You Done to Me," which put my mood into a unique perspective. *This must be how love is when someone is jealous of you. This is how they show you they care.* I rehearsed those words repeatedly as if to brainwash myself.

Over the next week, nausea came and went early in the morning before I got out of bed. I looked at the calendar on the wall and knew my menstrual cycle was late by 14 days. Last month out of desperation and puberty hormones, Momma turned the den into another bedroom. It was smaller than the other bedroom, but our little space was divine.

I sat up on the edge of my bed. I now shared a bedroom with Cara who was snoring loudly in her bed. My head dizzy and my throat watery. Unlike before, I would get sick and not vomit, but this time I had no choice; it was coming up anyway. I sprinted to the toilet and dropped my head into the clean porcelain bowl. I thanked the blue sky the lid was raised. I hurled hard a couple of times, and the toilet water splashed me in the face. There was no food coming up, merely green slimy acid stuff.

I flushed the green monster in the sewer. I held my belly as I stood up. I got a washcloth and wet it with lukewarm water. To my surprise, momma heard me throwing up and knocked on the bathroom door. "Candee, open this door."

I hesitated but knew she was coming in even if she had to break the door. She was a momma detective; seek, find, and solve the problem.

I unlocked the door, not knowing what she was going to say. She snapped, "Why you throwing up? You sick. Or worse – pregnant? When the last time you had a period?"

I sat on the toilet seat trying to regain my strength. I wanted to catch up with her questions, but she kept going.

"What did you throw up, was it green?" she asked, looking me right in my eyes.

"Yes, it was, why?" I asked.

"You might be pregnant. I know you and black ass Jermaine, screwing around. All the reason I wanted to get you on the pill. God knows you don't need a baby. I'm struggling as it is. Lord, another mouth to feed." She shook her head in disbelief and rubbed her hands through her long curls. "Get your clothes on now we're going up to the clinic."

I was wishing hard. My mouth was dry from pleading not to be pregnant. "No, no, not now. Please, I can't do this," I whispered to the air in my bedroom. I threw on a pair of velveteen jogging pants, a cotton T-shirt, and my tennis shoes. My hair braided with hundreds of colorful beads. I heard the beads tapping together as I hurried out the front door to get in the car with momma.

"Crystal, I am going to take Candee to the clinic, she act like she got a stomach bug. Look after your sisters. And do not leave this dang house!"

On the way to the car, my momma's steps were high and

forceful like a horse on steroids. I could see her face was disappointed. As she gripped the steering wheel hard turning her knuckles white.

"Buckle up." Her voice was cold. I am feeling guilty to put her through this. "If you are pregnant, I don't know how you are going to go to school and juggle a baby, but you are going to finish school. If your father was here..." she retorted and put the car in reverse and pressed on the accelerator. When we arrived at the clinic, it was empty. Momma made a beeline to the receptionist to sign us in.

"Good morning, do you have your insurance card today?" the young, round-faced woman asked with a half-smile.

"Yes, she does." Momma located the plastic card and handed it to the woman.

"Alright, please take these consent forms and if you have had any recent changes, make a note of it." She tapped the paper with her polished red nail.

It seemed as soon as we sat in the cold hard black chairs the nurse called my name. "Candee Black."

Momma stood up first. "Here she is."

I followed them to the examining room.

"Hi, my name is Nurse Tammy." The Nurse smiled and took my weight and height, and asked the reason for today's visit.

"She needs to take a pregnancy test. She been throwing up and I know those signs; I've had four babies," Momma shared, as she placed her hands on her hips.

"Alright, no problem. Candee, how long have you been sexually active?" The nurse outright asked me holding the clipboard with a pen ready to write the condemning answer.

"A few months." I lied, of course.

"Are you taking the birth control pills as instructed?" The next question warranted a true answer, but I fibbed a little. "I took a few later than I was supposed to this month, but not missing any." The truth, I skipped four days in a row because they were making me nauseated.

"I will be right back to take your blood and urine." She left the room.

The room was sterile, smelling like alcohol, and the floor was a dull yellow but appeared clean. When I was nervous, I found anything to count to pass the time. Therefore, I counted the tiles on the floor. Eleven rows of twelve tiles each equals 132. I stared up at the ceiling to see what else I could concentrate on – anything but my momma's face. In walked Nurse Tammy with a clear plastic cup with my name and birthdate scribbled on the label. She instructed me on how to wipe and where to place the cup after peeing in it. I followed her to the hall bathroom.

"If you have a hard time going, let me know. I can give you a cup of water."

"I should be fine, thanks." I closed the door.

I took a seat on the toilet and wanted to cry, but there was no time for a self-pity party. I placed the cup of warm golden urine in the hole in the wall. I washed my hands, and made silly faces in the mirror. I bite my nails as I sit in a trance staring at the cold linoleum floors. I must admit I was terrified about what the results might reveal. During the act of having intercourse, I did not worry about getting pregnant. I loved having sex, but a baby was not part of the equation. Next, I gave two tubes of blood, and the probing was over. The nurse explained the results would be available in about two hours and if positive, an appointment would be set up to see the doctor.

Back at the house, Momma sat by the telephone like a mother hen brooding over her little chickens. My dad who now lived about an hour away with his new woman dropped by to give momma child support money.

"My babies… daddy got y'all a lot of candy in this bag." He tossed the bag on the kitchen table; it made a thump on the wood. We loved candy. Therefore, we dashed to grab the bag at the same time. Crystal overtook Christian, the closest and the smallest of us, her little hands defeated.

"Stop it! Daddy, I had the bag first!" she whimpered, getting momma's attention.

"What in the world is going on now? Joseph, why the hell did you bring candy in this house?"

Daddy cowardly ducked into the bathroom to escape the raging lunatic.

"You should at least bring a gallon of damn milk, bread, and eggs for your growing daughters!" Momma sounded infuriated as she pounded on the bathroom door. I figured daddy had passed out because he did not respond to her. On the other hand, he was ignoring her once again. I intervened with the candy bag and passed out pieces.

As soon as the calm came, the storm was brewing again; the

phone rang. Momma a nervous wreck stumbled to pick it up. "Hello, yes, this is her mother. Really... thank you." She hung up the phone and yelled for me to come see her.

My momma talked with a no compassion in her voice. "The results say you are about five weeks pregnant. The doctor appointment is..." My mind went blank, and I could no longer hear her words. *Pregnant. No, I do not want to be.* I repeated these words, hoping it was a bad dream and when I woke up it would be over. My heart pumping, but not fast enough. I might pass out.

Dad emerged from the bathroom looking stunned. He was mute for about 30 seconds. Momma, however, was going on and on about how promiscuous I must be and what a bad mistake I had made.

He spoke up. "Listen, Charlene, I know we were taken by this news. I agree with your mom, this is not a smart choice to be having sex and getting pregnant at your age. However, we all make mistakes. You're my daughter, I am here for you." He gave me a quick one arm hug and announced to us he had to go back to work. Momma rolled her eyes at him and me.

I have cold feet about calling Jermaine and telling him the news. Nonetheless, my momma said she would call his mother if I did not tell him. I spoke to him two separate times and avoided telling him each time. On the third call to say goodnight, I blurted I had been sick and went to the clinic today, and I was pregnant. He was silent for about 10 seconds and blurted out, "Fuck, it ain't mine, you better call white ass Nicholas or one of them other dudes and tell them the shitty news!"

He hung up the phone. I redialed, and it was busy. I tried five times dialing the number and got a busy tone each time. I gave up playing the game of betrayal.

Chapter Eight: All Work and No Play

I was five months pregnant when Jermaine saw me again. We had sex without condoms since I could not get re-pregnant. He liked screwing me from behind, but I did not let him touch my booty hole. On several occasions, I contacted yeast infections. I was under the assumption it had to do with being pregnant a hormonal imbalance.

However, the other day at the clinic, I came across a pamphlet about STDs. The pamphlet explained they are caused by the overgrowth of a type of yeast called Candida. It's either Jermaine or me who was contaminated. I kept a calendar to track when we had sex and if I already had a yeast infection before or after sex. Yeast infections were torture. My coochie was raw, burned when I peed, and itched bad. I had to get this creamy white medication to cure it. My doctor was concerned the baby would contract a bacterial infection. He informed me to use condoms to protect the baby and me. This month I had treated two yeast infections.

From the looks of what I read from the calendar, Jermaine was cheating on me—again. I knew in my heart this baby was Jermaine's, but I was no fool. He seemed eager to see whom the baby would look like when it was born. My baby was due around the end of the June. I was not looking forward to the hot weather and being fat. I loved being pregnancy; except the morning sickness. I had to eat dry saltine crackers to coat my stomach before rising in the morning. My morning ritual was eating two crackers on my back, sitting up gradually, and waiting 5 to 10 minutes before shifting my body. I was afraid to eat breakfast because I threw it up within an hour of eating. I was normally hungry before the first-period class at school.

Today was a half-day at school because tomorrow was a teacher workday for the Good Friday holiday. After lunch period, I had my art class; I loved to draw and paint. I walked through the gym to cut a few minutes. As I got closer, I saw a familiar face I had not seen in months. It was nasty girl Francine. I heard a rumor while back she was expelled from a private school. It was hush, hush why it happened. She was eyeing me as if she had supernatural powers and could set me on fire.

"Girl, I see you poking out now. You know Jermaine say it ain't his. You look shocked to hear this... news." Her voice was low and brassy.

This whore had a gap front tooth. I wanted to slap another tooth out. I ignored her insults as I walked past her. A knot welling up in my throat. I could hear her roaring obscenities. Fear overwhelmed me. I professed to myself, this nasty cockroach gonna be squashed! Instead of going to class, I detoured to the restroom. I bat my eyes to fight the tears. I took a long huff and let out. "I hate that stanking bitch!"

I made it to class five minutes later. My teacher was a sympathetic person. He seen me coming in the class looking distraught. He assumed the baby was in trouble. "Candee, you don't look good. What's going on?"

I gathered my composure. "Mr. Shook, I'm weak. I've been nauseated today."

"Sure, no problem. I tell you what, you can stay in class and do what you can with the self-portrait assignment. Or you can go to the nurse's office and finish the project at home." He gave me a friendly smile. I chose to stay in class.

I took my seat next to my cousin Eunice aka 'Sugarbear', who identified herself as a Dyke or Lesbian. She was a stout girl with short Afro-style hair. Eunice had about ten tattoos on her body. She got the nickname Sugarbear from her first girlfriend. The story was, right before they kissed, Eunice was eating a sugar cookie and did not have time to chew on a mint. The girlfriend ended up with cookie in her teeth. Eunice could not get away from the story without getting a name for it. "What's up, cousin Candee? How is the baby? You two aight?"

I smiled at her, but it did not last.

I tried hard to concentrate on my drawing to fight back the tears. I am such a cry baby. I wiped my eyes with the tissue in my jacket and told her why I was upset. Her head bobs up and down as she listened to my frustrations. She leaned close to my face and whispered, "Cousin, you know blood is thicker than bullshit. I will say nothing else this situation will end today. No worries. It is going to be fine. Trust me." It was no surprise Eunice was pissed about Francine taunting me, to what degree was what concerns me.

As soon as class dismissed, Eunice acted as my bodyguard and walked me along the hallway to my locker. No, Francine in sight. I grabbed my book bag and headed to my last class of the day, good ole Social Studies. Eunice went in the opposite direction. It was the end of the day, and I was getting sleepy. It never failed, after I ate I was ready to lie somewhere with a pillow and blanket. I took a seat and got out my notebook, prepared to be bugged eyed bored. After we reviewed last night's homework the current event news, we focused on working on the study guides for the next assignment. I wanted to sleep, but instead, I wrote a letter to Jermaine to clear my head about Francine's remarks.

On the way to the bus, I saw a crowd of students gathered around the picnic benches next to the football field. There was howling and cursing loud enough to get the attention of several bus monitors and teachers. I was too drained to walk near the commotion. I got on my bus before the crowd came. Several of the students were talking about what was going on.

I found an empty seat near the front on the right side. I rested my head on the window and heard several students yell it was a fight between two girls!

"Did you see how Sugarbear slapped the piss out of Francine?"

I looked up. "Did you say Sugarbear is fighting?"

"Yep," a tall black boy replied. I smiled inside knowing the hussy would be out of my life.

On Sunday, I went to church with my family. It had been months since I'd been inside a church. I was sinful. I didn't want to face the church folks because I was pregnant. I forced a smile, held my head high, and found a seat on the third row with Crystal and Christian. The sermon touched my heart, and as usual, I fought back the tears. Much to my surprise, many greeted me with open arms during and after the service. I left engrossed about my mistakes and hoping God would forgive me. Reverend William's wife Delores followed me to the restroom to see how I was doing.

"Candee, how have you been? We have missed seeing you here." Her voice was soft and kind.

"Hi Mrs. Delores, I am doing as best as I can," I tried to sound positive.

"Praise God, if you need anything, please let us know." Her eyes glistened as she kept on talking. "A year ago, the church provided clothing and food for teen mothers. I cannot imagine being in your shoes." She gave me a tight hug and walked out. I swallowed her words. *In my shoes... I am walking alone after all.*

The baby was active during the day. I saw her knee sticking out my right side. I knew it was a girl. My mother and cousins agreed because of the way I carried her. I was round, and my stomach was high up close to my boobs. I gained 27 pounds and the morning sickness was getting better. Instead of having nausea daily, it was now a couple times a month. My skin was glowing, and my hair and fingernails were growing. I applied mineral oil over my tummy, butt, and breasts to prevent stretch marks.

After school, I spent most of my time at home writing baby names and collecting used baby clothes from my cousins who'd already had children. I missed hanging out with Vaughn and the others, though. I struggled with facing the truth I was a single teenage parent. My fun days were over. I tried to stay positive and sing and read books to my growing baby girl. I craved ice, salt, and pickles.

Therefore, I fixed a substantial cup of ice cubes, doused it with salt, and went to sit on the cemented front porch steps. My view is obstructed by sunflowers beaming bright and towering over 4ft. They are Momma's favorite blooming flowers in the summer. I got a glimpse of Vaughn, Lil FIFI, and Tiny, strutting up the street. I spoke to them, and they came over.

"Look at you. Puffy as a tick. Now I can tell you carrying a bun in the oven", Tiny joked.

"Girl, I am lucky to not be as wide as a house. Do you remember when my cousin Brittani was pregnant? Girl, she gained 50 pounds. She was miserable. Her baby weighed 6 pounds when he was born. Which means she carried 44 extra pounds for nothing." I smirked, rolling my neck and snapping my fingers.

"Do you know if it's a boy or girl?" Vaughn asked.

"I think it's a girl. You know my people believe in old wives' tales. I got no money for one of those sonograms. My boobs say it." I giggled. We chatted for a brief time to catch up with each other. Being identical twins was seldom misleading because Tiny had a piercings, and wore her favorite color; pink. Both girls had nutmeg skin color that oozed with pimples, but they were still pretty to me.

"Tiny, what in the world were you thinking to get such pain?"

She swung her beaded braids around her shoulder. "Lil FIFI and I had a bet over who would win the last football game. As you can see I lost." She giggled.

Lil FIFI continued to explain this madness. "She was getting her nose pierced and dared me to do it too, but I declined."

I snorted laughing holding my belly. "Good old sibling rivalry."

They both seemed excited about the school prom coming up next month. Tiny disclosed she was going alone this time. Vaughn said she had to go with Donovan since he liked boys, but was trying to hide the truth. A sense of dejection felt because I would not attend the high school prom. Vaughn offered to have a baby shower for me and hearing this news excited me. I told her she was welcome to arrange it because my mom was not overjoyed with my pregnancy.

Vaughn said, "Candee, we should do the shower a month before the due date because you cannot predict, you might go early."

"You are right, I guess. Let me know which Saturday is good for you. I will invite my cousins and a few other people," I said. I envied their life of freedom. I wanted to beg Father Time to rewind. Sadly, I was evolving into motherhood and had no room for playtime.

Over the next couple of months, my energy level was low, even though my appetite had slowly picked up. Jermaine had been busy working full-time at Eckerd's warehouse. He detested his job as a forklift operator, but it paid $175.00 a week, so he tried not to complain too much. After he graduated, he had hoped to get a scholarship for college football. Unluckily, even though he had applied to several universities, he did not get any appealing offers. I could see he was depressed about it, but he would not admit it. He had not denied the baby since Eunice whooped Francine's ass and she cussed Jermaine out about cheating on me. Time after time, he made smart remarks about me sleeping around on him too. I tore up the letter I wrote in class for fearing the worst could happen. I kept my frustrations concealed in my heart.

Lately, I had ignored his smart-ass mouth, but in reality, I wanted him to know I needed him. Last week, he gave me money to get my horse size vitamins and bought me a maternity top. I guess I should have been content and not have nagged him. I knew my cousin Sasha's baby daddy left her before she had her baby. It was no surprise momma had not shown me any favoritism by being pregnant. She flat out told me I was bringing another mouth to feed on a poor man's budget. I did not want to apply for welfare assistance because I was too prideful, but I did not have a choice when I added up the cost of formula and diapers. I comprehend I couldn't depend on Jermaine. I vowed my baby would have all it needed as long as I was alive.

The baby shower was held at my house. Jermaine did not come. He said he had to work, but would try to drop in later. I was not going to bet on it. For once, momma was in a decent mood. She invited my two aunts and her two neighbors to come over as well. She made delicious deviled eggs, chicken finger sandwiches, cookies, chips, and a bowl of sherbet punch. Do not ask me what was in this punch. All I knew was it was covered in white foam, and the liquid was green. It tasted good. I guessed because it was cold and it was burning up outside. I was sweating between my milky breasts and craving salt. My doctor told me I was anemic and I should avoid salty foods. However, this didn't deter my craving to suck on salty ice cubes.

"Crystal, can you get me a glass of ice water please?" I sounded like I was begging her. She was sitting next to me on the flowered covered couch as my guests arrived.

"Sure. Do you want me to add a little salt?" She winked back.

I shook my head; however, I asked her to bring me a pickle instead.

Vaughn and my mom were hosting the baby shower like professionals. I counted 16 people attending even though I invited at least 27. I zoned across the room to the small table where the gifts were and counted them. It looked like there were about ten of them. *Who did not bring a gift?* We played games like pick the baby name, a word puzzle about me, and name the baby picture. We laughed hysterically. I had to wobble to the bathroom twice. I hadn't had this much fun in a long, long time.

It was time to open the gifts. Vaughn handed me each gift to open or unwrap and I read each card if there was one. I opened ten gifts and four cards. My baby had two warm blankets, one yellow and one blue, four combs and hairbrush sets (*this was bad luck, my baby gonna be bald*), one pack of burping bibs, five packs of newborn disposable diapers, a pack of cloth diapers, several plastic bottles, washcloths, one bathing set, six onesies, and a car seat. There was money in the cards totaling $40.00. This baby shower was a blessing.

I woke up, as usual, prepared to go to school, but the baby had another plan. My back was in terrible pain. The baby was not due for three more weeks. I tried to sit up to go to the bathroom because my bladder was screaming. As soon as I stood up, a gush of warm water trickled on my legs. I was petrified. My mind went to a pamphlet I'd read in the clinic. It explained the details about what to expect when going into labor. In my mind, I checked off the warning signs; *Water breaking, check. Pain in my lower tummy or back, check. Tummy is hard, check.*

Fear overtook me and signaled my brain to get ready to deliver the baby. "Maaa, Maaa, the baby is coming out!" I wailed, holding my legs together and wobbling steady toward the bathroom. I heard someone running down the short hallway.

"Candee, where you at?" It was Mom, and she sounded nervous.

"I'm in the bathroom." I squatted on the toilet seat to see if more water would come out.

"No girl, get up from there. You want the baby to fall in the piss water? Get up, I need to see what's going on."

"Momma my water broke, and my back is hurting bad." My eyes teared up.

"It sounds like you may be in labor earlier than expected. Let's get you changed and head to the hospital." Mom's voice tone sounded concerned for once.

Mom left a message for dad at work to tell him what was going on. He was working two hours away on a job site. As I was dressing, I wanted to call Jermaine. I second guessed myself and asked, *is he going to act right? We are not on good speaking terms. Does he want to be there when the baby is born?* We were barely talking, and the pregnancy had made our relationship distant and cold.

I heard my mom speaking loudly, "You better call Jermaine and tell him to hightail his sorry ass to the hospital!" I did not want to deal with his rejection. I guessed I needed to face the truth he may not show up in time or not at all.

It was Thursday morning, the clock read 8:05. He should

already be at work. The phone rang two times, and the receptionist answered, "Good morning, how may I direct your call?"

"Hi, I have an emergency call for Jermaine McDoogle," I stated, trying to sound grown up.

"Please hold," she said civilly. Soft classical music played while I waited. After about two minutes she returned, "Yes ma'am his supervisor is going out to get him, it may take a few more minutes."

There was pressure in my vaginal area. I held back the flow of air and let out a low squeal. Mom walked in and gasped at my discomfort.

"Candee, hang up the damn phone! Let's go now before you have the baby here." I hung up before hearing Jermaine's voice.

There must have been a full moon because when we arrived at the hospital, we went to a waiting area for expectant mothers not ready to deliver because there were no available delivery rooms. My mom was not amused and asked to see a supervisor. I was aching all over. I wanted to scream, but it was too awkward in front of momma. She was pacing back and forth, chewing her pink polished fingernails. I had not seen this kind of reaction in her before. The wheelchair I was in was uncomfortable. It numbed my butt as if I was sitting on cardboard. I wanted to get up move around, but it hit me like a car. Pain – excruciating pain!

I panted in and out and focused on a hanging picture. A beautiful bouquet of flowers hung framed in mahogany wood; a mere distraction from the chaos in my tummy. I mouthed a silent plea. "God if you are real, please take this pain away. I cannot take it any longer. I am helpless." Tears flooded my eyes.

Momma grabbed a wad of tissues. "Shoot Candee, I am sorry you are going through this. You are but a child yourself. Where in the world is the baby daddy? He should be here too!" She sounded like she was losing her mind. I needed Daddy to be here instead of her. He was the calm one when chaos brewed.

A plump woman in a white nurse outfit approached my mom and spoke as if she smelled her upper lip. "Miss, we are trying to assist each person in the best way possible. We hope to have each new mother in her room shortly." She walked out of the room over to the tall whiteboard hanging on the wall. She scribbled on it and approached a young girl whose face was flushed and petrified. "The doctor is on his way. Your contractions are less than five minutes now. It shouldn't be much longer before you deliver."

I watched the nurse disappear as she walked farther from my view. The next hour went by like a blur because my labor pains were coming about 15 minutes apart. I was sharing a room with two other girls. Momma called home, and Auntie Belinda was there with my sisters. There was a small color TV playing on a tall armoire. The weatherman was talking, but I couldn't hear what he was saying. It was a good distraction to help me pretend not to be in the moment of torment. My mind cluttered with playing the game of guilt and regret. *I will not have any more babies coming out of my coochie! I hate myself for allowing this to happen! My future is ruined! Forget about going to college!*

I was shaved, stuck with an IV, and gave an enema within 10 minutes in the room. The hospital gown is for the birds because it exposed my ass. I motioned to my mom to help me to the restroom. I puked up green stuff and water at one end, and at the other end the poop poured out. The labor pains had me in a fetal position. The reality of my whole insides was coming out, must be an alien! My head hovered a pink plastic square bowl. Mom held it steady as I threw up my guts. I dared not look at her facial expression.

A white-headed older man with brown rimmed glasses entered the room, "Hi, my name is Dr. Smith. I will deliver your baby hopefully sometime today. I need to check you to see if you have dilated anymore since being admitted." He gave a quick smile and turned to put on the latex gloves. The worst thing about it was I had no control. There was no time to take a timeout. Contemplate if you want them to touch you. It was going to happen, ready or not. The doctor was standing in front of me. He had large hands. "Please relax your legs, Miss Black. I am now going to place my fingers inside your vagina to see how much you have dilated." His voice was calm. I held my breath for about five seconds, and another contraction came.

I panted like a dog in the desert. His voice was soft but firm like a loving, strict father. "Take deep breaths, you are about seven centimeters. We are going to prep you for delivery." He peered over his square glasses at the heart monitor. "The heart is strong, and the baby is in position. You may have one immediate family member and the baby's father in with you."

For the first time since she discovered I was pregnant, my momma gave me a smile and said, "Thank the good Lord, we gonna have us a healthy baby soon."

Chapter Nine: Counting Time

My baby boy came into the world at 4:26 p.m., on July 4, 1979, weighing 5 pounds, 10 ounces and 19 inches long. His skin tone was transparent and tan but smooth all over. His hair was thick and jet-black. His eyes closed as he screamed air into his lungs. Seeing his beautiful face completed my world. The pain and tears were worth it. While the doctor gave me four small stitches near my butt crack, I watched the nurses clean my baby. Mom was there too and told me he had 10 fingers and 10 toes. My heart filled with overflowing joy! The nurse did a few tests on him to make sure he didn't have any issues since he was three weeks early. The nurse reported my baby was in good health to be born early. She gave him to me to hold. I kissed the top of his soft, warm head. He sucked on his bottom lip. Soft tears flowed. I loved those tears!

Momma was overjoyed with tears. "Candee, you did an excellent job. He is beautiful."

I give him to Momma to hold before wheeling off to my room.

I was wiped out. Frankly, I was at peace even though Jermaine was not there to celebrate with me. I closed my eyes to rest them. When I awoke, I saw Jermaine and my Dad sitting on the tan tweed sofa. I shared the room with another girl, and she had company too.

Dad came over to say he was sorry to have missed the birth, but admitted he didn't have the stomach to watch.

"This little boy is going to be a football player. He looks strong already," he commented.

I smiled at his puff dream. Jermaine walked up grinning at first and took my right hand and kissed it. "I got here as fast as I could. I wanted to be here. You believe me, right?" His eyes were watery, and his voice was shaky. Dad got the hint we needed to talk, he excused himself. Jermaine made up excuses for what seemed like an hour for his mistakes and for missing the birth of our son.

When he stifled on his last words, I chimed in, "I hear you. I want us to get past the messy stuff. I love you." Those three words came out fast caused me to grasp. I could not take them back.

He put his hands around my face and gently kissed me and whispered, "I love you too. I have never stopped."

The following day, the baby scheduled for his circumcision. Jermaine paid for it because the government insurance would not. "No son of mine is ever going around with a dirty dick." Jermaine blurted out to Dr. Smith. The doctor had scheduled us to discharge after the baby cleared from surgery. We could go to the nursery to see him through the window before the procedure. Dr. Smith announced he did not give the baby boys any medication for the surgery. My heart fluttered envisioning his pain. A nurse reviewed with us how to give the aftercare to the delicate area. Jermaine was tight-lipped, but he grimaced.

Motherhood was a 24-hour job; it does not offer any money or benefits. I was learning each day how resilient I had become. Our baby favored Jermaine at first, but after about two weeks, he looked more like the both of us. When it came time to name our son, I named him Joshua. Simply, because I was pissed at Jermaine pretty much most of my pregnancy. Since he was acting stupid professing he was not my baby daddy, I wasn't about to name him anything close to his name. I called him 'Pooh' as a nickname. I gave him the nickname because of the way he slept with his little butt in the air. I had recovered as well as I could. My stomach disappeared right after giving birth. My tummy area was soft like a pillow. I did about ten sit-ups in my bed each day. I wanted my size 4 back!

I was soon exhausted from getting up in the middle of the night with the baby. He slept a couple of hours, and he was hungry, wet, and back to sleep. There was about two more weeks until I had to return to school when I heard hard knocks at the front door. I heard Cara talking to someone. She shouted out, "Candee, it's Jermaine and his mother!"

His mother? I had no idea they were dropping by. I hoped he brought diapers and milk with him. "Why is he showing up now?" I blasted at the wall. I heard Cara offering them a seat in the living room.

"Can I get you both a drink? Momma makes the best sweet tea."

"I do love sweet tea, but my blood sugar is occasionally too high. Can I have a glass of ice water?" his mother asked.

"Sure, it's no problem. Jermaine, you want water or tea to drink?"

"I'm good. Thanks, Cara."

I swaddled our newborn son up to meet his new grandmother Patricia McDoogle aka the town gossip. I had a personal issue with her. I heard she was the main person spreading rumors about Nicholas was my baby daddy and not Jermaine. I needed to address it with her but not today. I sighed deeply and walked into the room with a half-smile on my face. Jermaine knew me well enough to know it was my *'What the hell do you want?'* expression. His mother smiled and asked if she could hold her grandson. I said nothing and placed Joshua into her arms.

"He smells good, and he has Jermaine's nose and lips," she sounded proud and inspected him from head to toe. I took a seat next to Mrs. McDoogle, trying not to grit my teeth, as she smelled my baby like a plate of crispy bacon. I counted the lines in the wood grain on the wall to keep from boiling over with words of distaste. I glared up at Jermaine as he kept his eyes on Joshua.

"So how did you come up with his name?" his mother asked, looking right at me.

I cleared my throat. I knew her snake tongue would come out wagging, I lied. "It's a biblical name; it was my first choice."

Her face color vanished as she replied, "He should have been a junior. It's what most folks do when it is the first male born. But you young people do what you do, I guess."

I rolled my eyes. Before I could speak again, my sister brought the glass of ice water for the thirsty dragon.

"Candee, I want to give you some money," Jermaine assured and handed me a wad of cash. "I will make sure I give you money on a regular basis."

I was speechless at first but easily recovered. "Jermaine, that's good, but we need to talk about his daycare and how much it's going to be."

"Sounds good to me," he replied with a smirk on his face. I knew he wanted to get me alone and ask when could we have sex again. It was a freaking trap! I vowed not to fall into it until I was on a stronger birth control!

Later, Jermaine and I talked on the phone for two hours. For the first time, he talked like a mature man. We both expressed how much our lives were affected by becoming parents at such young ages. I let him know how doubtful I was about him taking care of his son. "My motherly instinct has kicked in non-stop while you have been breezing right along with your life as though we do not exist. The way I see it is this, you have been acting as though you don't want to see the baby unless you can get between my legs!" I blasted in his ears.

"Hold up, you know good damn well it's not about me wanting to have sex. Why should sex change because we got a baby now? I had a high sex drive before the baby, it ain't no surprise. I need a piece of your ass!" His voice was deep and condescending.

I was speechless since he did not get what I was saying. "I gotta go take care of my baby!" I hung up the phone with tears welling up. I refused to waste tears on his crap! It was 10:15 at night and time for me to wake Joshua for his night feeding. I was exhausted as usual and hoped to get in the bed before midnight. This was the reality Jermaine had yet to experience.

Vaughn was coming by this morning to see how we were

106

doing. She took a sick day from school and came to hang out with me. I was excited to see her. It seemed like forever since we had a gossiping moment. The house was tranquil with the smell of baby lotion lingering in the air. I enjoyed the quietness. I bundled Joshua in his soft yellow cotton blanket and sat in the rocking chair to put him to sleep. I was in love with him. He seemed content after his feeding and a warm bath. I winked at him and smiled. I loved singing to him a lullaby momma used to sing to me as a baby. "Go to sleep, go to sleep, go to sleep, my little baby. Sleepyhead goes to bed; may your cares go away. May your days be bright, your tomorrows be long. Happy land is here, goes traveling on."

His sweet eyes fluttered as if he was trying to fight sleep and he focused on my face. I cradled him close to my breast and rocked him until he fell asleep. I kissed him on top of his curly head and tiptoed to his bassinet. I removed his blue teddy bear and placed him om his back. It terrified me to hear sad stories about babies not waking up.

I heard someone at the front door. I creeped out of the bedroom and walked briskly and saw through the faded cream curtains it was Vaughn. She was wearing her shoulder-length no curls golden blonde wig. We all knew black people did not have blonde hair. In addition, curly hair if you were mixed with white people. Last time I checked, Vaughn was a full-bloodied black girl.

"Hi girl," she hugged me tight. I squeezed her back because I missed her dearly. "Were you busy? I meant to call you before dropping by."

I let out a sigh of exhaustion. "Girlfriend, I am one burned out momma. I laid Joshua in his bassinet for his morning nap. Somedays, I need to crawl up beside him in his bassinet." We both let out a few giggles, and within a few seconds, the conversation turned serious.

"How are you? I know this new baby must be an overload for your entire family," she voiced firmly. One thing about Vaughn she was like a momma hen to me. She seemed to know when I was not all right, even though I might say otherwise.

"Girl, I confess I hoped to be a supermom when the baby got here. I dreamed about breastfeeding him and using cloth diapers to prove I could be a great mommy. My head was in a cloud after reading the *How to Parent* books. The truth is, I am trying to survive," I admitted.

"How are you and your man?" Her facial expression revealed she knew he was being an ass.

"To tell you the truth V, our fairytale is in limbo. It has been for a long time. I know it, and he runs from the truth. I believe in my heart he had not been with just me. He would avoid confessing it, even when..." I catch myself before saying too much. "Even when I asked him he doesn't answer. Besides, I need to return to school, get my diploma, get a job, and take care of my baby." I was vulnerable, and my lips trembled. Soon the waterfall was dripping, and I needed to blow my nose. Crying was stupid! I need to stop wasting brain water.

Vaughn went into the bathroom and brought me a wad of tissues. She was speechless and did not know what to say to soothe me.

I gathered my raw and wry state of mind and spoke first. "I

know, I know, you warned me about him and I didn't listen. I lied to my parents and to myself defending Jermaine; saying he was good to me. I am reminded he is simply for himself and even with our son; Jermaine is selfish."

Vaughn sniffed. "Girl, I have to tell you a secret I have been holding onto for over a year. I thought I was pregnant by the jerk from Tower Heights Estates, Alton. I had been taking the birth control pills for a couple weeks, but they were making me sick." She sucked on her front teeth and pulled on the back of her hair as though it shifted.

I chimed in to keep the conversation going. "Yeah, I remember you telling me he was such a dog!"

Her eyes widened. "We did it, and girl, he had the smallest dick!"

We both giggled. "I took the pills whenever and one day I threw up! My momma panicked, and she told my dad we needed to go to the clinic. It was chaotic in my house. They both agreed if I was pregnant, I was going directly to the pregnant girl school in Charlotte. Deliver and let a rich couple adopt the baby. We went to the clinic, and I took the pregnancy test and praise Jesus, no baby! Talk about elated. I was the first saint to shout at church on Sunday morning. I knew at 15 years old; my life would've been horrible. I didn't like babies! I mean, your baby is sweet, but for me, I did not want one."

She sounded elated, and I was bewildered. *Vaughn kept a secret from me, and I have kept secrets too.* "V, I need to come clean with you about a secret I have kept too. You remember when we went to the football game with Mallory?"

"Yep, what happened?" She asked curiously.

"The same night, I caught Jermaine getting a blowjob from Francine."

Her mouth dropped open. "No, Candee."

"Yep, I wanted to tell you, but I was too distraught. I had recently lost my virginity to him and…" I took a pause. "It's no surmountable deal now, we talked about it, and he apologized to me."

She shook her head in disbelief. "Girl, you are a much better person than I will ever be. I am not one for violence, but I would have cut his dick off and made her eat it!" She busted out laughing.

"Girl, you know I was thinking it too," I laughed with her.

In an instant, she changed the subject. "Girlfriend, let me tell you the latest news about Mallory and new boyfriend, Walter Leeks. I heard he's old enough to be her daddy."

I sat upright and widened my eyes. "Shut up." I snickered holding my giggles to avoid laughing aloud. "And let me say this, her parents are upset. I heard her daddy might press criminal charges against the man. Girl, she has been acting like a wild child, as if wolves raised her. Sneaking out at night, skipping school, smoking cigarettes, and Lord knows what else. Her poor mother has been running the streets trying to find Mallory when she supposed to be at a friend girl's house. In truth, Mallory left with Walter in his red Porsche."

We laughed and giggled about Miss Goody Too-Shoes. We chatted for over an hour catching up on what else going on. "You know the other day guess who called me?" I asked.

"Brandon?"

I shook my head. "Nope, it would have been nice to hear his voice again, but it was Nicholas."

"Shut yo mouth," V said and covered her mouth.

"Yep, he asked me right out if the baby was his. I flat out told him Joshua was not his baby. Of course, he was relieved and said good luck with my life."

"Guys are a trip," she commented standing up to give me a hug. I object to seeing Vaughn leave; she had been such great company. Before she left, I could hear the whimpering sounds from Joshua. He was waking up from his two-hour nap. I went to get him to let Vaughn see him. Vaughn held him close to five minutes. She had no motherly instincts. We gave each other another hug, and like old times, we gave each other two fingers snaps and swirled around to leave.

Since I was on maternity leave from school, I had been able to keep up with my work by picking up schoolwork on Fridays. Most of my teachers had no problem with my situation, but there was Mrs. Donald, my Algebra teacher. For whatever reason other than being a snobby person, she seemed to forget to leave my assignments at the front office before 12 noon. I ended up sitting and waiting until after she returned from lunch. While I waited, one of my classmates, or a classmate of my friends would pop up in the office to peek at my baby boy. They commented, "He is cute, little, looks like you, and looks like Jermaine."

One day, Mason Johnson, who was my old boyfriend in the sixth grade, came to the office. "Hi Candee, I seen you through the glass window and wanted to come and speak to you. Is this your little man?"

Mason was tall, soft-spoken and nice to look at.

"Hi Mason, yes this is Joshua. He is four weeks old now," I said, pulling back the blanket for him to get a good look.

"He sure is a handsome baby. I guess you will be coming back soon?" he sounded like he misses me.

"Yeah, I have two more weeks. I hate to leave my baby with a babysitter, but I must graduate. My mom was kind enough to change her work schedule to the second shift to watch Joshua when I go back to school."

Seeing Mason reminded me, of how sweet and kind he was. We broke up simply because I had the hots for Brandon back in the day.

It was close to the fall, my favorite time of the year. I enjoyed the fresh, clean air and chilly temperatures. Even though the sun was shining today, I cannot fight doom and gloom. Life was draining for me as a teen mother going to school, and working part-time, and returning home to my baby. After applying to four different stores and going on four short interviews, and fingers crossed I got a job working at Mr. Pete's Grocery Store, which was close to the school. I worked Monday, Wednesday, Friday, and Saturday from 2 p.m. to 8 p.m. I was paid on Fridays. My paycheck was close to $55.00 after taxes. I also got government assistance with the baby milk.

When Joshua was close to six months, I would get a voucher for baby foods. Our next-door neighbor, Mrs. Sagitta Ortiz was originally from Tijuana, México. She lived with her two school-aged children and her mother. When she was working at the yarn mill last year, I was her afterschool babysitter. This all changed when she had to leave her job to stay home and care for her aging mother. It was several months later when her husband drowned during a freak fishing accident. She no longer worked outside the home. She had a home daycare. She typically had about five other children in the home. She greeted Joshua and me with a smile, and her home was nice and neat. She charged me $15.00 a week to take care of Joshua.

One Wednesday Joshua was fussy. He had the symptoms of catching a cold. I knew he was too young to be cutting teeth. I took his temperature, and it was the normal range 98.2. I decided to take him to the babysitter to not miss a day of work. I did my checklist. Diaper bag with bottles, milk, diapers, and extra changing clothes... check. I dressed him in his blue and brown teddy bear jumper outfit. It was one of his gifts at the baby shower. I bundled him up in his soft sky-blue fleece blanket and headed out the door.

At work, I was stocking canned goods for the first two hours and later, I would go on the register. I did not mind stocking, it gave me time to be alone, examine my life, and scribble my next to-do-list. I recalled the other day when I received a letter from one of my male cousins who was enlisted in the Marines. When we were kids, we talked about our dreams, about what we wanted to do after we graduated. He stayed on track and made his dreams come true. My goal to go to college and get a nursing degree did not go as planned with becoming a mommy before graduating high school.

In his last letter, he sent me pictures of his new wife and baby. He was stationed in Denver, Colorado. They looked content. I was a little envious. I knew he deserved all he had worked hard to have. I guessed I was having a long overdue pity party by myself.

"Excuse me, Miss. Miss, do you work here?"

I saw a brown-skinned heavy set, white-haired woman standing in front of me. I broke out of my trance.

"Yes, ma'am," I responded politely.

"Can you show me where to find a bag of dried prunes? I looked over there where they were last month." She pointed to the right side of the store.

"No problem, please follow me," I said trying to hold my smile.

My steps were swift and long, walking with a purpose. I observed the old woman walking with a cane and her steps labored and short. I slowed to walk beside her. We made small talk along the way to aisle 4. Time seemed to move in slow motion. Her name was Ms. Sadie Brown, widower and former schoolteacher, and had lived here for 65 years. I informed I was a single parent, student, and had a desire to go to college. She encouraged me not to give up on my dreams because they were what the heart desired. Hearing those words gave me a little hope I had not heard in a long time. After we approached our destination, I made sure she made it to check out. I walked her outside to a family member waiting in the car. It was time for me to clock in on the register. It was also the first of the month; which meant government checks needed to be cashed. This part of the job was draining, but it also made the time go by faster. Before I knew it, it was break time. I lived for those 15 minutes. I headed to the break room to find the first empty chair to relax and close my eyes.

I should've been trying to cram in some study time for my

Algebra test in the morning, but my eyes were heavy I needed a quick nap. I sprung up from what was supposed to be 10 minutes of shut-eye. I knew I had gone over my break-time. I was mad at myself. I raced to the register to find another coworker was slaving away at a line of customers. I walked over to ask how long she was going to be here and my supervisor, Mr. Marcus Pete, walked over and asked me to come to the office. He appeared taller than his 5 ft. My heart was racing with fear. *Is he going to fire me? I need this job.*

His cedar-colored face flushed from the neck up and he was not looking at me. His short-cropped haircut gave him a younger than 50-ish appearance. He stroked his thick mustache and shuffled the papers on his desk. "Candee, these past few weeks you have been doing an excellent job with no complaints from the customers." He looked up at me with a half-smile showing his dull-white stained teeth from drinking four cups of coffee most mornings. "I also find your job skills improving with little errors when balancing the cash register. However, I expect you to take your 15-minute break as scheduled. I recognize you are a teen mother and a full-time student, but let this be a verbal warning." He stretched his neck as though he was expecting a "Yes, master" from me.

"Mr. Pete, I do apologize for my tardiness. I-I- took a nap and...."

He stopped me right away. "No need to go there, I am certain you will take this as a learning experience and continue to do your job well. You do not know my story." His eyes rolled in his head. "I become a teen father when I was in the eleventh grade. I was not prepared. I had plans to leave this state to become an FBI agent." He

115

paused, and his mouth twitched. "I had to make some tough decisions as a young man. I stayed here and helped raise our son the best way we knew how. In time, the universe was on our sides, and I went to a local college, married my first and only sweetheart, and here I am today. I say this to encourage you. This job is not a stopping point for you. I can see you doing other things. Please go ahead and relieve Laverne from the cash register."

For the first time in a long time, I am rendered speechless from his kind and thoughtful words. I sensed a tug on my heart to say something. "I appreciate your story and your understanding."

Two people I barely knew spoke encouraging words of wisdom to me. After hearing Mr. Pete's story, it gave me another reason to push forward. The rest of the day at work went by with no more disruptions.

Chapter Ten: In and Out of L.O.V.E (Living On Vivid Emotions)

Each year during the holidays, my needs were less and less important. Joshua, he was my primary focus for celebrations. The upcoming Thanksgiving, as most of the previous Thanksgivings I could remember, we would go to my grandparents' house to join our close relatives. Jermaine invited us to his house for later. He promised he would come to pick up Joshua and me from my grandparents' house.

Thanksgiving was a wonderful time to relax, release, and regroup with my distant family who I loved being around because we had fun and we laugh a lot. It was a special year because Joshua was there and my two cousins had newborn babies as well. Tiffani and Brittani twin sisters are also teen mothers. Unfortunately, Brittani was raped. As a result, she got pregnant. Tiffani had a boyfriend who was an older man she met at a club and, after two months of dating, she got pregnant. We three could relate and shared mommy tips.

The weather was cold and wet. It had been drizzling during the morning. When we arrived at my grandparents' house, the driveway was running over with parked cars. I simply loved their enormous house! It was the last red brick house on the street. My grandfather Calvin built the house about 30 years ago. He and his family toiled the land and harvested crops and cattle. Nothing compared to living in the country. I missed visiting during summer breaks. I guessed I was too grown up now.

I saw my male cousins standing on the porch smoking cigarettes or cigars. "I need help with the food, don't jump out of the car as soon as I stop," Momma warned. Crystal was slumped against the passenger window, fast asleep. I grabbed my bundle of joy and wrapped him tightly. Inside the house, there was laughing and people spread throughout the house. My female cousins who hadn't seen Joshua yet bombard me.

"Hiya, Candee, how old is the baby?" my cousin Cici asked while taking him out of my arms.

"He is four months, 20 weeks, and 141 days and..."

She cut me off. "Girl, you a trip, you need to get out more." She burst out laughing and soon I was cracking up with her.

There was plenty of food to eat and a mouth-watering dessert. My belly was going to pop! We formed a large circle to bless the food and shared why we were thankful. The process generally took about thirty minutes, giving each person time to speak. The circle grew each year. The elders went in first to fix their plates, and the children and the rest of the folks piled in accordingly.

By 5:00 in the evening, I was ready to go and be with Jermaine, I called him to come and get us. His mother answered the phone and stated he had already left the house. I figure he was on his way to come and get us. I made my rounds to give hugs & kisses. When I hugged my grandmother Elaine, she told me how much she missed me. She wanted the baby and me to come back and visit for a weekend. The house had many sweet memories for me. Honestly, I missed spending time with my grandparents. "I give you my word Grandma Elaine, we will come back soon." I kissed her cheeks and gave my Grandpa Calvin a hug and kiss too.

I was full I decline to make a to-go plate. I had given out at least 12 hugs and kisses sensing it had been over an hour since I called Jermaine. *Where is he? What is taking him so long?* He lived less than thirty minutes from my grandparents. I worried, the worry turned to suspicion, and it all turned to anger. I heard my mom packing up plates to go and knew I might as well catch a ride home with her. The ride home was surprisingly nice for once because nobody was arguing or talking loudly. Joshua was sucking on his bottle of milk; he looked content. I stared out the back window and contemplated what and how I would curse Jermaine out for standing us up. I loathed him for making me look stupid! I could hear Brittani's voice interrogating me, "So why you not gone yet? Cuz, where is he? Did he forget about y'all?" Anger was engulfed in my throat. It was getting harder to hold back the burning tears.

As soon as we returned home, I went to check the answering machine in case he tried to contact me. The red light was blinking on the small screen. I pushed the play button and heard "click" no message. I listened to the next message, and it was another "click" and no message. *Who called?* I hoped it was Jermaine. I was too furious to call his house again.

It was the Saturday after Thanksgiving, and I was supposed to go to work, but Joshua was sick. I called my supervisor to inform him I needed to stay home today. He sounded less concerned but

119

understood and hoped my little man get well soon. As fast as I hang up the phone, it rang again. "Hello."

"Hi, Candee, what's going on with you and my son?"

I coughed to hold back using the 12-letter curse word. "What you mean? We are doing fine without yo black ass!" I screamed loud enough to blow his ears off.

"Babe, I apologize for the other day. You still pissed? I got with my homeboys they were home from college and time flew by. I want to see y'all," he said sounding sincere.

He went on and on trying to explain how they drank liquor, smoked pot, and he did not want to come around the baby. At some point, I tuned him out while he finished. "Yo... You on here?" he asked as though he already knew I had checked out.

"Yeah, I'm here," I responded dryly.

"Can I drop by today? I get off in another hour," he waited for me to answer.

I took in a slow suck and let it out. "I guess so." I conceive I gave in too easy and too soon. When I didn't like him, I hung up the phone without saying goodbye.

He arrived close to 6:00 in the evening and brought in a bag of diapers, four outfits, and $60.00 for me. I was highly impressed by his thoughtfulness. He pecked me on the forehead as if I was a baby chick. Joshua was lying in his bed, and Jermaine went into the room to get him. I put away the items and observed how Jermaine was interacting with Joshua.

"Hello, little man. Daddy is sorry he missed you on Thanksgiving." He gave Joshua a kiss on his cheeks and rocked him. It seems as though I was an intruder. I exited the room and went to the kitchen to fix my dinner plate. I offered Jermaine a plate too, but he said he was not hungry. *Good, because I was trying to be nice....* I said in my head.

I walked back to the room and saw he was rocking Joshua who had gone to sleep in his arms. I whispered softly, "He has been sick today. I called out sick from work."

Jermaine's eyes met mine. "Why didn't you call my mom ? She could have watched him for you to go to work."

I stare at him as though he was talking in a foreign language." I had no idea when you are available to help me." My body stiffened. I had to say why I was pissed before I slapped him. "Can you please put him in his crib; I need to talk to you," I said, not blinking.

We walked outside on the front porch and took a seat in the lawn chairs. I had already rehearsed in my mind what I needed to say. I wouldn't buckle from the nerve of him pointing the finger at me. "Jermaine, when you didn't show up Thanksgiving I told myself this would be the last time you would stand me up. You made me look like a fool! I am not satisfied with you. I haven't been for a long time." He wasn't giving me any eye contact. "We should break up again. We can try to be good parents without all the headaches."

He stood up and wiped his hands on his jeans as though they were wet. "Look, girl, I know we got trust issues! We both have slept around on each other. I noticed ever since the baby has been born you been trying to dump me. I have been trying to be there for you and him. I am not perfect. I do not want to break-up. I love you and him." He wiped his eyes. I didn't see any tears but seeing his

121

demeanor made me a little shamefaced in a strange way. He kept talking. "Christmas is right around the corner, and I want to spend it with you both. Can we wait until after the holidays to see if this break-up thing is what we need to do, for real?"

I listened and vowed to be civil and amicable during the holidays. "Sure, I guess it can wait. I've put up with this nonsense this long." Jermaine had once again changed my mind. Now I saw it wasn't about me, now Joshua was in the middle. He was now an important part of the equation too.

The weather had dropped 20 degrees since the night before, bringing in colder air two weeks before Christmas. The weather forecast was calling for freezing rain. I had made plans to go Christmas shopping, but changed my plans since the weather might be iffy. The good news was momma had found a nice-looking man who treated her like somebody. His name was Richard Shaw, and she met him at her second job. He was the mechanic who repaired the machinery. He had never been married. He had salt and pepper hair, and a thin mustache, and was dark skinned and about 6'3". He was from Austin, Texas and had lived in Jamestown for six years. At first, when my sisters and I met him we were standoffish. We wanted our daddy to come back home and make us a family again. We were disappointed to hear our parents did not support our opinions and informed us they were planning to divorce. After we heard the news, momma met Richard and he made our home his shortly after. Richard had a ten-year-old son from a previous relationship who lived in Washington D.C. with his mother. There was a chance the boy would visit for the holidays. I overheard Richard and momma discussing the plans.

Richard recused Joshua from the baby swing. I had left him in there to go and fix his breakfast. Joshua loved to eat! I gave him a couple spoons of baby cereal mixed in with his bottled milk. Mom said I should give him the cereal before bedtime to increase his sleep time. This advice was useful because I needed more than four hours of sleep. Therefore, my plan was to introduce the regimen at night.

I heard Richard shuffling towards the kitchen. "Candee, this boy is growing up quick! He is going to grow up and become a football player like his daddy."

I had heard it before, I giggled and said, "I don't agree 100% because his daddy is doing nothing with those football skills. I hope he develops a good common sense and plays football for fun." I got the warm bottle from the stove and offered to take Joshua, but Richard gently took the bottle from my hand and sat at the table to feed the giant baby. For a moment, I replaced Richard with Jermaine feeding our son. I yearned for it to be true.

The following day, my momma, my sisters, and Richard went to the American Legion building to buy a Christmas tree. The holiday was important to my family because we celebrated the birth of Jesus Christ and we believed in giving to the less fortunate. I stepped outside to see if the mail carrier had already come by.

I received my school report card in the mail. I opened it before putting it on mommas' bed for her viewing. I knew I had worked my butt off at least to have passing grades. I was passing all my classes, and it was a relief. I used to receive all A's and B's before getting pregnant, but thank goodness, I was able to make up the work along the way. I had 40 excused absences, which constituted my maternity leave. I saw I had a 76 in Science and Social Studies, both classes I disliked! My sisters received their report cards right before the winter school break. As far as I knew, my sisters were not flunking.

I heard the front door opening with loud talking. "Alright, as soon as Richard gets the tree up we can decorate it. Candee did you already prepare dinner?" my mother asked. We were having homemade soup with cornbread.

"Yes ma'am, the cornbread is half done, got about 10 more minutes," I said. I watched Richard struggling to pull the large and tall tree through our front door. He pulled and wiggled the branches one by one through the sides of the door. The sudden smell of pine took over the house. Richard wrestled and tussled with the tree. He stood it over in a corner in the living room. "Mannnn, the tree is massive. We picked out a good one, girls," he said smiling and wiping his forehead from the sweat.

We washed up and headed to the kitchen table. I loved homemade soup. There was nothing more soothing to eat in the winter. There was small talk at the table because we were anxious to decorate the tree. Therefore, there was less talking and more sipping on the soup. My ears were baby trained for any little noise. I listened intently in case it was Joshua. Sure enough, before I could suck up the last two spoonfuls he was crying and coughing. I made a dash to pick him up, and he was turning red and sweating profusely. His coughing sounded like he cannot get enough air in his lungs.

"Ma.... Come here! What is wrong with my baby?"

Acting like the police on a crime scene, momma and Richard

sprang into action. Momma took Joshua out of my arms, grabbed his quilted blanket, and headed for the back door. Richard was already on the phone calling 911 for assistance. My heart fluttered with fear my baby was sick and in serious trouble. I went outside to look for mom and Joshua. She had gone next door to Ms. Sagitta house. I followed, and Joshua was distressed.

I heard Ms. Sagitta saying, "The baby sick. Him coughing, poor baby. Is the ambulance on the way?" As soon as she said it, I heard the sirens getting closer to the house.

Richard knocked on Ms. Sagitta back door and walked right in with the Paramedics close behind. The paramedics asked questions about what he ate; drink, where he was at when the distress occurred. After a quick exam, they give Joshua a breathing treatment. They told me they needed to take him to the hospital to be re-examined by the Doctor to make sure he was better. A short blonde woman administering the treatment said Joshua might have had a bad reaction to food, medicines, or smells in the house. My first clue was the strong odor from the Christmas tree.

At the hospital, Jermaine met us in the emergency room. "Baby, how is my little man doing?"

"He is stable right now," I said hesitantly. I wanted to scream but knew this was not the time to lose my mind. Joshua was in a room on a bed for adults. I was close to him and rubbed his head to make sure he knew I was right here. "I love you, baby boy. It's going to be okay", I whispered to him and kissed his sweet face. I wanted to pray, but I had no idea what to say. Instead, I sang songs to soothe him before the first needle. We spent four hours at the hospital, and it was determined Joshua had a bad reaction to the pine tree.

The doctor said he could grow out of this, but his body's immune system was developing, and he was not able to fight off certain bacteria. He gave me a prescription for the coughing and runny nose and highly suggested we get rid of the tree before taking him into the house. I made a call to tell my family the good and bad news. Jermaine overheard me talking and interrupted with, "I got an idea. How about you and Joshua come and stay with mom and me until after the holidays? He can avoid another reaction, and the tree can stay in your house."

My mom overheard the suggestion. "Hmmm, don't get pregnant again. Let me ask Richard what he says, hold on."

I questioned why she needed to tell me what to do. I was not a kid anymore. Of course, I would not say this to her. Mom responded. "Alright, Richard thinks it's a decent idea for the baby's sake. We are fine with this unexpected situation because the baby needs to get better. Do you want me to pack your belongings and bring them to you?" Mom suggested.

"No thanks. I should get his prescription filled. Jermaine can bring me by. See you guys soon." I hung up the phone and said, "I have to work tomorrow. I need a ride there and a ride to the babysitter."

He rubbed his right hand across his round head. "I will call out at work tomorrow, and he can stay with me."

My eyebrows raised; problem solved.

I called Vaughn because she had heard the news about Joshua and sounded perplexed. "Hi V, we are good now. I am staying with

Jermaine until after the New Year. Joshua is fine. He is allergic to pine trees," I said, taking a full drag of oxygen.

"I thank sweet Jesus, he is much better! I can't believe his mom is allowing you to bed her son right under her roof", V giggled.

"Girl now you know I am biting my lip as we speak. She don't care for me, but she has been a good grandmother to Joshua. I'm trying to keep the peace."

"I hear ya girlfriend. I want to tell you I am dating again...but this time it is not about sex or the money. He is not from here. He has lived in Manhattan, New York most of his life and after he joined the Marines, he is everywhere. I do like him a lot. His name is Arnold Newton."

"You got you a man in a suit. I hope it works out for you," I responded joyfully.

"The other news I wanted to tell you is I am going to take training to become a travel agent. You know I would love to see the world for free!"

We busted out laughing and spent a few more minutes chatting to catch up. These moments I cherished because we gossiped to make us laugh. I missed hanging out with my best friend. I desired to have her life and her freedom. We are both growing up and going our separate ways. Kind of expectant, and bittersweet.

Mrs. McDoogle's house was empty of any celebrating Christmas because she was a Jehovah Witness and did not celebrate holidays, not even a birthday. Jermaine, on the other hand, embraced the holidays, but not around his mother. I made it window clear to him our son would know about holidays because I celebrated them.

127

The holiday I would not take part in was Halloween. Even though I was sure we conceived Joshua on that night. After coming back from work, I was exhausted. I took a hot bath and tried to make it to bed before midnight. Jermaine informed me Joshua was asleep and assured me he should sleep until the morning.

"What did you give him, Benadryl?" I said sarcastically.

"Girl, nah… I gave him a warm bath and fed him a good warm bottle with a tablespoon of baby food."

I was sure a look of amazement was written on my face. "I guess his little belly is full. I hope he would stay asleep," I said as I dragged myself to the bathroom.

Jermaine invited me to go with him to his employee Christmas party. I act as though I could care less about going my heart was excited. It seemed like forever since we went on a date. I found a cute red Vintage dress at the thrift store. It fit my apple shape bottom mighty fine. I fought with my hair for over two hours. I had to wash, dry, curl, and style it. I hardly ever wore shoes with heels, but tonight I wanted to look desirable. *Angels watch over me in these 4-inch black heels.* Jermaine's mom agreed to watch Joshua for us even though she was clearly against the reason for the fuss. I could smell the Polo cologne Jermaine was wearing. I envisioned how good-looking he was going to be. I admitted to myself how tasteful he was and hoped no other female would try to steal him away.

As I put the finish touches on my makeup, I heard his footsteps getting closer. "Yo baby, you ready? We have to leave in 5 minutes."

"Yep, coming right out," I said, blotting my face with a tissue to absorb the oily spots on my face. We kissed Joshua goodbye and headed to the front door.

"My, my, you two look very nice. Candee, it's cold outside you need a coat. This pretty dress kinda short on you. I hope it goes well." Mrs. McDoogle said as she kept on rocking our baby boy to sleep.

Although I disagreed about the shortness of my dress. I took her advice and grabbed my waist cut wool jacket. I had worn the same coat since 8th grade. I buttoned up, and it fit snuggly.

We chatted on the way to the party about nothing, but it helped pass the time. "I have been meditating about what is the next step for us. Having you and my son here I have enjoyed," he said, sounding as though he was auditioning for a sexy male role in a movie.

"I totally agree. It has been peaceful being around you and your mother. I have to admit, I was nervy about coming here."

"I know my mom can be unapproachable around new people, especially if they come to move in." He laughed, and I chimed in with my loud giggles. He whispered softly, "I love you, Candee girl. I see our lives are going to be much better. Now we are working out our issues and not running from them."

"I care about you too, and I want the same," I said putting my left hand on his right leg.

"Be careful with your hand," he said, smiling deliciously.

As soon as I stepped out of the car, the night air slapped me in the face. The sky was clear and crisp winter was here in full force. Jermaine came around to take my hand. He treated me like a Queen. We went inside the building where his coworkers embraced us with hugs and handshakes. A short, dark-skinned woman wearing a long loose fitting green dress, asked us to sign in at a small table. We were asked to follow the woman to our assigned table. The room beautifully decorated in sparkling colors. A huge Christmas tree was standing at the back of the room in a corner with blinking white lights. The ceiling had hundreds of hanging colorful glitter ornaments which made the room look more jovial. The music sounded nice; it was a live band. Our table was front and center of the band stage, so we got a pleasant view of the action. During the night, we got up to dance fast and slow to some great songs. I was having a fun time.

"Do you want another drink?" Jermaine asked as he pushed his chair back to get up before I could answer.

"I am good for now but could drink a glass of ice water," I replied.

"No problem, I'll be right back," he said and winked at me. As I sat there, my heart yearned to see Joshua. I missed him. It was strange being without him. Jermaine returned with a glass of ice water. I took a quick sip to clear my throat. A few coworkers dropped by our table to speak and introduce their significant others. Jermaine smiled each time as he introduced me as his future wife. This title gave me an assurance he was serious about us. The food was delicious. Honey ham, broccoli casserole, sweet yams, side salad, and homemade biscuits. The dessert was banana pudding and red velvet cake. I was so full I wanted to take a nap in the chair. My eyes were getting rock-heavy as I finished the last bite of cake.

I looked at Jermaine, and he said, "You act like you're about to tumble over."

"I am so full. I guess too much food is making me sleepy," I said as I put the fork on the plate.

"Let's say our goodbyes now," he suggested.

The next morning, we both got up early to finish Christmas shopping for Joshua and my family. We took Joshua with us and headed out the door before his mother got up. I did not like shopping at the mall, but when there was a clearance sale at JCPenney and Belk, I could not refuse the savings. As soon as we stepped inside JCPenney, Jermaine informed he needed to use the restroom and walked away. I went to the baby section and looked through the sales. I had no idea how long Jermaine had been away, but it has been long enough to use the restroom. I scanned the household goods in search of a new coffee maker for Mom. I spotted one on sale for $12.99. In line with my budget, so I grabbed one and headed to the girl's section.

My sisters were different in what they liked, so to make it easy on myself I bought them each a scarf and glove set. The store has solids and multiple colors. I grabbed three sets of the multiples. I looked up to see Jermaine walking with a bounce in his steps. "Baby sorry... I got distracted back there. There is so much stuff in the mall to check out. You got what you came for?"

I looked at him with cold eyes and answered, "Yeah, we can leave now." My insecurities were in high gear. *Was he off screwing a girl in the mall?* I changed my mood to think positive, and my heart softened. *Maybe, he was getting me a Christmas gift.*

Chapter Eleven: XOXO

Christmas Eve arrived, and we made sugar cookies and hot chocolate and watched *The Christmas Story* on television. I loved this movie! It tickles me each time I watched it. I grabbed a blanket from the hall closet and headed to the love seat to snuggle with my man. Joshua was fast asleep. I hoped he would sleep through the night. I could smell the cookies; they should be close to ready. Jermaine brought a plate with four medium sized warm cookies. He went back to the kitchen and brought over the cups of hot cocoa. Being so close, it was perfect. I was truly hopeful.

About halfway through the movie, Jermaine got up and walked to his bedroom. He came back with a small red box. "So, you know I love you. This represents how much you mean to me." He handed me the box.

I was speechless. My face flushed because he had never given me any gifts, not even for my birthday. I took the top off the small box and took out what looked like a ring case. I opened the case in slow motion. Inside was a beautiful, heart-shaped diamond ring. I covered my mouth and scream into my hand.

Jermaine dropped on one knee. "I want to make you mine, forever. Will you marry me, Candee Black?"

I squealed with tears flowing. He hugged me, picked me up, and spun me around the room. We kissed and hugged each other so tight. We made love as if it was the last time. I loved him so deeply I wept during my orgasm.

On Christmas day, we celebrated with Joshua, and I gave Jermaine his gift. I got him a gray sweater and Calvin Klein cologne. My family called to say, "Merry Christmas" and I told them I had their presents. Mom informed me the stomach virus was ruining their Christmas. Crystal contacted it first and from there it attacked everyone in the house. She said they could come over on New Year's Day; if all were feeling better. I was perturbed to hear this news. I kept my news a secret because I wanted to show off my engagement ring.

Mrs. McDoogle expressed how she disagreed about it over breakfast. "So, you two prepared to get married? Marriage is not easy. It would be better to wait for a couple years and see if this is what you both want. People fall out of love quicker than a blink of an eye." She sounded negative as usual.

Jermaine spoke up, "Mom we are serious about getting married. We do love each other, and we are ready. My son needs both parents in his life." I sat still my face remained impassive from what had transpired.

We stayed at his house on New Year's Eve even though we were invited to his cousin's house party. We stayed up until midnight playing a game of spades. He opened the cold 40 ounces of Coors Light beer and poured us a glass. "To us, baby. Looking forward to spending my life with you until your pussy turns gray." We both

133

snickered over his smart-ass mouth.

It was my turn, "To you, my first love. I look forward to the future knowing I will wake up each day looking at you."

"Aww, baby thanks," he said, intensely into my eyes. I was melting. He kissed me and popped me on the booty. "It's a new year let's do it right. You know the old saying, whatever you are doing on New Year's is how your year would be," he whispered. He was so strong; he picked me up and carried me to the bedroom. We made love so hard my toes curled up, and goosebumps ran up my back!

When my family arrived at the home, my stomach was in knots anxious about telling them my news. I had a sense momma and dad liked Jermaine as a person. Richard had not said anything negative about Jermaine, at least not to me. The truth of the matter was momma could see through the games and lies we had played on each other. Since momma was in love with Richard, her mood had been pleasant. Therefore, the relationship between them had been great! Jermaine heard firm knocks at the side door.

"It's Charlene and family," I heard momma say cheerfully.

Mom had a large fruit basket bundled in her arms. Mrs. McDoogle strolled in from the back of the house and greeted them with a half southern and half "who cares" smile. "Please, come inside and have a seat in the den area by the fireplace."

Mom gave me a warm hug and whispered, "I miss you and my grandson."

I whispered back I missed them too. The atmosphere was nonchalant; simple conversations exchanged amongst us. The air sucked out of the room like a fierce tornado swooping to grab whatever is in its path. "So, it seems my son and your daughter has interesting yet disturbing news to tell you." Mrs. McDoogle held nothing back when she wanted to put a hot bulb on your head.

I glared at her but caught my pose and sat still not giving any eye contact. I heard Jermaine clearing his throat to take the lead in this dramatic scene of events. "Richard and Ms. Charlene, I-I...I want to tell you both I care a lot for Candee and my son. We engaged now, and we plan to marry someday soon."

Silence was not golden in this situation. I want to jump up and run out of the room, but it would imply I was too immature to become his wife. It took all the strength I had to sedate my anger. My fingers were tapping on the side of my legs to ease the tension.

Mom and Richard spoke at once. "You both are too young!" They looked at each other and stopped at the same time.

This was no different from the ages she and dad married, though. "Mom, listen. I know this may not seem like the greatest news to you, but it is what we want to do. You have said on numerous occasions we need to get our act in check for Joshua's sake. Getting married is what we are ready to do." I rose up to be excused and wiped my eyes before the tears gushed out.

Crystal followed close behind me. "Please don't cry sis, it's going to work out. You know mom, Richard, and even daddy don't want you to rush into anything."

I wiped my nose and sniffed. "I hate they are judging us without a cause. We both know our relationship has been in trouble, but we love each other." She gave me a hug, and I was relieved someone was on my side this time.

135

From the bathroom, I heard Mrs. McDoogle agreeing with them and telling Jermaine we should wait until I at least graduated from high school. I walked back in the room, but I did not take a seat. My knees were shaking because I was getting angry. I could not hold it in any longer. "We don't want your approval! It is our business, not yours!" My face turning red because a wave of heat came over me.

"Candee, you better not talk to us this way!" Mom chimed in and reprimanded me. "When you get older, you will look back on this day and regret being so hasty to get married. Where will you live? You gonna finish school?"

I wanted to spit out the answers, but I refused to say another word. It was as though no matter what we said they were not going to support our decision. Richard stood up and said he needed to go outside and smoke a cigarette. He didn't give me any eye contact.

During the commotion, Joshua woke up and Cara was attending to him. "Candee, he is hungry. Make his bottle, and I will feed him for you." She sounded so grown up.

After about 20 minutes, the conversations changed to lighten the mood, and it was calm. Our bags were packed and ready to go, so Jermaine loaded them in Richard's truck. I put Joshua in his blue cotton coat Jermaine bought for Christmas. I looked at my little man who was growing so fast his cheeks were fat like a little piggy. I kissed his warm nose. "Mommy loves you so much." He responded with a little grin; it warmed my heart. Jermaine walked us out to the car where my family was waiting.

"I guess we talk later baby. I love you", he said and kissed me gently on the lips.

Back to reality. School is back in session, and I was sleepy. I zoned out in my science class. I daydreamed about our wedding day. I saw my lace dress long and white with a 6-foot train lined with beads of pearls. I imagined how handsome Jermaine would be in his black tuxedo. His sexy smile melts my heart as we stood in front of family and friends. There were flowers arranged throughout the church like bright colored tulips, my favorite type of flowers. The whole thing looked perfect! Daydreaming interrupted when I heard a strange voice.

"Class, you will need to write a two-page essay about the damage to the ecosystem as a result of the pollution in the US." Ms. Gantz popped my sweet bubble with her blah, blah, blah voice. I snapped out of my daze and rubbed my eyes to focus long enough to jot at least a sentence or two before the bell rang.

It was lunchtime, and I stayed on campus to eat lunch with Vaughn. I missed hanging out with her as we used to and she had not seen my engagement ring yet. I spotted her coming towards me as I stood in line. She was smiling, as she got closer to me. "Hi girl, I am glad to see you!" We gave each other a tight squeeze. Lunch was seldom a king's' meal, it was more like a prisoner's delight. The menu today was a choice between a sloppy joe sandwich or chicken patty, raw carrots or an apple, and tasteless mashed potatoes. I took my picks and told the lunch woman my lunch program ID#. I'd had the same number since kindergarten. It was another way to track the cattle.

We took a seat near the right side windows to feel the warm sunshine, for it was chilly in the cafeteria. "So how was your holiday?

Did you guys do anything special?" Vaughn asked as she took a bite of her sandwich.

I had so much news to tell her. To get the conversation juiced up, I picked up a carrot with my left hand and nibbled on it bit by bit, hoping she will notice the ring. "Yeah, we did go to a Christmas party hosted by his job. I wore a red Vintage short dress. He said I looked sexy. We had a wonderful time." I finished the carrot and took a sip of my chocolate milk.

Vaughn looked like she had seen a ghost. She was speechless, staring at my hand. She blurted out, "Whoa...what in the world? You got an engagement ring?"

I grinned like a monkey in a banana tree and said, "Yessss, he asked me on Christmas eve. We haven't made a date yet, but I know it will be soon."

"Girlfriend, you need time to get your perfect dress. A church wedding is a lot of work, girl; you need about a year to get it together." Vaughn sounded serious.

"I can't wait a year. It is going to be this year. I would love a church wedding! It will be simple enough for us to afford. You know, V, our parents are not delighted about this, and they have been trying to talk us out of it. After Mom told my dad about the blow up on Christmas Day, he has not had much to say to me. I assume they don't want me to be with Jermaine."

"You know how parents are they know better than we do. You remember when Cedric Bostic gave me a friendship ring back in the 6th grade. My dad went to his house and told his parents on him. I was so mad at him. You know, I reckon he was protective over his little girl. I get it now." Vaughn had me examining it was not a terrible gesture my parents were trying to protect me too.

During the winter season, my sinuses were terrible! My nose was red and throbbed as if it would explode. My head hurting, my stomach is queasy. I wanted to stay in bed and rest, but mommy duties did not come with a sick day pass. I dragged myself out of bed at 5:30 a.m. to get ready for school and get Joshua to the sitter. It dawned on me we are practicing for the Scholastic Aptitude Test (SAT). The test used for entrance into college. I abhorred tests! Same I distasted mayonnaise. I had test anxiety. With each test I have ever taken, I overworked my brain on information I already knew. I would second-guess my answer and spend too much time contemplating about it. I saw Joshua was already awake lying in his crib, but he seemed content watching the baby mobile dangling over his head. Perfect timing for me to do as much as I can. I heard mom in the bathroom shouting to Crystal to come and get her dirty clothes off the bathroom floor. I bypassed and headed to the kitchen to get a glass of water to take my allergy medicine. Richard was dressed for work and sitting at the table with a newspaper under his nose and sipping on his third cup of coffee. I truly believed he was addicted to the black mud. Ever since he stopped drinking alcohol, he drank a great deal of black coffee, no sugar, or cream.

"Good morning Richard."

He looked up. "Morning." He was not a morning person. It was obvious after many times trying to engage him in a conversation before 8 a.m. I fixed a bowl of Captain Crunch cereal and instead of sitting at the table; I walked back toward my room.

Baby fussy butt, mustering up a good cry, was becoming bored with his mobile. I am learning to allow him to soothe himself more as he got older. Therefore, instead of rushing over to rescue him from his tears, I ignored him and finished my cereal. I went through the checklist. My Clothes. My book bag. Diaper bag. Bottles made. I dressed and headed to the bathroom to wash my face, took the rollers out of my hair, and brushed my teeth. This was done in less than 10 minutes. One thing has made me a better person as a teen mother is time management. Next up was getting baby dressed, fed, and getting his diaper bag out the door before 6:30 a.m. Ms. Sagitta has told me if I do not have time to feed him, she would do it for me. Truthfully, she was good to my baby, but I wanted to make sure he was fed before leaving my arms. Baby in tow and dropped off with a full tummy. Mommy was pleased. Now off to the bus stop.

When the bus arrived at school, the parking lot packed with students and teachers lined up near the fence. There was a Policewoman directing the bus to park near the gym; which was located at the back entrance of the school. The students on the bus whispered what might be going on inside the school. Ms. Walker, the bus driver, instructed us to stay seated because we could not go inside the school. Thank goodness, it was cold outside and not sweltering hot because I could not stand to smell funkiness. Today I was sitting with the twins younger brother, Toliver, whom I heard liked Cara, but was too reserved to talk to her.

"I hope this messes up the schedule to take the SAT test," I mumbled softly.

He looked at me with his warm chestnut eyes and said, "I

know what you mean. I had an exam in Language Arts I didn't study for." His face was stoic, looking out the window. He is tapping his right fingers on his knees. I heard he was a bookworm and skipped a grade or two. I leaned back in my seat to see who else had ridden the bus I might know. In the last row on my left side, Jemma had an expression of heaviness on her face. I recall when I ate lunch with Vaughn; she mentioned Jemma might be pregnant by the married man she is seeing.

Like a mother hen, I rose from my seat, and Ms. Walker chastised me. I could tell Jemma was upset and I wanted to find out if I could help her. I took a sheet of paper out of my notebook and wrote her a note. I folded it up enough to cover what it said and passed it back to her. The note had to go through five different sets of hands before reaching Jemma. I knew it was risky, but I sent it back anyway. I whispered to the blonde-haired white boy named Justin, who was sitting behind me to pass it to Jemma. He complied and off it went from one hand to the next. I watched the toss off like a hurdle track race. It had one more hand to go to before making it to Jemma, but it stopped. My heart sped up puzzled about who was holding on to the note. If I got back up, I was bound to get in trouble.

The bus driver was prejudice because she tends to call out the black students before the white ones. A sense of urgency shadows me to protect the note. I stood up to get a better view over the seats and to see who had the note. It was the shit face Roger Pickens! Before I could get his attention, he was reading the note aloud. *"Jemma, I hope you are okay. If you are pregnant, it will all work out. If there is anything I can do to make you smile, please let me know. Your friend, Candee."* Everyone became stagnant and all eyes beamed at Jemma. Before I stopped, I was at Roger's seat to snatch the note out of his hand. He was a white redheaded six-foot giant with a physique like a linebacker. He stood up and dared me to take it out of his hands. I was so furious. I knew this was not going to end peacefully.

"You pecker head piece of shit! Give me that fucking note!" I bellowed at him spewing hot air. Ms. Walker yelled at us both to sit! The noise level heightened, and we did not listen. Roger had his right fist up as if he is going to punch me if I get close enough. I knew he could beat me with one hand, but I was too mad to stop. Out of nowhere, Jemma stood up and snatched the note out of Roger's left hand. He turned his fury towards her with a raised fist. I punched him so hard in his back my knuckles cracked. Students were out of their seats trying to see what was going on. A hand pulled me back, and someone stepped in front of me as if to take over the situation.

It was Toliver; he grabbed Roger by his shirt collar. Roger faced him, and Toliver pops him in his nose. Blood oozed down the left side of Roger's face. He appeared stunned as he stumbled back in his seat. Before Roger could retaliate in rushed the football coach Mr. Phillips, pulled Toliver back and hollered, "Go to your seat young man!" The coach knew Roger, so he told him to get off the bus with him. I watched the fool cover his nose with his bloody T-shirt.

Jemma's eyes were on me, so I placed my left hand over my heart and mouthed the words, "I am sorry." She put up two fingers up for the peace sign and smiled.

It was another 15 minutes before the rest of us could unload the bus and go to our first-period class. The talk around the school campus was there was a bomb threat, which caused the distraction this morning. As soon as I sat at my desk, I heard over the intercom system I needed to go to the office. I smirked at the possibility of suspension off the bus. In all my 10 school years, I avoided a physical fight on school property. I did not look at choking my elementary bully/friend Alyssa as a fight. I normally tried to settle my differences by talking or ignoring the instigator. This time was different because I had a run in with Roger in the seventh grade it left me bitter.

He was in my gym class, and we were paired up to train for the President's Sports Award. This award was for students' who passed physical fitness challenges in different areas such as push-ups, sit-ups, one-mile run, and jumping jacks, etc. The purpose of the award was to motivate the students to maintain fitness to prevent certain health risks, such as obesity. Roger was already fit for this training from playing football, so he seemed annoyed to deal with me. I knew the one-mile run was going to be a challenge for me because I dreaded running the distance. I could run fast in the 50 and 100-yard dash with no problems. We both got through the exercise routines with average to excellent record scores. During the difficult times, we both pushed each other along and made it through to the finish.

It was during the one-mile run when Roger acted as if he did not need a partner. We jogged at a steady pace. From training together, he knew I would get a cramp in my right side within 5 minutes of running. Therefore, I paced to a crawl to push through the pain in which he willingly slowed too. Not that day, he kept on running. He did not trot enough for me to at least to try to catch up with him. Of course, I made it to the finish line 15 minutes later than most of my peers! He had the nerve to be standing at the finish line with this look of, *"It's about time you got your slow ass here."* My mood stomped by his actions and I did not speak to him again. Therefore, a punch in his back was well worth a suspension or whatever consequence I had coming.

When I opened the front office door, I saw Jemma, Toliver sitting, and Roger standing on the opposite side, closer to the Principal's office. Mrs. Gibson had been the Principal for over 8 years and known for being firm when disciplining students. She could not care less if your parents are on the PTO committee and sold a thousand boxes of doughnuts for fundraising. If you broke school rules, you would suffer the consequences.

I stood near Jemma, but do not exchange words. The gray wooden door was ajar and out stepped Mrs. Gibson, wearing a two-piece Navy skirt set with six large black buttons in the center of the jacket. She had fresh shoulder-length dreadlocks and wore dark brown trimmed eyeglasses sitting on the edge of her nose. "Let me talk with Candee first, and the Roger will be next." Her voice was monotone and stern. She gestured for me to come in her office and have a seat.

I imagined I was someplace else to take whatever was coming. She took a sip from a silver mug and pressed her lips together. "Candee I want your side of what happened on the bus." My right foot was shaking because I was anxious. I had already rehearsed what I was going to say, and I planned to tell the truth.

"I wrote a note to Jemma because I saw she looked upset. We knew to stay in our seats, so I sent a note back to her. Roger read the note aloud. I tried to intercept the note, and all the fighting started."

She blinked and sat back in her tall black leather chair. "I had no idea you were a licensed professional," she responded sarcastically. "Did you see her balling her eyes out on the bus?" I tried to answer but, she abruptly cut me off. "I appreciate your information. You may go to your next class." She dismissed me with her right hand pointing to the door. "Please ask Roger to come in next. Thank you." I walked out and pointed to the asshole who was holding up the wall.

The rest of the school day was a blur. I went from class to class, lunch, boring ass Social Studies, and it was over. While in my homeroom classroom, I copied my homework assignments for the week. More Shakespearean literature to read, *does the madness ever stop?* I moaned to myself. I had to work an extra day at the store to cover my bills. Juggling work and education was not ideal as a teen mother.

I faintly heard my teacher calling my name. "Candee…, Candee, please gather your belongings for dismissal. You need to stop by the office before the bus leaves." I walked the halls, knowing my sentence was coming. I did not see my partners in crime, so I took a seat in the usual spot. Within a few seconds, Mrs. Putnam, the Assistant Principal came to get me to follow her into another office.

"No need to sit, I have your copy of the consequence for the incident on the bus. You have received a 5-day suspension starting tomorrow. I notified your parents about the consequence by telephone. Please sign here." She pointed to a line at the bottom. I scribbled my name. She pulled off the yellow copy and handed it to me. "The bell should be ringing in two minutes," she said and walked over to a prehistoric file cabinet hidden in the corner. I guessed it could've been worse. I would take the consequence, spend time with my son, my man, and catch up on homework. I would take it as a mini vacation after the vacation.

Mom locked her eyes on me as I entered the house. "Your daddy said to call him on your lunch break, young lady," she said with a bad attitude. It would be nice to be able to snap my fingers to change into my work clothes. I normally had time to go and give Pooh a kiss before leaving, but today I needed to keep going.

"Candee, get in here before you leave," momma directed me.

"Give me a minute please," I said respectfully.

"Candee, I am more disappointed than anything right now. You were fighting on the bus! What in the heavens is your problem?" she kept going non-stop. "Look here, you are a freaking mother now, and I have no room on my plate to deal with you acting like a wild animal. Get your ass in check! Do I make myself clear?" I dared not speak. She shut up and walked out of the room. I glanced at my watch; I need to get going fast. I dashed out the back door to get on my bike. I could call a cab, but I told myself only if the weather was bad. It was a balmy 76 degrees with no clouds in sight. I waved at a few neighbors on my way to work. While peddling, I heard my mom's angry voice blazing. 'Candee get your act together! You have a baby now, grow the hell up!' ' I talked to myself. "If I was married I wouldn't live in her house. I am sick of her getting on my case. I am grown! She cannot tell me how to act. It is too late for a speech."

Riding the bike to work helped me process back burner

memories. It also allowed me to reflect on what else was going on. It dawned on me Crystal was starting to get boy crazy. I saw her sneaking out one night to meet the boy across the street. She was fifteen now. I was curious to ask if she was still a virgin. I would make it my business to ask her. I did not look forward to calling dad either, but he was more lucid than mom was. Cara got her period at age 13, a late bloomer. The doctor has discussed her eating habits. She needs to avoid eating sweets and chips. This put a damper on the rest of us who were not fat and loved to eat snacks. Poor Christian started her period too at 11 years old. She was chosen to go to the state spelling bee contest.

Puffy clouds with words swirled through my head as I rode. I was close to work, another half a mile to go. I had one more stop sign before turning right. Then a sharp left and my destination on the right.

By riding the bike, it was shaping my body right. I motivated myself because most times I avoided a mirror. The baby weight had my stomach soft, and my thighs jiggled like a bowl of jelly. Jermaine had made some stupid jokes when I was naked, but he apologized before wanting to have sex. Typical dang male!

Chapter Twelve: Follow the Breadcrumbs

After Mom and Dad separated for fifteen months, they legally divorced and shared joint custody. Since we were not babies anymore, we would tell when we wanted to see dad and his wife-to-be. Christian was the one who seemed to miss him. Many nights she cried herself to sleep. Especially if there was a week when daddy had not called or dropped by to see us. It was a good thing Richard was not the crazy jealous type like the boyfriend mom had before him. Talk about a cuckoo bird in the flesh, a joker from the devil! Momma had to put a restraining order on him because he had threatened to beat her up if she stopped seeing him. It was a scary time for all of us. I thanked God for Richard.

It was 1980, and I would be turning 17 years old on April 26 – the next day. Vaughn and I had the hots for the young and upcoming musician, Prince. The Fire It Up Tour was in town with Prince, and another artist named Rick James. I had not paid much attention to Rick James, so I did not know what to expect from him. Prince was so freaking handsome, though! I played a fantasy when Jermaine and I were having sex. I craved for Jermaine to get buck wild in the bed. I imagined us screwing on the floor, on a table, anywhere exciting! Prince lyrics talked about liberating your mind and sexuality. I could listen to his music in my sleep. He was a musical genius. He made great jamming music for dancing and erotic lovemaking music. He was the one man who looked alluring wearing women's clothing.

Vaughn invited me to go to his concert when he came to the Charlotte Coliseum. She said it was my birthday present and I was in blitz obsessed about seeing Prince perform. I heard he jumped off speakers as tall as I was – which was close to five feet tall. I had to twist Jermaine's arm to be okay with me going without him. I knew he was jealous, but he didn't want me to know it. Momma bought me a new pair of dark blue Wrangler jeans for my birthday. I already had a jean jacket, which would complement the jeans. I chose to wear my red V-cut knit shirt. I was so thankful I didn't spend half a day doing my hair. A perm was a Godsend for black girls with thick hair like mine. All I did was comb lightly through the curls and all done. Momma offered to watch Joshua for me since Jermaine had to go to work. Vaughn had her own car. It was a white Volkswagen Beetle. It looked practically new. There were no dents or scratches on it. It had the new car smell.

Vaughn picked me up an hour and a half before show time to avoid the late traffic. She was dressed in a cute short black front zipper dress with her go-go girl stiletto heel boots and fishnet stockings. Today she was wearing a short brunette curls wig, which I had not seen on her in over a year. Vaughn was the one girl I knew who had a name for all her wigs. "Girl, who you rocking today? Thelma," I said, teasing her.

"Now you know I got to change it up; especially tonight. Now, do not judge me when I say there is going to be fresh meat staring at this pretty face. I am not available – but there's no harm in looking."

149

I second that motion.

As soon as we got about a halfway from the coliseum, the traffic flow slowed to a crawl. The local radio was playing Prince's new and old songs to put us in the right mood. I wiggled my booty and snapped my fingers to the beats. "I hope he sings *Soft & Wet*. Yes, it's my jam!" I shouted excitedly.

We went up a couple times getting closer to the Charlotte Coliseum. At that pace, we figured we were going to miss the first act to start in 30 minutes. We both panicked missing a minute of the sexy Prince. It took about 20 more minutes to get inside the parking lot. We parked after handing the tall parking attendant the $2.00 parking fee. I gathered my small black wallet with my lip-gloss and concert ticket.

"V, should we carry an umbrella? I heard it may rain after midnight," I asked.

"Naw, we should be out before it comes."

The crowds lined up at the entrance doors waiting to go inside the arena. We had floor tickets, so it meant we were standing all night. There was loud music coming through the heavy metal doors. It's crowded like a herd of cattle pushed to get branded on the ass. I feared getting stomped on by a mob of out of control people. I got anxious and grabbed Vaughn's hand and pledged, "Whatever happens, do not let go of my hand!"

"I gotcha girl!" she responds back. It was pitch black dark except for the bright lights coming from the stage. A worker escorted us to the standing area center of the stage. The air was thick with white smoke and lit cigarettes. The smell of cigarettes is despicable!

It would get in my clothes, hair, and up my coochie before we got out of here. The crowd was going wild singing, clapping hands and hollering words incomprehensible. Vaughn and I joined in to act normal, and before long, we were smiling and grooving to the beats too. Within a matter of minutes, the lights come on, and the announcer reported this was intermission time for 15 minutes. It was my first concert, so I had no idea what was going on.

"V, is the concert over already?"

"No, this is when they set up for the next act. It had better be Prince. We can run to the restroom or get a drink if you want to."

"I am glad we got this spot. I would hate to leave and have to stand way back there," I said hoping to persuade her.

While the bright lights beamed, I scanned the floor looking to see any familiar faces in the crowd. Good, I did not see anyone here I knew. I saw a large crowd clapping and cheering for a man dressed in an all-white suit who was dancing near the back wall. We ended up staying in the spot, and after about 20 minutes, the lights went dark. *Did someone purposely tap my ass?* This was why I avoid crowds. The excited mob clapped loudly, jumping, and shouting, "Prince, Prince!"

We joined in jumping up and down as if we were about to lose our minds. Prince was shorter than I knew, so I was hopping like a bunny on acid.

"What's up sweet thang, do you want to sit on my back?" It was a brown-skinned dude with a front gold-tooth, dreadlocks, wearing a black leather outfit. I was tempted to take his offer.

"Sure," I said, smiling at V. The view was much better. I could see my Prince step out on the stage playing a white guitar, dressed in black pants and white ruffled blouse. I see his chest full of hair. Hoping he would shave it off one day. His hair was a thick black Afro. He played his new song *Soft & Wet* and about eight other songs. He danced, did splits, and dove off tall speakers in those high heel shoes! He was a beautiful man. I was awe-struck. He was sexier in person than on an album cover. I melted inside looking at how amazing he was on stage. I hollered so much I could barely talk. V was swamped standing. I was a little guilty about being higher. I got back on two-legs and enjoy the rest of the show with my best friend. He was a serious entertainer. The crowd was going wild as he finished the last set and took a bow.

"Encore, Encore, Encore!" we all chanted and cheered for him to return. He was such an artist at heart. He returned twice to satisfy the hungry fanatics. I guess I was included as well because each time he left I vociferated for more! No more returns. The lights came back on, and the crowds dispersed. In the lobby area, there were posters, music albums, T-shirts, etc. Vaughn bought a poster and I bought a T-shirt – to sleep in.

The next day, I planned to take Joshua to see my grandparents. Jermaine would pick us up by 4:00 p.m., drop us off, and return early Saturday. We were going to the mountains and would return on Sunday evening. Jermaine and I were not married yet. However, we went to find an apartment so we could live together first. It was like doing a trial run to get the kinks out before being stuck with the goods. Even if none of our parents supported our decisions, we agreed we were ready. Joshua was nine months old and had six teeth. I got nervous when he got around the house in the baby walker. His little feet and hands were everywhere.

At my grandparents' house, I kicked off my stuffy tennis shoes and let them air outside. Grandma and me and took a seat in the white plastic lawn chairs on the back screened porch.
"So, tell me, how have you been, Candee apple?" A nickname my grandparents gave to me.

The fresh spring smell was clean and crisp in the country. I held in as much as my lungs could take and released. "Grandma Elaine, my world has been like a tidal wave. I get my bearings, and another wave comes back again."

Her black eyes had small fine lines around them as she smiled and patted my right knee. I saw up close how my mom resembled her. She wore her thick long hair in a bun. Her blue apron had flour on the front. It was obvious she had made my birthday cake earlier. "I reckon, Candee apple, it sounds like life to me. You know when Calvin and I got married we were young 15 years old. The early years were different," she disclosed as she picked up the flyswatter and killed flies on the floor. "He got a job cleaning horse stables, and I did house cleaning for a white doctor. Not long after, the babies came. Before we knew it, we got five youngins under the age of six. We both stayed busy before the sun came up."

I gasped hearing how many babies she had to care for.

She continued, "We learned much, and there was no time to point fingers. Life was tough it is seldom easy." She broke fresh green beans in half and tossed them in the white plastic bowl between her legs. "I reckon, the good Lord just gives you time to relax and enjoy the good moments. The tough times are the best times; you see what you made of. It will all come together in time."

Grandma dipped tobacco snuff. She used an empty tobacco tin can to spit out the tobacco juice. She took a spit.

"Did momma tell you me and Jermaine would be living together?" I asked, wanting to hear her advice, if any.

"Yes, she mentioned it the other day. I reckon you two have counted the cost and want to make a life together, before marriage. My views are different because I got married first. Being you got a baby already by this young fella, twist your life around as such. Do you love him?" she asked and spit in the can again.

"I do – very much," I expressed, smiling.

"Well, if so, you gonna follow your heart no matter what we say. You can't blame anybody else if it fails." She commented no more about it. Those words settled in my head. I found myself accepting them. We finished breaking up green beans from the garden for canning her famous vegetable soup.

My Grandpa Calvin took Joshua with him to feed the chickens, two horses and a slew of hogs. I was grateful for so many teachable moments growing up around them. When they returned, it was suppertime, and the smell from Grandma's cooking made my mouth salivate.

"Well… shoot fire! This little one helped me feed all dem animals, and he was not afraid." Grandpa exclaimed, holding Joshua in his arms. I remembered when I was small around three; it was my job too. One thing I knew Grandma loved to do is cook! She made barbeque chicken, collard greens, mashed potatoes and gravy, homemade biscuits, and a chocolate cake with vanilla frosting for my birthday.

Grandpa blessed the food, and we dove right in. Joshua loved mashed potatoes and gravy. I had been giving him chopped meats, mostly grilled and fried chicken. I fed him the baby foods for the vegetables. He was drinking from a sippy cup. No more bottles. Thank the moon, stars, and planets! I was ready to potty train him before he turned two. Later on, we settled inside to watch TV and eat more cake with vanilla ice cream. It had been a wonderful visit.

Jermaine arrived at 4 p.m. sharp, looking joyful to see us. "Good afternoon, my babies." He kissed me on the lips and Joshua on his cheeks. He shook Grandpa's hand and gave Grandma a quick hug. They told us to be safe and to have a good time.

The drive to the mountains was a good distance, so it was a challenge to keep ourselves entertained. We discussed our plans for getting our own place. "So, I found two apartments which are pretty reasonable in the price range we can handle," he announced as I opened a bag of salted pretzels to feed my boredom. I munched as he talked about both places. 'No deposit' and '1 month free' got my attention.

"Hold up. So, which has these perks?"

"The apartments closer to my job," he replied and added, "From the advertisement, they look decent. They are a lot older than the apartments near the downtown area."

I crunched on pretzels and said, "I should go check the ones out near your job. They are at least twenty minutes from my job, but I guess I can look for another job once we are settled." He agreed to the plan.

We got unpacked at the hotel, which was high up on the mountains. The view was beautiful. The bright colors displayed from the trees appeared like heaven on earth. Being so high up gave me a sense of being close to heaven. We got dressed to go hiking up on the trails to the waterfalls. I applied sunscreen lightly on the little one. Jermaine laughed at me and joked he was 'too black' to worry about being sunburned. Me, on the other hand, I applied plenty to my pale skin. Joshua was on Jermaine's back in a baby riding sack; he looked so handsome with his baseball cap on his perfect meatball shape head. He was smiling as if he knew he was going on a fun ride. We gathered the water, snacks, backpacks, and headed out. Time flew by when your life was going well. I couldn't believe my little boy was turning one-year-old in three months. I had been secretly planning his birthday party with my sisters. Even though he was too young to understand the concept of the party, we wanted to show him love. Jermaine was raised a Jehovah's Witness. He does not celebrate birthdays, but after we met, he chose to celebrate Christmas with us. He never mentioned what day he was born-only the month, which is October. We had a quick conversation about what we believe about religion. We agreed not to force the issue upon each other. My family has been involved in a church before I was born. He knows I was adamant about raising Joshua to celebrate his birthday. He made no qualms about it until I started planning his 1-year-old birthday. "The boy has no idea what is going on and what is the big deal anyway? He is too young." He bickered when I explained the details of the party. "Jermaine, I have not asked you for one freaking dime! This is a big deal to my family and me and eventually, it would be to Joshua as he grows up." I handled telling him to shove it in a civil manner. Since his birthday was on July 4, this made the colors and theme so simple. I bet when he got older he will speak up and tell us, *"Enough already with the red, white, & blue."*

We got to the waterfall in about 45 minutes with no stops. There were several other people standing at the edge. The weather was perfect. Plenty of warm sunshine, but the massive trees had abundance of shade. I was hypnotized by the flow of the water slapping the rocks. The tranquil sounds coming from the waterfall. It was serene. It was hard to look in any other direction.

"Babe, let's take out the blanket and sit over here. I got my new Polaroid camera so we can freeze this moment," Jermaine instructed. A *camera... when did he get it?*

"Let's chill here, I responded trying to focus on the moment.

"Say cheese," he suggested, aiming it right at Pooh and me. I came back to earth from daydreaming and held my face near Joshua. He pulled my earring out of my left ear.

"Ouch!" I wailed. "Pooh, mommy needs her earrings to stay in her ears." He was such a loving boy, smiling wide as though he had done no wrong. Jermaine was on a snapping frenzy and took at least four pictures in one location. I took out the cold-water bottles, took a few sips, and poured the rest in Joshua's sippy cup. He gulped the water as though he was dehydrated. I was glad he drank regular water. I remembered when Cara was a baby she would not drink water unless momma added sugar in it to give it a flavor. I held up a cold-water bottle for Jermaine in hopes he would come and get it.

"Babe, I got one more shot to get of the waterfall. Can you and

Pooh come over here?" he asked, showing his pretty teeth.

I was comfortable and did not want to move. However, I knew moments like this were hard to come by. So, I grabbed my little man and headed over there. "You need to be in this picture because you not in any of the pictures." I begged him to ask some people to take it for him. An elderly Asian man overheard me and offered to help us take the picture. We thanked him for the suggestion. We took off our shoes and put our feet in the water. It was cold to the touch, but refreshing to our sweaty feet. I was reluctant to put Pooh's feet in; he might not do well to the temperature change. I took his plump little hands and wet them instead. He seemed to enjoy it, giggled, and splashed the water around. After about 10 more minutes, we gathered our backpacks and strolled down the mountain.

For the first time in a long time, Jermaine took my hand as we strolled on the trail. "I have enjoyed being here. I have to admit, I assumed I would be bored in these woods," He laughed.

"Don't tell me us getting busy in these woods have not crossed your dirty mind," I muttered sarcastically.

"Since you inquired; I did visualize you standing naked under the waterfall. I would come from behind you, and it'd be doggie style for sure!" He was cracking up. I took my free hand and slapped him lightly on the chest.

"You are such a dog!" I say, laughing.

Chapter Thirteen: False Hope

We made it back down the mountain with no problems. I had a little fear of going up the mountain and running out of drinking water or getting lost. With Jermaine, we were safe. I knew he would be level-headed enough to save the day if an emergency happened. We stayed inside instead of going out to eat because we were drained from the hiking. We ordered a large Pepperoni pizza for delivery. He already had 12-pack cans of Coors Light beers. His cousin bought the beers since Jermaine would not be 21 years old until next October. "I got us a smoke too, baby. My cousin Nate bragged it's the choking shit, I meant *stuff*."

After correcting his language, he rolled the joint up in the white tobacco paper. He lit one end and took a long pull, let out a large cloud of smoke. He passed it to me, and I could not suck in the hot smoke as he did, so I blew it right out.

"Dang, Candee girl, you waste this shit... I meant smoke." He fumbled again. He told me a few weeks ago, he wanted to avoid using curse words around the baby. I told him it was about time because one-day Joshua was going to repeat what he heard and the worst thing to happen was the boy would pick up cuss words and skips right over da-da and ma-ma. I was guilty too. We both pledged to hold each other accountable.

159

The night was ripe with the sweetness of affections we gave to each other. To celebrate my birthday, he bought me a necklace with two red hearts. He informed he wanted to get our initials on them, but the process would have taken too long. He also gave me a beautiful card with a red heart on the front of it read, "No words can express the depth of my love." Inside the card was where he wrote his own words. ***Where do I begin to tell you how much you mean to me? You connect the dots in my lonely world, which made a loving heart. My heart ready to give and receive love. I didn't know love could feel so good. Thank you for our son. You are my world ... Always and forever, Jermaine.*** I was astounded.

We took a bubble bath together in the huge bathtub. He lit candles, and the aroma scent was vanilla. The portable radio was playing low with love songs by Anita Baker, Luther Vandross, and Freddie Jackson. Those songs were baby-making songs. Thank goodness for birth control. God, I loved this man right here. My heart was exploding with joy. It was amazing to be in love. Our bodies were in harmony in the king-size bed. Joshua was sleeping in the large dresser drawer I made for him. Jermaine and I had oral sex. It was good to my body and soul. There was not any reason to be self-conscious about what we liked to do for each other. All pleasure points were in full effect.

The following day, we went to view the apartment, and we both liked it. Shacking day was the next day, and I packed each free moment I had. Momma was giving me the silent treatment, which was fine with me. I refused to argue with her about my life. While I was folding up my clean laundry, Crystal walked in and told me she got a job cleaning the church.

"Candee, I can't wait to get my first check. I know how I want to spend it. I am going to buy me a study guide for the college entrance exam."

"Honey chile aren't you the smarty pants," I smiled and gave her a high-five. "I know you will do fine on the exam. Have you decided which college to apply to?" I asked.

"Yes, I got my eyes on the University of North Carolina at Charlotte and Western Carolina University in Cullowhee," she bellowed, sounding proud of herself.

"Sounds like you have a plan, my dear sister."

I stopped folding my shirt to give her my full attention. "I may not say this to you enough, but please know I am so proud of you. I see so much potential in you. I guess I see in you what I could've accomplished if I had stayed focus on my goals."

Her eyes filled up with tears and mine followed close behind. We embraced for the first time as sisters we didn't hug each other enough. I was the oldest I should model affection. I promised to give my sisters a hug when I saw them. For the rest of the day, I spent time giving away possessions I would not be taking with me. I see Joshua's baby clothes needed to go too. Therefore, I bagged it all up and called Jemma to offer her his stuff. She had her baby boy a month ago. It was unfortunate she had been struggling to support him since the baby daddy was MIA. The rumor was he was a married man. He left the city as soon as she told him she was pregnant. He was such a bastard!

It was cloudy with an 80% chance of rain. I had begged Mother Nature to hold the H20 back until we finished using the U-

Haul moving truck. We had already made two trips to load both of our belongings. We had to make one more stop at my house. Nate was waiting at the apartment to help us unload. I could see small raindrops covering the truck's' windshield at a steady pace. I knew the heavy rain was close behind. When we pulled up in my mom's' driveway, I saw my dad's truck parked on the side street. My heart raced, fearing he was there to sway my decision to move-out.

"Baby, stay in the truck, I can handle the box I need to get," I expressed nervously to Jermaine. He mouthed no words as I got out of the truck and went to the front door.

As soon as I went inside, Richard came fleecing from the kitchen with a glass of tea in his hand. His eyes were cold and fixated on my movements. I had to respect him, so I spoke first. "Hi Richard, I need to grab my last box in my…old room."

He questioned, "Are you 100% sure this is the right move to make?"

Him giving me the third degree what I was trying to avoid. I avoided eye contact and shifted my body weight to the left side. "Yes, we are going to be alright." I gave him a slight hug, grabbed my box, and left before he fired up again.

The outside of the apartments appeared more attractive than the inside. The place had a musty odor as well as damp sensation to it. I assumed it is the fault of the tall red maple trees. They expanded from the back to the right side of the building, shading our apartment. This might create comfortable days and nights for the summer months and nippy to freezing temperatures in the wintertime.

To my surprise, we are doing well after living there for a few months. We found a small daycare center about five miles from the apartment, and it was on the way to Jermaine's job. We were able to get a few pieces of furniture from the Goodwill Center, now we had a fold out table, two chairs, and brown suede couch and love seat. Jermaine was picking up overtime two days a week. I was holding out on asking for extra hours at work. First, I needed to get another sitter for Joshua because his daycare closed at 6:00 p.m., Monday-Friday. As I toiled over making grown-up decisions; my mind drifts to talking with the gang a few days ago about the upcoming high school graduation. They all seemed to have their own plans to either make a living by working or enrolled in college. I planned to attend their graduation ceremony even though I would be jealous it wasn't for me.

For the most part, Jermaine and I had been getting along great. With the exception of him throwing his dirty clothes on the bedroom floor soon as he got home from work. I cursed him out for leaving his sweaty, funky drawers on the floor. I was not his freaking house cleaner!

On Memorial Day holiday, we chilled at home and cooked out on our cheap grill on the back patio. Jermaine was off too, but left out before 9:00 a.m. to go by his mom's house and help her rearrange the living room furniture. There was normally a chore to do around the apartment since I had become a clean fanatic. Mental health people would label my actions as OCD, due to me excessively wiping the kitchen and bathroom with bleach when I saw hairs, toothpaste, or anything out of sorts. It drove me crazy!

I heard the phone ringing and sprinted to get it before it woke up my sleeping boy. "Hello." I softly mumbled.

163

"Hi Candee, how is it going?" Crystal asked.

"Hi sis, we are good. Is all good with the family?"

"I guess…it's why I'm calling. Listen, no way to drag around this; its Grandpa…. Calvin." Her voice was shaky. I could tell she was choking up trying to tell me what is wrong.

My heart flutters causing me to brace myself, "What, what is it? Is he okay?"

She stammered. "Nooo, he's gone… Grandpa didn't wake up this morning!" She was sobbing so hard. The news made my knees buckle, and I collapsed to the floor. I covered my mouth, trying to block the screams. I questioned if I was in a nightmare.

My heart raced, and I got dizzy. "Where is mama?" I asked, choking back the tears.

"Uncle Paul, came… and drove her… to be with the family," she choked crying profusely.

"Okay…good…," I was sniffling now. "I want to come over there now, but Jermaine is at his mom's house. Let me call over there. I'll call you right back."

She hung up, and I fumbled over dialing the numbers. "McDoogle residence." She answered on the second ring.

I cleared my throat, "Mrs. McDoogle, I don't mean to bother you, is Jermaine hanging out there?"

"Sweetie, he left over an hour ago. You sound different; are you and the baby okay?" For once, she sounded sincere.

"Joshua is good he's napping. I got a call…my Grandpa Calvin …passed away in his sleep last night."

Tears came pouring like a waterfall. I could barely hear her condolences because my mind was numb. Within a few seconds, I drift back to the present when I heard the front door opening.

"He's here," I blurted, and hung up the phone. He looked past me, standing in the living room. He walked towards the kitchen and spoke.

"Good morning, what's wrong? Have you been… crying?"

I stared at him and shot back, "Where the hell have you been?" I wanted to blast more nasty words at him, but I could not. "It's my Grandpa, he's gone…. I-I need to go to my mom's. Please take me right now." I called Crystal and told her I was on my way. By the next month, I'd have my freaking driver's license and then the car. *No more waiting on him!*

I was on the schedule to work the next five days. I contacted Mr. Pete and requested to take off for bereavement. He granted my request but reminded me I did not qualify for the bereavement pay since I was part-time. I figured missing three days was surely going to hurt our tight ass budget. "If I can, I will come in for one day," I muttered.

"No problem let me know. I am sorry for your loss, my condolences to you, and the family," he responded sincerely. Before hanging up, he asked for the name of the church to send flowers.

"Thank you," I whispered. My mind jacked up to worrying about school. My school attendance miserably stained so I would take one day off. School would be out for the summer in another month. So ready for a break.

One thing about Grandpa Calvin, he loved his church and was well respected in the community. My Grandpa was 77 years old when he died. He and my Grandma Elaine has been married for 62 years and had five children, 14 grandchildren, and three great-grands. He was a hard worker and loved his family, but most of all he loved God and helped the needy. The family dressed him in a black suit with a cream dress shirt and a navy-blue necktie with cream dots. I dreamed I would kiss his face when I got close to the casket. I touched his face it was ice cold and hard. My lips trembled seeing him in the white casket. It was my first funeral and the older I got I understood this would not be the last. As we took our seats on the second pew, I saw momma falling apart, leaning on Uncle Paul. I held hands with Christian, and she was balling her eyes out. I struggled to keep my composure. I sucked air through my nose and out my mouth to soothe my nerves. I thanked God Jermaine stayed home with Joshua because this was no place for small children. The eulogy was beautiful, and there were several speakers reminiscing about what a great husband, father, and brother Grandpa was.

The last surviving close relative Grandpa had was his twin brother, Dennis, who lived in Baltimore, Maryland. Uncle Dennis was single and had no children. I heard momma say years ago he was gay. I was unable to get to know him since he lived out of state, but I did know Grandpa had a good relationship with him. He spoke into the microphone and told a funny story about how he and Grandpa got into trouble when they did not tell their parents they were going fishing. Dennis recalled how Grandpa convinced his parents' it was his idea to leave without permission. When it was time to get his punishment, which was picking an extra bale of cotton, Grandpa ludicrously changed his story. Uncle Dennis smiled as he went on to explain they both got the belt, but they laughed the next day about the incident. The heaviness in the church is lighter for those few minutes.

After the graveside service, me, my sisters, and a few other family members watched the crane lower the casket into the ground. There were so many beautiful flower arrangements around the grave. I needed to take one home with me. I spotted Grandma standing on the other side of the church looking in my direction. She had a blank look on her face. I went up to her and gave her a hug.

"Grandma, do you need anything?"

She recalled, "No baby, I'm alive. I know my Calvin, in my heart is at peace. He is with God, and I know he will be waiting for me when God calls me home too."

"I hate to ask, but I did not want to take one without asking. Can I take one of the peace lily flowers?"

She bowed her head silently.

I met up with my family in the food hall, ready to eat the meal prepared by the church members. The mood was upbeat, and people were laughing and chatty. I got my plate and detoured, sitting with my family and finding a seat with Jemma and Donovan. Vaughn and Mallory could not make it because they both had new jobs out of town. It had been months since they had seen me, so I was eager to catch-up with them. We all went back and forth exchanging information about our lives and the new gossip! Dad walked over to see me and gave me a tight hug. I was reserved and didn't say much, but let him know I was glad to see him. He offered to take me home. I accepted so he could know where we were living.

167

The ride home with dad was different as a young woman since the last time I was with him we were a family going to the campgrounds three years ago. "So how do you like married life before the marriage?" he grinned.

My mind went to the day Grandpa passed and the look on Jermaine's face when he came home. "Things are good between us. We try to make it work as best we can. Somedays are tougher than others."

"Candee, I may not tell you this enough, or I don't know if I have ever, but I am proud of you for at least trying to grow up and make a life for yourself." His words meant a lot to me since this was the first time he had confessed this to me. I had to admit to myself since he had been away from us he seemed like a changed person. In a safe way, he had softened in how he interacted with my sisters, momma, and me.

"Thanks, dad," I replied, wanting to say more, but I held back before I admitted the truth.

At home, the communication was stale between Jermaine and me, so I practically ignored him and spent more time with Joshua.

"Look at my little man!" Joshua was taking steps. His arms extended, as Jermaine cheered to keep him coming.

"Go, little man, you are doing it," I heard Jermaine say as he stood in the bedroom doorway. I rolled my eyes at him, and he saw me. "I guess you got an attitude about some crazy bull crap. You gonna tell me what's up, now?"

I ignored him and picked up Joshua to get him ready for bed.

"Candee girl, we not going to bed until you talk to me!" His voice was loud, and he looked desperate for an answer. I was seething through my skin from the madness of his presence. I knew he was cheating again. I found condoms in his jeans a week ago, and we had not had good sex in two weeks. On Fridays, he had been coming in later than normal. All signs I was familiar with as his typical cheating pattern.

"We can talk as soon as I put him in bed," I answered calmly as I sauntered out of the room.

I found him lying across our used king-size waterbed from his old neighbor. I was not a huge fan of the bed because it moved like waves. It seemed to take me too long to fall asleep most nights. I sat in a chair next to the closet door. We both were mute for about 15 seconds, and we spoke at the same time. We both stopped.

"You go first," he echoed.

"First, I need to say I sense a noticeable change between us since we been here. It is different. Call me paranoid or whatever, what's wrong?" I asked.

He was sitting up now. His facial expression was flat. "You could be right, we are different. I must admit, I am trapped. I get bored easily and...look for exciting things to do. You do you, and deal with Joshua, school, work, and have little time for me."

I interrupted him. "Wait a minute, you bored, with what?"

He ignored my question. "I had hoped you could figure out where I'm coming from." He shook his head and ran his right hand across his face.

My face on fire, eyes watering, and a tight knot forming in my throat. The words discharged as if they were streams of lightning.

"You, you, you? What the…? All you do is whine about you and what you want, and when do you want it! The truth is, I could care less about your selfish black ass! And you can kiss my ass!" I stood up, wanting to grab the broom and hit him with it, but instead; I ended up leaving the scene. I needed to use my hands. I now see why people smoked cigarettes when they were upset. I rubbed my hands together, and I tried to crack my knuckles. I was so mad. I fought back the tears. I needed to go back and talk to him. I needed answers. I paced back to the bedroom. When I returned, he was standing and looking irritated.

When he spoke, again his voice tone was sarcastic. "See, if you were a grown ass woman by now, you'd figure out missionary is not the only way to fuck! I am fed-up of dealing with this childish bullshit. Fuck it, I'm sleeping on the couch!" He hustled out of the room. Hearing those remarks hurt me to the core. I had nothing else to even the score. I licked my wounds, tucked my tail, crawled into bed, and buried my head under the sheets. I sniveled into my already tear stained pillowcase.

It was four weeks after our last blow-up, and we had barely said a sentence to each other. He slept on the couch to avoid me. Meanwhile, I put Joshua in the bed with me off and on although I knew better, so I stopped. I did not want to confuse him and mess up his bed routine. I was going back to school as well. My head hurt from musing about my messed-up life. It was getting the best of me. I needed some advice on what to do about my life. Whom could I trust? During English class, I tuned out the substitute teacher to make a list of those in my circle. One side of the page the names, and on the opposite side, I ranked each one from 1-10. With one meaning, "I could not trust" and ten "I trust with my life." By doing the ranking; I could clearly see my immediate family ranked between five and seven. Grandma Elaine and my best friend were at number ten.

I skipped Biology class to take a nap in the restroom. It sounded hideous because the girls' restroom was filthy. I was fighting sleep, and I returned to work the afternoon. I found an empty stall, covered the seats with double layers of tissues, propped my butt on it, and feet on the seat. Resting my head was relaxing. There is no ventilation in here. I was trying to avoid the smells as much as possible. I took more tissues and covered my nose and mouth. This was much better; the dead trees smell. It was about an hour when I jerked awake from the nap at the sound of the loud school bell. I wanted to skip homeroom too but pulled myself together. I got a few sips of lukewarm water from the water fountain.

I asked myself, *do I have everything?* I remembered I left my Literature book in my locker. I headed toward the lockers, and before I got in the middle, I saw Francine standing at her locker. It's been a while since the last time I laid eyes on her. I was confident we had nothing to beef about, so I walked casually by her. Her head followed my movement.

"Candee, Candee."

I did 90 degrees and faced her. "Yes."

"I know we are not on speaking terms, but I have changed my life and need to clear up any confusion."

She paused, and before she could speak, I interrupted her, "Look, Francine, I'm over this dumb shit. I do not hold any grudges.

171

Let's leave it alone." Begrudgingly, I hoped she would move along and get out of my way, but she didn't move. Her face was flush, and her lips trembled.

"I-I-I.... want to get this off my chest. Can...we catch up later?" she asked wiping her face with the back of her left hand. I pleaded, *if God is listening, can he please come here, swipe her up, and keep her. She is making my life miserable on earth!*

I agreed to allow Francine to meet me at work on my lunch break. Since Jermaine and I were barely speaking, I purposely did not tell him. The pace at work was slow for a change, and after counting the drawer for the next shift change, I clocked out for the 30-minute break. I informed Mr. Pete I had a visitor coming by and to escort them to the breakroom. I headed to get my brown paper bag from the stuffed fridge. I had a blueberry yogurt, ham sandwich, and pickle. The weather was relaxing today, around 68 degrees. I ate out on the patio to ditch the smoky break room. Like an alarm clock, here came Mr. Pete's with Francine close behind.

As soon as we sat, her gums are flapping. "Candee, first off I want to say I am truly sorry for all the hurt and pain I caused you during and after your pregnancy. My intentions were purely evil and wrong." She cleared her throat. I apologized for eating in front of her. I bit into the dry sandwich, but she was not fazed and continued apologizing. "Jermaine was with me and you screwing around, and I got pregnant first. My parents were furious with me, so they took me to have an abortion."

She wiped her eyes and blew her nose. I, on the other hand, was in the zone from hearing her apology, which sounded like a horror story. "About eight months ago, we watched porn flicks, and he implied he wanted to have an orgy. At first, I told him no, but I cared for him, so I went along with his request. We did it one time." Her gaze shifted to the floor as she kept spilling her guts. "I caught him out with two other girls from the cheerleading squad. When confronted, he admitted he had slept with them both. "

I notice my lip was bleeding enough for me to taste the bitterness in my mouth. I dropped the half-eaten sandwich on the paper towel. My appetite was gone.

I wanted to grab her neck and choke her until she passed out! I saw red...which scared me. I had to remember where I was and show her no anger. Work. I needed this damn job! I collected my composure even though my ego was hurting.

"So, you are sorry for what?" I asked directly. "Jermaine and I are not married, and back then we were not engaged, so no harm done." I retorted, convincing myself.

"So, you accept him, the way he is?" she asked this with an attitude.

"What do you mean, the way he is?" I asked as if I would regret it.

"I-I don't know if I should be the one....to say anymore. I recently converted to Buddhism. I no longer practice sexual perversion. Candee, you are a decent person. Jermaine does not deserve you." She stood up and asked to give me a hug. I did not want a hug.

"Sit and tell me what you talking about," I demanded, gritting my teeth.

She was like a frightened kitten in the rain looking around for somewhere to run and hide. "Well... me and Jermaine have been together regularly up until....one month ago. It was all sex, no love, and no connection. After embracing my spiritual awakening, I craved more knowledge to follow my path towards enlightenment. I had come to terms we needed to go our separate ways. He has not made any contact with me to hook-up since Memorial Day. We were sneaking around because my parents loathed him. Please forgive me, I was wrong." She sounded sincere, but she was the one who had found religion in a fat man, not me. I was a work in progress... because I was livid and wanted to strangle her.

I took a cab home from work. My head was weighty from what Francine had confessed. For once, I was so numb I did not care if I made it out of the cab alive. The cab driver was talking, but I could not care less what he was saying. I stared ahead and mull over how many times Jermaine screwed me and went to her on the same day! Why did he treat me like crap? He professed he loved me. He claimed he wanted to marry me. I tried not to use obscenities because of Joshua, but my baby was not in the cab. I scream, "Fuck this motherfucker! Piece of shit! Dammit!" I slapped the passenger seat repeatedly, until my voice goes out, startling the driver.

The cab driver frowned at me and threw one hand up. "Yo... lady, what is your problem?"

I snapped back at him. "I am pissed! Drive this cab as fast as you can. I need to get home!" The cab driver seemed to sympathize with my overgrown tantrum, and when I asked how much the fee was, he waved his right hand at me and sighed, "It's on me, no worry."

I did not expect the act of random kindness. I thanked him and exited the cab.

It was fifteen minutes past eight and Jermaine should already have Joshua fed and ready for bed. As expected, I saw Jermaine lying on the love seat with Joshua fast asleep on his chest; snoring like bears. I detoured to the kitchen to see if there were any leftovers from dinner. I spotted a bowl of week-old homemade soup from Grandma Elaine. A memory of Grandpa bringing in the ingredients from the garden warmed my cold and barren heart. I tried to make the slightest noise as I heated up the soup.

As soon as I sat at the table, I saw Jermaine waking up looking around as if he was unaware of his surroundings. I froze to avoid startling him. He stood up with Joshua snuggled in his arms like an infant. He saw me, and stated faintly, "Hi baby, you home, great. Little man has been a good boy."

I made eye contact to show I heard him. He took Joshua to his bed and returned. He yawned, stretched his arms out, leaned in and gave me a hug. I abhorred it, but pretended to receive it in love. I was stewing all the lies, betrayals, and cheating. There were so many disappointments I wanted to scream again....but I couldn't. Not right now...not yet.

I wanted to pick up a plate or glass to throw at him and hit him so hard to put him in a daze. I wanted to cut his skin and cause him to bleed. My blood is boiling. I could slap the shit out of him! I ached to do it...anything but sit there and regret ever hooking up with him altogether. I got up from the table to wash my plate and avoided eye contact with him. He knew me well and could sense a problem by

175

the tension in my body language. I raised my shoulders up close to my ears as though I was carrying a pile of bricks.

I heard him talking, but it sounded like gurgles. I turned around to say, goodnight and he grabbed my right arm. "You seem distant, what's the matter? Was work bad today?"

I winked to throw him off. "I'm okay a little fatigued," I answered, as I turned away from him and went to take a shower. The shower was my weeping place. I mourned so hard, my heart was pounding through my chest. I moaned inaudibly into the warm wet washcloth. I sat in the shower and mourned more and more until my throat was burning in agony.

Chapter Fourteen: Irreparable

Beep... beep... beep! My alarm was going off. The alarm clock read 5:45 a.m. I wanted to press the snooze button for five more minutes, but instead, I motivated myself out of bed. Thank goodness, it was Friday. School would be a breeze with no homework. I had to work four hours at the grocery store, which meant I could get home before 8:00 tonight. As I sat up in the bed, I heard no noise from Joshua. Rather odd because he ordinarily woke me up before the alarm rang. I walked over to the crib, and he was not in it. Jermaine was not in bed either. A whiff of bacon crawls up my nose with a smell of coffee close behind. I crept toward the kitchen, which was about 15 steps away.

I saw Joshua sitting tall in his cream-colored high chair. His yellow plastic bowl was upside down on the tray. Jermaine had his back toward me as he stood in front of the fridge. "Good morning, Pooh." I gave Joshua a kiss on his nose because his cheeks covered with oatmeal. He stuck his fingers into the blob of oatmeal on the tray into his mouth.

"Good morning, Baby. Our little man is feeding himself this morning. How did you sleep? You almost kicked me right outta the bed," Jermaine insinuated, laughing.

I looked at him and own up, "I must have been having a

nightmare or dreaming weird things. Sorry, I can't remember," I lied. I did remember kicking him.

"I wanted to cook for us. I could tell last night you were kind of out of it." His voice sounded so sweet and caring. I was familiar with this trifling gesture. It meant one thing; he was up to no good and being helpful was his weapon of choice to slay the dragon. I thanked him for the meal but continued my morning routine.

Since we both had day schedules, Jermaine dropped me off at school and Joshua at daycare. To detour from any conversations, I pretended I needed to study for a pop quiz. Jermaine turned off the radio and concentrated on driving. About five minutes went by before he said, "Excuse me, baby, I gotta ask you quick."

I looked over at him, *with what the hell is it now* expression.

"I picked up a driver's handbook for you the other day. I placed it in the kitchen drawer next to the stove." He sounded genuine.

"Thanks," I remarked, as I looked back over at the notebook.

"I can help you study and test drive when you ready," he continued.

I was silent and gave him no attention. His eyes glared at me while we sat at the traffic stop sign.

Therefore, I purposely agreed, "We will work on it." I took a deep sigh to let him know he was bothering me. He tapped the steering wheel as though he was listening to music. Being silent was not a normal thing for him to do. He loved talking and being heard. I, on the other hand, could do without them both. A memory of the third grade, when my teacher would yell my name for talking too loud while working at a table with other students. To this day, I can hear her yell, "Candee Black! You are talking too loud and too much! Close your mouth and get to work!" I was teased each time she caught me. I got the hint to lower my voice. With each school year, when working in groups, I would whisper so much my friends in middle school spread a rumor I was hard of hearing. Back to reality, we are now crossing over the bridge to the school. I needed to talk to someone before I exploded with words of venom.

I put my notebook inside my dull blue book bag with a broken strap. I peeked at Joshua in the back seat; he was fast asleep. I adored watching him suck on his bottom lip as if he was sucking on a bottle. I kissed my right index finger and touched his left leg. As soon as the car stopped Jermaine stated, "See you tonight baby." He leaned over and kissed me on the lips. I was deeply in love with his kisses. His lips were smooth and moist. For a few seconds, I forgot how much I was displeased with him.

"Yep, see you tonight." I chimed as I exited the passenger door.

Right now, I trusted two people with the details of my messed up life; Vaughn and Grandma Elaine. I should run into Vaughn when exchanging classes, but not enough time to vent my rage. I could write her a note to let her know we needed to talk today. This time around, I would hand it to her myself. I remembered what happened to the last note I handed off…. *Intercepted. Yep, non-delivery.*

In English Lit, we were discussing *The Lord of the Rings* by J.R.R. Tolkien. I enjoyed it more than the other previous readings, which had already slipped my memory. With this particular book, I get entwined in the storyline with its many twists and turns. I drifted off into a fantasy world filled with a cascade of magic and wonderment. For a short moment, I could forget about the pains, disappointments, and betrayals of a man I loved with all my heart.

"Class, please turn to page…," the teacher requested. My cue to pretend to follow along.

Instead, I wrote the note to Vaughn. I wrote two serious sentences to show her how urgent this was. *V, if ever I need you it is now! I need to talk to you ASAP! Please meet me at the girl's restroom during lunch period. C-*

To my surprise, the teacher didn't assign any homework after the discussion was over, but she did inform us there would be a pop quiz before the end of the week. *These pop quizzes are a pain in the ass! They should go out to the students who have nothing better to do!* On the way to my next class, I kept a lookout for Vaughn, hoping she would not lollygag around. Like a familiar tune, she waltzed near the yellow double doors heading in my direction. I smiled at her, walked toward her, and gave her a quick hug.

She hugged me back. "Good morning."

I swiftly planted the note in her right hand. "Morning V, check this out when you get a chance. See ya soon", I uttered and sprinted off to make the next class. I did not look back.

I was practically jogging as I headed to the girls' restroom. I focused ahead like a horse wearing blinders. It appeared I was trotting in slow motion. I tried not to knock into anyone. I waited for about two minutes before I saw Vaughn prancing up to me. She looked concerned. She whispered, "Let's go outside so we can talk." I followed aimlessly before the tears surfaced. I was heartbroken about what I was about to tell her. We found an empty bench away from other students.

As soon as I sat down, I spoke. "V, Jermaine has been sleeping around with Francine. She got pregnant, had an abortion, and he was with her last month. He had other girls too. I am so disgusted!" I blasted. "I am such a fool!" I already had the tissues ready. I wiped my nose and dabbed my eyes.

Vaughn sympathized saying. "I am sorry to hear this, Candee. I hate to say this now, but you do remember when he first cheated on you? If I were you, I wouldn't give him any more ass. Jermaine has not changed. What are you going to do?"

Hearing the truth from my best friend did not help me. Although I needed to believe the truth, I knew Vaughn wasn't trying to hurt me. "I don't know what to do. I do not want to live with him anymore. I am thankful we are not married."

"Can you move back home? Have you told your parents? How did you find out?" Vaughn asked. I want to sidetrack from all the questions but answered them anyway.

"Francine came by my work. I told her she could. She confessed she has changed and she needed to tell me so she can ask for forgiveness." I blew my nose and sniffed one more time.

"So…she found God, Buddha, shit maybe Muhammad! She is a whore and needs her ass kicked! You mean she told you they been sleeping around even after you got engaged?" Vaughn was livid.

"Yep, she ain't lying. Jermaine has been coming in late. Sex with me is close to obsolete. He claims he is too worn-out to get busy like we used to. I didn't fuss about it, but I guess I was in denial about our relationship. I'll call my mom sometime today."

The sound of the dull lunch bell rang through the air, and we both stood up. We hugged each other and walked together until we split up to go to the next class.

After school, I headed to work in a cab. My usual driver was not available, so I had to wait 10 extra minutes for another cab. I took a seat at the end of the school driveway, but not for long.

"Excuse me; you cannot sit there. You should sit near the front of the school. It's the school policy." The sun was shining directly in my eyes as I glared in the direction of the soft-spoken teacher.

"No problem," I answered standing up stretching to carry the one strap book bag up the hill. I was waiting for the other strap to break off before buying another one.

As soon as I plopped my badonkadonk on the cemented sidewalk, a horn beeped and there was my ride. I slogged downhill dragging my heavy feet. The cab driver had a friendly face. A beige cap covered his long black hair. He had a thin black beard, and his skin tone was bronze. He hopped out to open the back door for me.

"Good evening, young lady. I'll get the door for you." I grinned, chivalry wasn't dead after all.

"Thank you so much. I am going to Pete's Grocery Store on Mulberry Street," I voiced, as I got comfortable for the fifteen-minute drive. I saw the clock and could see I would be at 10 minutes late clocking in.

The driver made small talk. "Shall I wait while you pick up groceries?" His accent sharp and foreign; he was not from around here. His eyes looked right at me from the rear-view mirror.

"No, I am on my way to work."

"Should I pick you up at what time?" He was persistent. I let out a soft giggle, "No thank you. I have someone coming to get me."

He was silent for about twenty seconds. "You go to school and work. Must be tough, yes?"

"Not at all when you have to do what you gotta do."

"Sure, family needs help, huh?" Now he was getting too nosey, but seemed harmless so I answered him.

"Yep, I got a baby boy and...an apartment to take care of." I left out Jermaine on purpose.

"It sounds good, a young woman doing well."

I took his words to heart. In my mind, I patted myself on the back. Soon he pulled up to the store. "It is $3.75," he informed.

I gave him $4.00 dollars. He gave me my change and a business card. "I hope you have a safe night," he stated.

"Thank you." I squinted at the card and tried to pronounce his name. "Rau-u-l Ba-naan-bar." I got it out without chopping it up too bad.

"Most people call me Ralph." He smiled showing his less than perfect teeth.

"Good-night, Ralph. Thanks again."

It took me close to four months to acclimate to the smells from the meat department. The smell of raw meat gave me the heebie-jeebies. My skin crawled when I first saw the red meats not wrapped in the plastic. I see the dried dirt buried between the cracks of dull white tiles on the floors, It is obvious the night shift overlooks deep cleaning. I counted and tagged thousands of neatly stacked canned goods. As soon as I had the groove for my counting system, a customer interrupted me.

"Excuse me miss…" Could he not see I was counting? *Dammit!* I huffed and made eye contact.

"Yes, sir, how can I help you?" I asked relaxing my shoulders.

"I seem to have forgotten where the loaves of bread are." He was an elderly Caucasian man wearing thick-rimmed glasses. He appeared thin and frail. He is wearing a pair of oversized gray pants and beige sweater. I knew the weather was pushing close to 80 degrees outside.

I stood up to assist him so he would get out of my hair. "Sure, it's no problem. Follow me, please." I could tell he was taking short strides but at a moderate pace. "The bread is on aisle 15; the store has been remodeled, and some things have been shuffled around," I implied, smiling back at him.

He spoke again but stopped. "I-I-I, who… are you?"

He was looking right at me in utter confusion.

"Sir, I am a worker at Pete's. My name is Candee." I pointed to my nametag clipped on the right side of my white shirt. His crystal blue eyes were lined with aging wrinkles. A flashback came to me of my great-great grandmother Dorothea; she was stricken with Alzheimer's' disease at the age of 70.

One day she was laughing and talking at a family reunion, and the next week she was walking along a busy road in her pajamas, dazed and not remembering where she lived. Momma told me the signs of the disease had been showing here and there for several years in Grandma Doretha, but she refused to get a checkup.

Therefore, it progressed and took her away one bitter snowy winter before I was six years old. I had not met her husband because he had died many years before from a heart attack.

"Sir, what is your name? Do you live close by?"

The man was dumbfounded as I watched him patting his right pants pockets as if he was a little panicky. I knew I could do more harm if I touched him because he could attack me from fear. I saw I was closer to the deli than the back of the store where Mr. Pete was doing inventory. I motioned to Amber, the clerk in the deli, to come assist with the situation. She must have seen the urgency in my expression because she dashed right over.

I whispered to her, "I have no idea who he is, and it seems he has no idea why he is here. Please call 911 so we can get some help."

Amber smiled at the man and spoke, "Mr. Ben, do you know where you at?"

The man responded with some jumbled words. His eyes widened, and he stepped back as though he was frightened.

Amber turned back to me. "Candee, this is Mr. Ben Hamilton. He fought in the Vietnam War. His mind is pretty messed up. He walked off from the nursing home again. This is his second field trip here this year." She spoke softly to him. "Mr. Ben, you going to get your workers fired." She shook her head at him, gently took him by his left hand, and told me she would call the nursing home.

I thanked Amber and moseyed on back to my assigned duties. For some reason, I could not get Mr. Ben out of my head. I had concern for him and could not fathom how staff had not missed him.

After counting 12,520 cans, it was time for my fifteen-minute

185

break. I was thirsty, so I grabbed my water bottle and some coins to get a cold can of Dr. Pepper from the drink machine. I used the free phone in the canteen to call my mom. It had been a couple of weeks since I have spoken to her. I was looking forward to hearing her voice.

"Hello. Charlene speaking."

"Momma, hey…it's Candee, how is the family doing?"

"Hi Candee, we are good. I hope you and Joshua doing well. Is everything alright?"

I pause for about five seconds, "Momma it's not going well with Jermaine and me. I need to move back home and figure this out."

She was quiescence and all of a sudden huffed. "Well now, home is not the same with Richard getting joint custody of his son, RJ. He will be coming here during the summer, school breaks, and the holidays too."

I was speechless. *She told me no, I cannot come back home because her man's son has taken my place.* My world was breaking piece by piece, and I was crumbling with it. "Ma, please let us come home. I can't stay here anymore." I begged and pleaded to no avail.

Momma was firm and ended the conversation with, "You two can work this out. You both are stubborn; sit down and talk things out."

I was self-conscience to admit our problems, but now I was desperate. "Ma, Jermaine is cheating on me and has been for a long time."

She cleared her throat before speaking. "Candee, as a woman you have to bear it and ask a man what can you do to make him desire you more. It is all about giving and taking. Jermaine loves you because he is with you. Those other women are pawns."

I shook my head to make sure I was alive hearing these crazy words! I tuned out my mother's voice. I was numb from hearing her say we needed to work out our problems. Most humiliating, she wanted me to overlook his trifling ways and continue to take his shit. I did not like her right now and did not want to listen to her crappy advice either. "Ma I gotta get back to work." I wanted to slam the phone on the hook. Instead, I hung-up without saying good-bye.

After I finished the inventory, I did not go back to the cash register. Instead, I had cleaning duties. It was another way for me to escape and not have to entertain the customers. I toss around the idea of going to stay with Grandma Elaine or Auntie Bernice. And regretfully Mrs. McDoogle, if I became desperate. I had a conversation with my low self-esteem. I blamed myself for Jermaine's wrongdoings and the reason he slept around. I guessed I should have paid more attention to him and my body. I admitted it was not as lean as it was before my pregnancy a year ago. A part of me agreed momma was right, I needed to change and forgive him. Besides, it could have been worse – he could have left me before the baby was born. I finished cleaning the break room and bathrooms and sweeping in the freezer area. The store was closing at 7:30 p.m., so the night shift could finish the inventory. I gathered my belongings and headed to sit at the front of the store to wait for Jermaine.

I had been waiting for over ten minutes when I asked for a ride home from my co-worker Amber. She lived four blocks past me so I was hoping she would not mind. Amber and I were casual at work, so I found it easy to chat with her on the way home. She drove a clean blue van. There are two car seats in the back row.

"You have two children?" I asked.

"Yes, honey I got me one-year-old twins' a boy and a girl. I was determined to give them strong names – Kassandra and Kirkland."

I pictured her children were as beautiful as she was. Amber had a dark caramel skin tone accentuated her shoulder length black hair. She had to cover and wear it in a bun when working in the deli. She once told me her ethnicity was Cherokee Indian and Black. The large size dreamcatcher dangling from the rearview mirror distracted me. My eyes followed it swinging back and forth.

"How old is your baby now?" she asked.

"Joshua is fifteen months now. He has most of his teeth too," I boasted, laughing. We chatted for a few minutes about the love of our lives. I switched gears and asked. "Does Mr. Hamilton have any relatives to check on him at the nursing home? He seems like a nice man."

"Yeah, he has a couple of sisters and brothers, but they hardly go there. I think most of them live out of town. He was married before, and they divorced, no kids though." She looked at me. "I used to date one of his nephews when I was in high school. I know a lot about Ben. He taught high school Algebra after he came back from the war. He was the serenest teacher we had. He did not believe in exams so he would give us mini quizzes throughout the week. It was the last time I made an 'A' in math." She burst out laughing, and I joined in.

To my surprise, I didn't see Jermaine's truck in its parking space. I hope he stopped by the store to pick up some diapers, milk, or toilet paper because we were out. Most nights, I didn't have any fear of walking up to my apartment in the dark. However, tonight for some reason it was spooky. It was motionless, and it appeared two streetlights were out. As soon as I turned the key in the door, I saw headlights on the front door. I turned around, and it was Jermaine. I went inside, dropped my book bag and jacket on the square wooden lamp table, and turned around to go meet him.

As soon as I head back out, Jermaine was walking inside with Joshua on his shoulders. Joshua looked drowsy; his head flopping side to side like a rag doll.

"Aww, my baby is pooped." I took him gently from Jermaine's arms. "What happened? I waited for you. Did you forget about me?"

He did not answer. Jermaine was not looking at me; his eyes were gazing at the floor. I knew him well enough to know when something was bothering him. He was not easy to dissect, especially if he was guilty of wrongdoing. I could see and sense it even when he was upset.

"I got some stuff in the truck. I be right back", he announced dryly and walked out. I tucked Joshua in his bed.

Jermaine returned with two bags of groceries and his work duffle bag. Within a few seconds, he disclosed, "I got fired today because I had an accident at work and they piss tested me. I tested positive for weed. No surprise, right?"

My mouth dropped wide open. I went numb. My blood ran ice cold. I was going to lose my freaking mind! I picked up the first thing I got my hands on and threw one of Joshua's shoes at the wall. I couldn't deal with his stupid ass!

"What... fired? You told me after you got the job you would stop smoking. You gave me your word to not fu...uk.....screw this up!"

He popped up and leaped right in front of me, pointing his middle finger right in my face. "Yeah, I did say it. I tried to quit. Hell... I needed a high to go into that shitty place to work my ass off for that little ass money!" His eyes were dark and wide. My heart was beating fast. "Without the weed, I would have hauled ass outta there a long time ago! I should be playing pro football with my time! My last check should cover the rent after its paid .... fuck it!" As usual, he stomped off like a two-year-old needing a damn nap.

The next day, I planned how to say I was fed up! There was no uncomplicated way to tell him I was leaving him or to confront him about his deceitful ways. I needed to spit it out and let him deal with the repercussions. I could get ten extra hours at work, and it helped make ends meet. On the other hand, I had dropped out of school going on a month now. I was overwhelmed with work, and I was wounded and depressed. I had not told my family yet. I was regretful. One good thing was I got my driver's' license. Dad had been forthcoming to help more now he knew Jermaine was not working. Dad mentioned he would look out for a piece of a car and I would not have to worry about paying him back. Jermaine declared he had been busy looking for jobs in the daytime. I told him he could donate his blood and plasma any day of the week. He did not respond to the comment.

The day came when he received his last paycheck. "I got a

money order for the rent, and I got a few groceries with what's left," Jermaine reported as he put the four brown paper bags on the kitchen table. I pretended to have deaf ears as I stepped past him on my way to the bathroom. I could hear him smack his lips as a sign of dismissing me. I should have been glad he kept his word about paying the rent. My little paycheck would barely pay for the utilities, daycare, and whatever left for cabs and lunches. I glared at this lie on my left hand and contemplated not if, but when to pawn it.

I ran right into Jermaine as I scurried to check on Joshua. He had been playing in his playpen in the living room area. "Dang, sorry," I apologized, looking through him. "Listen, we need to have this conversation now because we are not going to get past our issues." I gave him the dead eye contact. He followed me into the living room. I huffed and puffed as I picked up all the toys Joshua had thrown on the floor from the playpen.

"Dada." Joshua reached for his daddy. Jermaine picked him up and hugged him close.

"Hey, little man, what you want?" Joshua grinned, showing a mouth full of teeth. He looked so sweet and handsome. I had braided up his soft black hair to help him not sweat so much.

Jermaine took a seat on the used couch. He cleared his throat. "I'm leaving next month. Back to moms unless my boy Deon let me chill at his place until I get another job. I will help you with little man, take you to school, but it is going to be tight to take you elsewhere."

I cut him off, "So you want to run home to your mother?" I stared right into his eyes to see if he was going to be a wuss and gaze at the floor. To my surprise, his eyes stared back at me, not even a blink.

"Yes, I do. I know my getting fired has put a wedge between us and…"

I interrupted with an attitude. I pointed and waved my index finger back and forth. "No, no, hold up!" My voice was loud. I saw Joshua's bottom lip poking out, so I gathered myself and tamed it.

"Look, Jermaine, it's not about you being fired. It is the other shit going on since we been together. Yes, I know about you and Francine, she got pregnant, had the abortion. She said you have orgies and sex with all these stank asses." I was exhausted and nauseous at the same time. His face was blank, no reaction. No words…silent. My chest was aching from my heart beating intensely through my shirt. Hot tears were forming up in my eyes and spilling over like a dam bursting at the seams. "I can't believe you! I must be a complete fool….I want nothing more to do with you."

Jermaine glanced at me with a look of shock. He stood with Joshua and took him back to his playpen. He grabbed Joshua's sippy cup and filled it with cold milk from the fridge. Joshua took the cup and sucked big gulps. "My son is thirsty." He said to Joshua.

"Yeah, Francine, confessed about y'all and the fucking you been doing behind my back!" I blared. I stomped off toward the bathroom to blow my nose because it was full of snots. My gut instinct was to avoid contact with him, but not today, no today I had plenty to say. I strutted back into the living room where I saw him laid back on the love seat staring at the ceiling. He looked relaxed, calm, and tolerably chilled. I needed his attention so instead of screaming I picked up an old magazine and threw it at him, hitting him on his right leg.

"What?" he jerked, looking dazed. I bit my tongue. I did not notice any pain. "You make me sick! We deserve better. I know I can have much better. Joshua does not need a whore for a daddy. Yea, we are done. And I don't want you anywhere near me!"

Blood rushed to my head. My body hot like an oven cooking a fat ham. I paced back and forth as if I was in a boxing match sketching out my next move. And he watched me like a hawk. Now I had his attention fully, so I kept talking. "For years...I wanted to believe you weren't fucking around. Even when Vaughn use to tell me she seen you riding around town with some girls...I was in denial. I would make up excuses. You were helping a cousin or a friend. I told myself repeatedly you were trying to do right by our son, and no, no, hell naw! You had your dick in someone else, some nasty heifer! Jesus, Mary, and Joseph, I need to get checked for diseases!"

I looked up to the ceiling with my eyes closed. In my head I screamed, *I hate him. I want to kill him. I want to hurt him so bad!* I could not spend time in jail for this piece of dick.

My knees were weak from shaking. My throat closing from holding in the scream. I got up enough strength, dragged my sagging body to the bedroom, and collapsed on the bed. I let out a deep groan, which soon turned into un-controlling sobbing. I grabbed a pillow and let go... hurting from wanting momma to hold me and tell me it would get better. I needed my daddy to tell me he would kick Jermaine's ass because he hurt his little girl. I needed someone to care. The engagement broken from words spoken. Words dipped, covered, and smeared across my heart in deception. It was all lies hidden from the truth.

I woke up in a stupor; the effects of total oppression, it has shattered me. I saw the bathroom light was on. I heard no noise. No TV, no Joshua's pitter-patter, or any evidence of life. I slapped my face lightly to make sure I was alive. I made my way looking for my baby boy. I checked his bed; it was empty. I checked the kitchen; it was empty too. I saw a note on the walnut table propped up between the salt and pepper shakers. It read, *Candee, you ain't feeling me. Joshua and me at mom's. When you up call me.* I dropped the note back where I found it. I went into the bathroom and washed my face with cold water. I saw my loose curls matted to my head, I guessed from the tears and sweat.

I called Grandma Elaine to ask her if I could spend some time at her house. The phone rang four times before she picked it up. "Hell...lo-o-o." Her voice sounded dry and wearisome.

"Hi Grandma, it's Candee. You sound as though you might be coming down with a cold."

"Hi dear, no it's about getting old. You know my birthday is in two weeks. God grants me that day I will be 78."

"I had you on my mind. I was hoping you would want some company."

"Candee apple, you know I love to see you and my great-grandson. What day you talking bout?" I wanted to blurt, *right now*, but did not want to sound frantic.

"Soon, I need to reflect, time to refresh, and get some wise advice."

Saying those words crumbled my *shameful wall* into small

194

pieces exposing the brokenness. I covered my mouth with my right hand, unable to keep the conversation going. Grandma Elaine was my gift from God. She did not ask any unnecessary questions or blame me for the mistakes I had made. She listened and prayed quietly. After a few cricket minutes, she responded, "I tell ya what- you call me when you on your way. Can I expect ya before my birthday?"

I sniffed and cleared my throat. "Yes Ma'am." We chimed good-bye, and my mind conjured up a lie for my boss to approve my short notice to take off.

It had been about two hours since I read Jermaine's note; I missed my little boy. I called him and asked him to bring Joshua home. I made dinner even though I had no appetite. I knew my baby had to eat regardless. There was the delightful smell of spaghetti sauce with sprinkles of minced garlic. I toasted a few slices of white bread with my homemade garlic butter. The salad was a little plain looking without tomatoes but looked appealing with the romaine lettuce, cucumbers, and onions. I learned to make my own dressing from momma's recipe. Ketchup, mayonnaise, and few chopped sweet pickles. I did not care for the last two ingredients, but it had a decent flavor. I heard the keys jingling the front door, so I opened it. The sun was setting in the background, and the air had cooled down. Jermaine was holding Joshua's hand as they both stepped inside.

"Pooh, hungry? I made your favorite, spaghetti." I served dinner with love for my child. Although my heart was heavy with anguish for my ex-lover, baby daddy, and once upon a time fake husband, I would feed him one last time.

Chapter Fifteen: Considering All Things

For the next few weeks, he slept wherever and we avoided each other as if one of us had a deadly virus. It seemed our movement was locked in slow motion. I was sick of seeing, smelling, and hearing him. He had hoped to move in with his boy, but it did not work out. Now he said he was going back home to mommy dearest. It was Saturday, and I had the weekend off, which helped my mood.

I had picked up the nasty habit of biting my nails when my mind drifts. I got a voice message from Vaughn, Dad, and the clinic for Joshua's 15-month immunizations shots. I prioritized whom to call first. I chose the clinic.

In another week, millions of American couples who were in love would celebrate Valentine's Day. I would spend this V-Day without a grown-up sweetheart. Forgotten memories crept back to celebrating Valentine's Day at my elementary school. Back then, I had a boyfriend or a crush on some boy who liked someone else. I feasted on collecting the different cards, and I loved the candy heart suckers! Back in grade school, it was not a major deal if you had someone special it was more important to receive the most cards. A couple of times I cheated because I did not want to be the one with the least number of cards. Therefore, if I had any extra cards left over, I would write it was from someone else. Reminiscing about those days, I now saw how desperate I needed the validation of being worthy to be loved. I had made plenty of friends. Valentine's Day would prove otherwise; as I looked in my brown decorated paper bag with those silly red, pink, and white hearts glued all over and those so-called friends hadn't even given me a card!

I had to admit, it hurt. I took those moments and logged them in my memory bank. Over the school years, I removed those so-called friends out of my circle. It did seem with each school year my circle became smaller. I did not admit it bothered me because I had Vaughn in my circle. As we grew older, she and I were becoming distant. She was off traveling, and I was here being a mother. She had no children and actively dating. I had no social life. As I compared our worlds, I was miserable and lonely. Remembering the old days, reminds me I need to call her back.

The front windowpane thickly covered in crystal-white frost. Outside was freezing temperature at 32 degrees. I used my right index finger to scribble some lines through the frost as I listened to the phone rings.

"This is Vaughn" she answered on the fourth ring.

"Hey, V. It's Candee. I apologize for taking so long to return your call. Shit has been crazy around here lately."

Before I said another word, she chimed in. "I had you on my mind. What's going on now?" she sounded annoyed. I hesitated to give her all the juicy details and nonstop to the punch line.

"I am fed up with Jermaine, and he is sick of me. Yeah, we split up."

She paused, but I could hear her making noise in the

background. "V, you there?"

"Girlfriend, what are you gonna do? Can you survive without him? I mean he was helping you get around and watching the lil one."

I needed to catch her up on a few changes. "Yes, I did need him, but I got a driver's license now, and daddy is looking around for me a car. I plan to pay him back when I file my income taxes." I was proud to be held accountable.

"My girl, you are such a trooper! I have to admit if I was in your shoes; I think I would be at a nuthouse by now." She giggled, but I didn't. A few seconds go by, and she says, "Anyhow... I am glad you called. I am coming to town next week – on Valentine's Day to be exact. However, I had plans to spend a few days with my baby Arnie, he's taken off from work. I'm giving you a heads up so we can hang out and have fun."

My head throbbing from stress. Overloaded about how we would make it without begging for help. My pride was thicker than a mattress, so I responded, "Sure sounds as if we got ourselves a plan. I can't wait to see you; it's been too long."

She agreed, and we chatted a few more minutes before I heard a pitter-patter, and saw Joshua standing with his diaper hanging half off his brown buttocks. "V, girl, I gotta get off here. This boy got his ass out..." I busted out laughing.

"I hope he wet and not pooped," she giggled.

"Rightly so... Mom implied he might be ready to be potty-trained because he has been pulling the diaper off."

V was dying laughing. "Hahaha, we talk later. See you soon!"

I detested wintry weather! The icy wind cut through my bony

legs as I stepped outside to check the mailbox because Grandma Elaine had sent me a money order to help pay next month's rent. My heart warmed as I saw the familiar sky blue colored envelope Grandma used. My smile erased as soon as I opened a **FINAL NOTICE** from the electric company. It read, '**Please pay your bill in FULL within 7 days to avoid disconnection.**' The bill was two months behind, and the total due was *$ 175.00.* This was my sign it was time to pawn the sparkling piece of jewelry. A small solution to conquer one problem. I had no quick fixes or plans on how to pay all the bills with my poverty level income. It was going to be impossible another defeated moment. I watched the thick white smoke from my mouth dissipate as soon as the frigid wind carried it away. I walked briskly back to the apartment, remembering I had left Joshua in his high chair eating his favorite food, macaroni and cheese for lunch. As soon as I returned to the kitchen, he whined, "Juju" for juice.

"No sweetie you need 'wa-wa', I mean water. Too much juice is bad for those pretty white teeth." I puckered up and blew him a kiss. He smiled as I handed him his drink. He loved those yellow noodles! I had to trick him into eating other foods by using macaroni to hide it. He had not figured it out yet. He dived right into the plate with his little fat fingers and shoved the noodles in his mouth. I planned to introduce him to the spoon soon.

I wiped his hands off and took him out of the chair. He walked over to play with his ball. As I finished cleaning up the kitchen, I heard two hard knocks at the front door. It startled me a little because I was not expecting anyone. I peeked through the peephole and saw it was daddy. I opened the door and saw he is not alone.

He smiled. "Hi sweetie, we were close to the neighborhood and figured we'd drop by to see how y'all doing."

I stared at the woman with him.

"I am sorry. This is Ursula, my lady. Ursula, this is Candee, my oldest daughter."

We greeted each other cordially.

I invited them in, and within two seconds, Joshua appeared, grinning like the Cheshire cat. He adored my daddy. He hobbled over to him and gave him a sweet hug. My eyes shifted to the Ursula woman. She was cute and had a petite shape. Her skin was tawny with ruby cheekbones, and I saw her long jet-black shiny curls escaping from under the fake fur lining of her brown hooded jacket. I could tell she had a large butt as well. Clearly, daddy was still an ass man. My dad knew me too well and could sense when I was stressed because my facial expression showed it.

"Candee, can I use your restroom? Your father missed the last exit for a pit stop," Ursula announced in a monotone voice.

"Sure, go to the right of the hallway." I pointed.

"Sweetie, what's wrong?" My dad wasted no time asking. I try to shun from lying, but most of all I hated begging.

"Dad the bills are coming due before I have enough money it's getting hard. Sorry," I finished with watery eyes.

"Sweetheart, I get the picture before you lose hope have you considered Social Services assistance? They got money for cut-offs, evictions, heating bills...you gotta apply," he instructed with calmness and gave me an 'I miss you' hug. He kissed me on the top forehead and released me. Joshua came toddling over towards us, grasping his large blue ball. Dad encouraged him to throw it. "Throw the ball, lil man." Joshua smiled and walked closer to dad and dropped the ball. After they left, I called Social Services to inquire about my bills. I was relieved when a live person answered the phone.

On Valentine's' Day I brought home vanilla ice cream and chocolate chip cookies from work to celebrate with my son. He was too young to be eating hard candy, but he loved ice cream! At the last minute, Jermaine called and declared his truck would not start up and he could not get me. I instantly called my dad and begged him to come instead. He had returned after working out of town. He sounded drained, but I overlooked the fact. I had no money for a cab. I had walked out the front door when he arrived.

"Hi sweetie," he responded sheepishly.

"Hi daddy, Happy Valentine's Day," I leaned over to kiss him on the right cheek. I sensed the smell of cigarettes on his skin. I carefully reminded him to pick Joshua up at daycare. "Happy Valentine to you sweetheart. Okay, tell me where to turn," he responded.

I stared out the passenger window and listened to Barry White playing on the radio. My dad loved Barry. He loved all of his music. A memory came to mind when he was trying to surprise momma on her 30th birthday. He cooked dinner, set up the table with candles, and we cleaned the house with extra bleach to get a clean smell. Momma came from work fatigued she entered the dark house; we lunged with "Surprise!" Dad sang, *You Are the First, My Last, My Everything,* into his right thumb with his low-baritone voice. Mom seemed jubilant. It might have been the last time I saw them both on the clouds. I informed dad my appointment with Social Services went well for me. They agreed to pay the cut-off notice for the utilities, increased the food stamps, and added Joshua's name to the Christmas Bureau for toys assistance. "I'm glad you asked for help before it got too bad," dad responded.

"Yep me too." My pride was gone.

At the daycare, Mrs. Ruth greeted me at the front office with a note in one hand and Joshua's hand in the other. He smiled wide when he saw me standing there. I squatted to meet his big mocha colored eyes. He looked so much like his daddy I wanted to pinch him.

"Miss Candee, your little one has been busy today." Mrs. Ruth sounded annoyed. I picked him up and remembered how heavy he was as his long legs attempted to grab me around the waist.

"Maaa, Maaa," he squealed, hugging my neck.

"Joshua, what you been doing?"

Mrs. Ruth explained he had been throwing toys at the other children when he didn't want to share. "We are sending him to a time-out chair for two minutes when he does this. We encourage our parents to do the same discipline to help the child learn consequences."

I stood quietly and crossed my eyes after hearing this. I shook off the icy demeanor and faked a warm smile. "I am sorry to hear he misbehaved. I will work with him at home." Fumes filled my head, *He is a dang baby! He might be a terrible two, but he is all mine.* I swiftly snapped back to mommy attitude, gently took the note, and snatched his navy-blue diaper bag from the floor.

As soon as we got inside the car, daddy turned around to speak, and Joshua leaped out of his car seat. Joshua loved my dad and dad loved him back. It was a beautiful relationship because dad longed for a baby boy.

Even though the temperature outside had dropped, it warmed my heart seeing them love each other as if they were the only two alive. It dawned on me how much I had missed my dad's affection and attention for a long time. "Candee, the other day I drove by a sky-blue 1975 Pontiac Grand Prix for sale. It is up off HWY 85 near Charlotte. I stopped, and the fella there said he would let it go for $1,200.00. It has high miles, but the engine is clean, new wheels, and inside looks brand new." He paused for a few seconds.

Before he could speak again, I squealed like a kid on a sugar rush. "Yes-s-s-s, daddy, get it!"

He laughed sluggishly and chuckled, "Okay, chill out. After driving it, I talked the fella down to $1,000.00. So first thing Saturday morning we need to go and get it."

My cheeks filled with exuberant joy. My own sweet ride. I already had a name for it: Sally. As I glanced out the passenger window, my smile was visible in the glass. I had not been so excited in a long time, and it soothed my soul!

Dad arrived at 7:00 a.m. to pick me up. His girlfriend Ursula agreed to watch Joshua at the apartment. She did not have any little ones but had a ten-year-old daughter. I am against leaving him with a stranger, but I needed to get the car before someone else did. I kissed Joshua's tender cheeks before handing him off to Ursula. Her daughter's name was Shaquita, and she brought some bubbles to blow with him. His eyes appeared excited; my cue to leave. During the hour and a half drive, different situations ran rampant about the car. *What do I do if it breaks down? Who will change the oil? How much is the insurance? I am not an experienced driver yet. I had my license for a month.* My body jerked from hearing dad blare my name in my left ear.

"Candee! You awake?"

"Of course, I'm stunned. It's hitting me all of a sudden I will soon be a car owner."

"I hope it's a good first starter. It should get you back and forth without problems. You know I don't know a lot about cars. I depend on this guy to be straightforward about the car. But you know how folks are after a quick dollar."

I agreed anxious, but there was no turning back now.

Later, during my weekend visit with Grandma Elaine, we celebrated her birthday with family and a few of her Bingo friends. Grandma seemed to have enjoyed her celebration even though she whispered to me she missed Grandpa. I kept silent. Mrs. Lucille's Home Cooked Meals had catered dinner. The food was delicious! The barbeque ribs practically fell off the bones. I licked my fingers clean and went for seconds. The collard greens spiced with red peppers and bacon bits, and potato casserole coated my taste buds similar to a warm blanket. Some gave presents, hugs, kisses, and I.O.U.'s to Grandma and too soon it was time to leave. Mom and I had not talked much since Jermaine left. Her body language showed she was jealous about daddy getting me a car. I giggled inside. As I transferred to the kitchen to clean up, Mom and Christian were standing near the bathroom.

"Sis, when you gonna take us for a ride in your stylish car?" Christian asked, showing off her perfect smile. "Girl, you know I will get around to it soon as my hectic life becomes peaceful. You know I am trying to do it all without a baby daddy."

Mom stared and sighed. "Candee, how is the car doing?"

"It is a gas guzzler, 8 cylinders and it's a fast car too. So far so good." I informed her, visualizing a pat on the back.

"I hope you can come over for dinner next week after church. You are welcome to come with us." Mom sounded serious.

Richard waltzed in with a glass of tea and an empty plate. "Hi Candee, I see Joshua is getting taller. Whatcha feeding the boy?"

I laughed softly. "He is eating more protein and starches, loves macaroni and cheese. I got extra food stamps to keep up with his growing appetite." We all broke out laughing.

We hugged and kissed as they were leaving. Soon the house was calm. I found Grandma humming with Joshua in Grandpa Calvin's maple rocking chair in the den area near the fireplace. The song sounded familiar. "Candee girl, you remember me singing you this tune?"

I smiled and made my way to the tan colored loveseat. I stretched out to rest my worn-out body, and within seconds sleep took over. A few minutes went by, and Grandma tapped my shoulder. "I put him in the bed. You should go on to bed now." Her voice was low, her face supple, even at her age. I sat up and thanked her for taking care of Joshua.

"How you doing baby?" Her voice was concerned, and I

couldn't lie to her. My heart raced because it was time to face my fears. Tears filled my eyes, stinging the corneas. "I don't get it. Why did this happen? It hurts so much. He confessed he loved…. me and would be there for us. We were engaged. I hate…. him and never want to see him again." I covered my face from shame and wept.

Her arms cradled my head and shoulders. She hummed for few seconds. "Love does not hurt my child. Love does not boast. Love is not selfish. Love forgives. You read the scriptures, I Corinthians 13. God loves you, child. Wipe your tears. God's gonna work it out." She softly rubbed my back. In my heart, I told myself to believe Grandma's words and go to bed.

The next morning, we made it to church. It was not as if I had a choice in the matter. Church was a priority in Grandma's house. The sermon was long as usual, but it was interesting. The Pastor preached on forgiveness, how we must learn to forgive others to have peace in our lives. I enjoyed listening to the choir; the singing inspirited me to a trusting place. My problems seemed so small, and I believed I could face anything. At the close, Pastor Paul D. Wright, the guest speaker, orchestrated the alter call to those who were sinners. We all stood and bowed our heads while the Pastor prayed. My heart fluttered as though someone was tugging at it. Tears welled up in my eyes, and I fought myself not to allow them to fall.

Grandma had the gift of an angel. She tapped my leg and whispered, "Go on down for prayer." I was reluctant because the congregation would know I got problems only God could fix.

I peeped at her with a look of disgrace, *No; I do not want to go in front of everybody.* It was as if she read my mind. She cradled my right hand and carefully stepped over members to get out of the pew. I resembled a small child going to the bathroom. Snots and tears took over my face before my knees hit the carpet. My heart was racing so fast. Grandma squeezed my hand tight.

"Yes Jesus, I thank you now," she confirmed tearfully wiping her face with a white handkerchief. My mind was talking loud. *You should not confess. You not going to change. You should get up before the Pastor speaks. Run out now!*

As soon as the Pastor laid his hands on my shoulders, the voice goes mute. My eyes closed as he prayed. I did not discern the language. It seemed weird; I do not remember hearing prayers this way. A warm tingling came over me, and I was at peace. My heart was back to normal, and the tears were gone. He spoke softly, "You are not alone in this battle. He is with you always. Surrender your will to His. It's time to trust God, child, trust Him for He is able."

I opened my eyes, and for once in my life, my mind was calm. I wanted to thank the Pastor for praying for me. However, he went right into asking the people to repeat the sinner's prayer. I repeated it, and today I meant it. After church dismissed, I was encouraged to sign up for the new convert class because I had given my heart to Jesus. I agreed without an excuse.

I drove Grandma to my mom's house to eat dinner as planned. I missed my mom's home-cooked meals. I had trouble making homemade biscuits or frying chicken that didn't bleed out of the hot frying pan. For some reason, the house appeared smaller than I remembered. The oversized brown leather furniture in the living area had an effect. On the other hand, it could've been the way the furniture was arranged. I also spotted a new family portrait hanging high over the cedar lamp table near the back wall. Richard and his son had replaced the pictures of daddy and me. Mom made my favorite pie – chocolate custard. I devoured the first piece and hoped she made my own to take home. As we enjoyed dessert, a small conversation followed.

Crystal cleared her throat. "I would like to say I passed the SAT scores and have my heart set on applying to the University of North Carolina at Wilmington. I would love to become a Special Education teacher, and Minor in English." She took a short sip of the glass of ice tea and scooted back into the hard, wooden chair.

The applause and congratulations seemed to go on forever. Cara emphasized, "Bravo… I was nervous about my news, but thank you, Crystal, for setting the mood." She stood up. "I dream of traveling the world because Jamestown is too small for me." She giggled, and we do too. "I want to take JROTC to explore my options and work on my college education as well. After graduation, I plan to enlist in the Air Force." She continued standing as if waiting for applause, but the room was eerily silent. No immediate family has ever enlisted in the armed forces. I wanted to congratulate her because she is serious about her health and staying in good shape. I heard the thudding beats of my heart.

Richard saved the day and broke the ice by offering a toast to the good news. I was itching to tell my good news about being saved from the pit of Hades, but my news seems miNUTE. As soon as our glasses tapped, the phone rang. Cara reacted as if she was paid to answer it.

"Cara speaking how can I help you?" she blasted in the phone. "Oh sure, no problem, Mrs. Tessie. Thank you, good-bye."

Mom looks directly at Cara. "What did Mrs. Nosey body want?"

Cara bust out laughing, "Ma, she said Dexter, the vacuum man coming around with some cheap electric blankets. He charges $5.00 for each one."

Momma's frown turned into a clown smile. "You joking, go get my pocketbook. Richard, we need to grab at least five blankets. Candee, you want a blanket?" I shook my head, "No we got one it works."

"Well, I could use another one I reckon for the guest room. It tends to get cold back there." Grandma announced and dug into her wallet looking for her cash.

My sisters reminded me to come rain or shine to take them for a quick ride in my blue machine, Sally. Christian and Cara bounced in the back seat and Crystal glided in the front. I drove them around the block to show off the rough humming engine. I cranked up the radio, and we belted loud to the song, "We Are Family" by Sister Sledge. I loved my sisters.

"Candee I sure do miss having you around the house," Crystal admitted.

"I miss you all too," I spoke softly. Here I go, this was a proper time to share my news. "I went to church with grandma and gave my life to Jesus today. I know I am different already."

"Wonderful, Candee!" Cara blared loudly.

"Sis, you did it without any pressure from Grandma?" Christian asked giggling.

"Sure silly, I know she can be serious about spending eternity with Satan. It was my time. I need help, and Jesus is going to fix it all for me." My heart skipped a beat. My guilty conscience pinched me. *Did I do this for the right reason?*

As soon as I pulled back up to Mom's house, I saw some people gathering on the front porch. A Monopoly game was in full swing. I enjoyed playing too, but the game could take hours to finish so I opted out. I found Joshua playing in the backyard with Richard's son RJ. When I called his name, he expressed he was not pleased to see me by poking his bottom lip out. His way of saying, he was not ready to stop playing. "Shucks, Joshua, sorry to stop the fun. RJ, thank you for playing with him"

"You welcome. He is pretty good at throwing the ball," he commented, walking over to pat Joshua on the back. "We play next time okay?" RJ reassured him.

Mom made us some leftover plates, and we loaded up. On the way home, Grandma and I talked about how nice the dinner went and how good it was to be around family. "You know, Candee apple, I miss Calvin allot it hurts. I know he is at peace with God, but we were together for so long it's like missing a body part that's hard to live without." She rubbed her hands together as if to warm them.

I turned the heat up in the car. Grandma was habitually talkative, but today she seemed reserved. "I could not imagine how you go on Grandma Elaine. Grandpa could not be replaced. I hope with time your heart will not ache as much." I kept my eyes focused on the road.

"I hope so too, baby," she replied softly.

After dropping Grandma off, I rushed to make it home before sunset. I worried about driving in the dark. I seemed to use the high beams more than I needed to. I am overdue for an eye exam. Jolt that on my ongoing to-do-list. I glimpsed in the rear-view mirror and saw Joshua knocked out. He was so adorable with his mouth open. It dawned on me the radio was off. The *Quiet Storm* marathon was playing back-to-back love songs. I wanted to change the channel, but I believed in love and refused to keep running from memories. It seemed like most of the songs playing reminded me of Jermaine. It might have been me stewing about him. He dropped by two weeks ago to have a short visit with Joshua. He acted as though his life was going great. He did not inform me what he was doing for cash when he handed me $70.00.

We were home, and Joshua's weight was close to carrying a sack of bricks. I put his head on my left shoulder to carry him inside. His thick coat snuggled his chubby body. I also grabbed our duffel bag and the leftover plates. The street lights were dim, and I was vigilant when walking briskly to the front door at night. I had my cub in tow, so do not mess with momma bear. From the sidewalk, a couple of guys are standing around smoking weed. I eye-balled them as I passed by.

"Ah... Girl, you need some help?"

I stammered slightly but firmly, "No... thank you. I am good."

"Huh, I bet you are," another one replied. I heard them chuckling as I got closer to my door. I touched the keys, which were normally already in my right hand, but today they were in my right coat pocket.

There was a white note sticking inside my door. My thoughts automatically go to the bills. It was a weekend; no service people came out today. I sat the note, bags, and plate on the table and put my boy in his bed. I fussed about him wearing pajamas at night. I changed him into his Mickey Mouse pajamas and tucked him in without a whimper. I was anxious to read the note. As soon as I saw the handwriting, I knew it was from Jermaine. His scribbling was choppy, especially when he wanted to make a point. *"Candee-girl, I hope you and Pooh are ok. Look, I gotta go out of town. I got a job. Will call when back. Call mom tomorrow, left you some green papers. You was not here. – Later, J*

I dropped the letter and watched it float in slow motion to the floor. I took a few moments to digest his words. I told myself it was good he had found work. A heaviness overshadowed me from the burden he would not be there for our son.

I had a new goal, and it was to stay busy! I joined the church choir and the New Babes in Christ Bible study. Choir rehearsal was on Friday's @ 6:30 p.m. and Bible study was on Tuesday's @ 7:00 p.m. It helped me forget about Jermaine. I met some decent females I called my sister's in Christ. I talked with Sister Robbie-Ann about my life in general, and she offered me advice on how to budget. She also offered to show me how to use a sewing machine. There were some good used sewing machines at the Goodwill store. I planned to save up for one.

Some days, the pressures of balancing work and church seemed impossible, but I knew I needed to press on. I would enroll at the Community College next month to work on my GED. I was working hard to stay strong even though many times I was weak. I read the Bible, and it gave me hope. Mr. Pete offered me a promotion as the Deli Manager. I got a nice raise along with daytime working hours 7:30 a.m.- 3:30 p.m., M-F. I recruited Crystal as the new babysitter for Joshua when I return to school.

At work one day, the lunch hour transitioned at a steady pace. The deli had roast beef and turkey for half off prices. While doing the inventory for the week, I temporarily zoned in and out about life in general. My mind drifted back to life before the talent show. It was so simple back in the day. I was in such a hurry to grow up and do my own thing. I had no idea life could be cold and heartbreaking. I could not recall my parents' having a heart-to-heart talk with me about growing up. I bet they talked with my other sisters and regretfully overlooked me. The last time Vaughn and I had plans to get together, it did not happen because Joshua was sick. It was six months ago; thankfully, she was back in town this weekend until Monday morning. We planned to go to see the movie *Bustin Loose* with funnyman Richard Pryor. I could not wait to cut-up with her. I had so much I wanted to say to her. I missed our close friendship. Every so often, I wished it were us without grown-up problems.

My trance broke by Dillon Holmes, the new hire. He was my height, so his russet brown eyes locked right on me as he spoke, "Ms. Black, can you help me with this order from the Jamestown Rest Home on Main Street? I haven't been trained on how to ring-up so much food."

I glared at him for interrupting my peaceful moment. "Sure, Dillon, I'm coming right out." I dug into my scalp with a pencil to loosen up the tight curls. I glared at the lead to see if there was any evidence of dandruff. Nope, its built up hair grease. Training people was my best quality as a manager, but it seemed identical to being tortured.

Dillon watched me as I washed my hands with the orange disinfectant soap and slipped on the transparent plastic gloves. I gazed over the order sheet presented to me. I showed Dillon how to check the billing invoice to make sure the items were already paid. The order was prepared one hour before pick-up time. I watched him nod as a sign he at least heard what I stated. "Are you confident you can handle this now?" I asked, clearing my throat.

"Sure, I have no issue with the cash register; it's the paperwork. It makes me dizzy." He smirked and walked off with both hands in his front pockets.

My left eyebrow raised as I had to remind myself why I hired the kid. He was my next-door neighbor's son. A black kid, seventeen years old, high school dropout with no criminal background, and a baby on the way. I could relate to his situation, so I hired him.

After I finished payroll, I made an appointment to refill my birth control pills. Right before Jermaine left for good, we did a quickie on my lunch break. I had not had sex for close to a month. I envision my Jewel had closed. The memory of being a virgin again scared the crap out of me. I would pull out Mr. Rod tonight to make sure it didn't happen! I now had private health insurance, so I had a new doctor. She was mixed-race, and her name was Dr. Vivian Schuler. Her office was downtown near the Bank of America. I scheduled the appointment for the next week.

It was springtime, and the weather was beautiful! The sunbeams illuminate my bedroom resembling stars from heaven.

I took a quick inventory of my outfit and makeup. My Gloria Vanderbilt tight blue jeans accentuated my round booty. I put on a purple paisley printed blouse from Momma. She informed she was ready to throw it away. I was so ready to meet Vaughn. Momma was dropping Crystal off to babysit. I was anxious because she was running 15 minutes late. It seemed like forever since the last time I had entertained myself. I placed my blue jean jacket and brown pleather purse on the lamp table near the front door and re-checked Joshua to see if he was about finished with lunch. He was able to eat with a spoon now, so there was less mess. He had devoured the rice and boiled chicken I made. I got the wet rag prepared to clean him up.

The doorbell rang. A quick check out the peephole and I saw Crystal's puffy hairdo. As soon as I opened the door, I heard a horn beeping. Mom was waving good-bye, and Vaughn was pulling in at the end of the lot. She tooted her horn too. Good timing! I handed the wet rag to Crystal and sprinted over to Joshua to kiss him on the forehead. "I love you. Thanks, Crystal."

"Have a good time," she said as I pranced out the door.

Instead of buckling my seat belt first, I leaned over to give my best friend a tight hug and kiss on the cheek. "I missed you, V! I am so glad to see you."

She smiled with those cute dimples. "Girl, I could not agree with you more. I told my baby, I was counting the days until I got to NC. You look wonderful!" she expressed excitedly, looking at me like a word search puzzle. "Your hair has grown so much! I love your hair

215

like this. Did you do it yourself?"

"No girl, I went to *Hair Your Way* beauty shop. You know it's where Jermaine's cousin, Shayla works," I recounted buckling my seatbelt and adjusting the seat.

"So what's up with Jermaine?" she asked, but I ignored the question. I went on to explain my new hairdo. "It is the new hair thing called a 'Perm.' A chemical foul-smelling creamy stuff looks like mayonnaise straightens thick hair. Best thing out there for us black folks," I smirked. "I see you have a new look too."

"Yes girl, I gave up the wig phase about four months back, and now I added hair to my hair. This is called a weave." She swung the long brunette tresses to the right shoulder.

"It's you, girlfriend, without a doubt adds a bold appeal," I complimented her.

The conversation dead for about ten seconds and she had to go there. "So back to MIA, Jermaine, what's up with him?" she asked smacking her tired old chewing gum.

"All I know is he left me a Dear John, note a while back in the front door. He left out where he was going, but claimed he got a job out of town. He has been sending money to his Mom. She invited us over to visit and was mouth shut about where he at." I stared out the passenger window.

"I know your life has been up and sideways since your man has left town. How are you doing money wise?" she looked me in the eyes as if to hypnotize me.

I shook my head. "One good thing is I got a job promotion with a nice pay raise. We are making it as best as we can. Jermaine writes his mother, and if possible, he sends a few dollars for me. Which reminds me; I had some money waiting for me at Mrs. McDoogle's house. I been so busy I forgot about those few dollars." I shared I had been in therapy for a couple of weeks because I was deeply depressed.

"Oh, my goodness! I had no idea." Vaughn sounded shocked to hear my sadness. Lastly, I shared about the activities at church and told her how it lifted my mood.

As we walked into the movie theatre, the smell of the buttery popcorn crept ups our nostrils. We laughed aloud, ate a humongous tub of artery-clogging popcorn, and washed it with bladder regretting cups of sodas. The movie was hilarious. I needed the laughter, and she might not admit it, but Vaughn needed it too. We left the movie theater and headed to eat at the Waffle House because they had the best meals for the bucks. A waiter greeted us without a smile, but was polite and gestured where we could have a seat. We grabbed the first booth in the back of the restaurant. This place was not large, so seating was limited. We chatted a little about the menu, and both wanted the waffles, ham, grits with cheese, and eggs with sweet ice teas.

I was anxious to catch up on her news. "Now my gloomy story is out, what in the world have you been up to?"

She was beaming. "Girl I love my job! I am blessed to be able to get on a plane or ship and go wherever my heart desires. I truly want you to come with me someday when you are better moneywise. You can pick the place." Her smile was immense. I am privileged to have her as my dearest friend. It made my heart warm.

"V, ever since kindergarten you have been the same little girl who had my back. Do you remember the time we snuck out the window in Mrs. Bloomsdale's classroom in the seventh grade?" We both crack up laughing so hard our voices disturbed a middle-aged man sitting alone reading a newspaper.

"Excuse us." V waved at him. He threw up a hand accepting the apology. The food arrived, smelling delicious. We bowed our heads, prayed, and attacked our plates.

As she drove me home, I admitted I had kept a dark secret to myself, long enough. "V, before I gave my heart to Jesus, I was depleted and desperate, and I did not want to live anymore. I was hurting so bad." Here came the lump in my darn throat. I swallowed hard to stop it.

"Ah…, sis, I am so sorry. I was not there for you," she responded sincerely.

My eyes glazed with tears. "I don't think it would have mattered. I fantasized about taking pills, falling asleep, and not waking up. I ached for Joshua and snapped out of it, but on some days, the temptation would invade my mind like a swarm of bees on honey. I would cry myself to sleep. I could not eat for several days. It was so bad. I knew I needed help."

She handed me some tissues from her purse. "What did you end up doing to get help?"

"I went to Grandma Elaine's, and it was as if God knew what I needed. I went to church, and my life has changed for the better. Not all my problems are gone, but I do not think about taking my life. I want to live for myself and for my little man."

Vaughn was silent for a few seconds. "I know my life is far from perfect, but I know I need to change some things too. I am not a churchgoer as I used to be, but I pray and read the Bible when I have a chance. My parents taught me at nine years old once you give your heart to God, you belong to him always."

Vaughn came inside the apartment to see Joshua and Crystal. She stayed for half an hour before looking at her watch. It was time for her to go. We did two snaps and a twirl before she drove away. I had a smile so wide the universe could see it.

Chapter Sixteen: Better Days

My check-up appointment was at 10:00 a.m., and my wristwatch read 9:42 a.m. The downtown traffic was moderate at in the morning. I pumped brakes to the 20-mph speed limit and carefully glanced for the building's address. I spotted the tall glass building and saw it had a private parking lot. I pulled into an empty spot near the front double glass door, found the elevators, and the location board to see where Dr. Schuler's office was. She was on the fourth-floor in office 407. I was not fond of elevators, but going up four floors was not too bad. At least six people unloaded from the elevator. As soon as I stepped into the open elevator, and pushed the number four button, a hand interrupted the closing door.

It was an attractive middle-aged man wearing a black turtleneck sweater and black jeans. He caught my attention in a good way. Without delay, I pushed the stop button for him. He thanked me. "We appreciate this, thanks. We going to the fourth floor." He stepped in; he is holding a woman's hand. She appeared to be noticeably pregnant. Her face flushed from walking briskly.

"Baby, I told you we going to be late." She smiled at me. "Thanks for holding the door." She unwrapped a blue scarf from her thick Afro puff. Seeing her baby bump reminded me to take a pregnancy test during my check-up. I had been keeping a secret… my period was over three weeks late. I frowned at the idea of being pregnant again. I did not want to abort if it was true, but God knew I couldn't handle another baby. The elevator door opened and the couple stepped off first. "Have a good day," the woman said.

"Same to you both," I replied as I walked to the right looking for 407.

As soon as I opened the office door, a whiff of cinnamon soothed my nostrils. The check-in process was a bit daunting because I was a new patient. I had to fill out forms about my family history and any current ailments. I didn't care to give my medical background for fear of the doctor doing unnecessary tests. So most of those answers were N/A. After the receptionist took my insurance information, I sat to wait for the nurse to call me back. Within thirty minutes, a thin white woman greeted me. "Miss Candee Black? Hi, my name is Nurse Chelsea, come on back." She seemed friendly, asking me how I was doing.

I was cordial. "As good as can be, hope you are too."

"Yes, thank you," she replied and pointed to the scale. I fret the power of this thing as she moves the right side to balance at 144.

She asked if anything was bothering me today and proceeded to take my blood pressure and temperature. My mind was stuck on those 14 pounds I had gained within the last three months.

"Although I have had no symptoms, I need to take a pregnancy test. My period is three weeks late."

Nurse Chelsea asked when my last unprotected sex date, and the last time I was on birth control pills.

"It's been over six weeks since last sex encounter, and I have been out of pills four weeks." She scribbled my information on the blue chart board in her hand. She turned and said Dr. Schuler would be right in. She instructed me to sit on the examination table.

I found a *Cosmopolitan* magazine to pass the time. Skinny white girls were on the front cover. *Were they as beautiful in person?* It was not long afterward I heard a knock on the door.

"Hi, I'm Dr. Schuler nice to meet you, Miss Black."

Dr. Schuler was a short, robust woman with smooth light skin, and short wavy hair. We shook hands.

"Nice to meet you as well," I replied.

She asked those get in your business questions, and I avoided answering by stating, "Not that I know of," she asked me about taking the pregnancy test and if positive, what my plans were. I gave her the short bits and pieces about my life as a single parent. I even admitted I had been battling depression. I informed her I would not be thrilled to be pregnant right now. The nurse came back in and gave me the urine cup to take into the restroom. Before peeing, I whispered a quick prayer, *"God, I know you can hear me. I do not want another baby. Maybe later, not now. If you can do a miracle, please do it for me. I ask in Jesus' name. Amen."* I placed the cup inside the square white window in the wall.

Dr. Schuler expressed if I was not pregnant she would prescribe the newly improved pills in which weight gain was not a side effect. She explained the current pills were known to cause weight gain in 70% of the women taking them. I was relieved to know my weight gain could be tamed. After washing my hands, I lifted my shirt up in front of the mirror. I rubbed my belly and said, "No baby please." I bit my nails while waiting on the pee results. Reading magazines did not block baby blues. I looked up and seen Dr. Schuler coming back in the room.

She smiled. "Test result shows you are not pregnant. From what you have told me about all you got going on, it is possible you been highly stressed. Some people can cope with stress better than others can, but the body will show signs of it. In women, the menstrual cycle is interrupted or stopped for a while because of elevated levels of stress." She scribbled on the yellow notepad.

"So, what you are saying? My period will regulate soon?"

She cleared her throat with a short cough. "Yes. I want you to take these pills tomorrow morning. Remember to use protection if you have sex ; even after you start the pills. Your period should regulate within 2-4 weeks. I do recommend continuing with counseling, and I wrote a prescription for the depression. I want to see you again in two months." I left the office and headed to work; beaming all the way.

Work was a breeze for once! The five employees on the day shift were in harmony with one another, and this allowed me to catch up the paperwork. I took a fifteen-minute break and went to pick up a few snack items for class. As soon as I hit the corner of the snack aisle, I saw a familiar face. It was Brandon!

I walked briskly up to him. He was startled when I spoke. "Hi, Brandon."

His eyes widened. "Hi...Candee, you took me by surprise! How have you been? It seems like forever since I've seen you."

I wanted to give him a quick hug but figured this was not the place. "We are doing well. My son Joshua and me; he is two years old now." His speech impediment was gone although he wore wires in his teeth.

He blinked his eyes as though he needed to focus them. "Time sure do fly. You look great! So, you still with Jermaine?"

I hated this question but answered without hesitating. "We broke up a few months ago. We've moved on."

He was quiet as if I could read his mind. He thinks *I knew it would not last long.* "Sorry to hear. I saw your sisters Crystal and Cara last week when I visited my parents."

"So happy for you!" I pretended to be ecstatic for him as well.

"You know I am in college at AT&T University. My major is Criminal Justice. In two more years, I graduate. I want to become a police officer." He sounded serious for once in his life.

"I recall hearing from Sylvia you were doing well in college. Congratulations."

He went on to catch up with me. I gave him a speedy overview of my life. He likewise congratulated me on being a manager and alleged he too had been going to church regularly. Before parting, I told him I could not hug him but would welcome a high-five. Seeing Brandon brought back the early memories of tender love. I was so desperate to find it. I tried not to have any regrets because I admitted it was a learning process.

In class, we took our first of several mini quizzes in English, and I was not prepared. Class was a bust! I knew I should prepare for the stupid quizzes, but what was done is done. When I got close to the car, the front passenger tire was flat! *Lord not now, it's too dark out here*. Thank goodness for the dim streetlights. This moment made me vulnerable, and my brain went blank on what to do next. I heard talking from a couple of white classmates strolling by me. One of the girls asked me if I needed help. I was reluctant to respond because they didn't talk to me in class.

"Yes, I don't know if I have a spare."

I went over to open the trunk with the key. To my surprise, there was a spare tire. Within a few minutes, the college security man drove through the parking lot on a golf cart.

"Do you have a spare?" he asked.

"I do, it looks fair," I alleged as I put my book bag in the back seat.

I thanked the girls and the tall one, Marsha, suggested they should hang around while the security man changed the tire. I thanked her with a smile. It was a cold night, and the wind chill was cutting through my blue jeans. I introduced myself to the girls, and they likewise did the same. We made small talk about the quiz. I was relieved to find out I was not the single one caught off guard. The security guard was able to change a tire and suggested I get a new one.

"Your tire has dry rotted, so it will be a good idea to have them all checked as soon as possible. The ole weatherman is calling for sleet and snow next week." He seemed to be a concerned older white man. He had a salt & pepper sideburns and his voice tone reminds of Grandpa Calvin's, nurturing and caring. I watched him around campus smiling and talking to other students. I thanked him and told him I would have them checked. I drove away thankful someone was looking out for me. This sort of hiccup, having a dependable man is essential.

I said a silent prayer for the security man. I am jealous of those young girls. I envied their freedom. They were talking about stopping by the mall to do some window-shopping. Neither one of them had any children. Shortly, I was on my way home. I was annoyed with myself when there is downtime. I turned on the radio. *The Quiet Storm* was brewing slow jams. I had no time to be in a woe is me headspace. I turned past it and ended up listening to the Classical music station. The music soothed my mind and lately, I studied and slept to it most nights. I could tell a slight difference in how the car rode with the spare tire on. The car shook on the passenger side. I slowed down my speed to see if it made a difference. Driving at 40 mph on the highway was not a good idea, especially when the speed limit was 55 mph. The shaking was less noticeable, so I pulled into the right lane to coast to my exit.

As I entered the apartment, I heard the TV, but I didn't see Crystal. "Crystal, I'm home. Where you at?" I walked back to my bedroom, which was dark. I flipped the light switch on the wall and saw her bundled up in my bed. Joshua was snuggled up alongside his stuffed chocolate puppy dog he called *doggie.* Since I had no bed to sleep in, I went to the hall closet, rustled up a fleece blanket, and headed to the couch. I needed my pillow, but it had a drool spot where Crystal's mouth was open. Therefore, I looked for another blanket to fold into a makeshift pillow. It dawned on me I should call Momma to inform her Crystal was staying overnight. I would drop her off at school on my way to work. I thanked God for my home telephone. I did not know how I had survived without one this long. Momma answered but sounded as though she was sleep talking. "Ok, ok." She hung up. I could lay down and try to sleep out of my comfort zone. No music, no pillow, and no bed; sleepy spirit come fast.

Our morning routine juggled since Crystal had stayed the night. Although her presence was new, she was a great helper. I did not have to get Joshua dressed, she already took care of it. Her helpful gesture added a whole ten minutes for me. When I got to the kitchen, Joshua was sitting in high chair chomping on some sliced apples.

"Good morning, sis," Crystal voiced cheerily.

"Good morning to you both. Girl, you are a lifesaver. After last night, being able to coast through the morning without any more setbacks, I am thankful." I went on to tell her about the flat tire and how bad I had done on the quiz. We continued to chitchat about non-related topics to pass a few minutes before leaving out. I went outside to warm up the car. There was frost built up on the windshield. I found the red plastic ice scraper in the dashboard. This was not my favorite thing to do in the cold, but the defroster did a half-ass job.

After dropping Joshua at daycare and Crystal at school, I remember what the security guard mentioned about checking all my tires. I pulled into the gas station near my job to see if I could leave the car and pick it up later. The cashier told me they had one person working on the oil changes and brakes today. She encouraged me to come by tomorrow before noon. I was not delighted to hear it, but I had no time to go to another place. As soon as I got one foot in the front door at work, Shelly the day shift deli assistant came up to me and asserted she needed to talk to me right away.

I walked methodically to my office door. She closed the door behind me as I am apprehensive but asked, "Should I sit for this?"

She brushed her long red hair to her back and motioned with her right hand for me to take a seat. "This morning, when I got in, I did not see Dillon. He worked a couple hours over last night. He was scheduled today at 8:00 a.m. I went to balance the register, and it came up short again."

My neck stretched in an awkward position. "What do you mean *again*?"

She paced to the right side of the room. "Last week, we were short by $50.00 on second shift when he volunteered to stay until closing. He worked with Jo-Lynn and Mary who both did most of the stocking. I asked him about the shortage, and he denied knowing anything about it."

I stood up and placed my hands on my hips. Heat surrounded my neck. "$50.00 is missing. Not good, I guess I need to talk with him."

She cuts me off. "This morning after I balanced the drawer, it came up short $150.00, and all the food stamps were missing too."

I gasped. "What the heck is going on with this out of control boy? I am going to call the police to have him arrested." As soon as I blurted those words I stopped and said, "I should talk with him to hear his side of the story first. I guess I should not assume the worst and call him."

Shelly's gaze went to the floor, and her white face turned red, which gives me a sick response. "You won't be able to contact him, not today or tomorrow." Her voice went flatter with each word spoken. I jerked when someone pounded on the door.

"Yes, who's there?"

"Candee, it's Mary. It's an emergency." Another problem, my heart skipped a beat hearing the urgency in her voice. I stepped toward the door to open it. "The police are here they need to talk to you and Shelly." The police? My mind went to my immediate family members. I prayed for strength.

I saw Mr. Pete walking towards us. He glanced right at Shelly and me. "Mr. Pete's what is going on? Why are the police here?"

"Candee, last night Dillon was shot and terribly wounded while trying to rob the 7 Eleven store on Main Street. The police are trying to put the pieces together." He stepped away when the short black officer spoke to me.

"Ma'am, what is your relationship with Dillon Holmes?"

I was speechless. Tears overtook my eyes, and I tried hard to act as though it didn't affect me. "I hired Dillon six months ago. He lives in my apartment complex with his mother and some siblings." I sniffed up the mucus sliding down my throat. After several hours of employee interviews, I struggled the rest of the day to hold my somber attitude together in front of others. Shelly was not the lamentable type, but even she teared up a couple times. From what the police had gathered Dillon might have been connected to other local store robberies. There was gossip he was involved in gang activity. A typical reason to explain the shortages from the cash drawers. I am compelled to extend my sympathy. Although he worked at the store a brief time, when he was here, he did a decent job. I wanted to make sure his family heard about the good in him.

I met with Mr. Pete before I left to ask if I could use the family funds to send food to the family. "Candee, I know your heart is in the right place with this devastating news, but this kid was stealing from my store, and God knows what else. I will not approve any funds, I am sorry." He rubbed his left hand across his face as if he wanted to take those words back. I paused for a few seconds. He sat in his high back black leather chair and swirled around to pull papers from the fax machine. I dropped my head, stopped talking, and turned around to leave. I paused because I heard a soft voice say, *Remind him of his youthful days and his mistakes along the way.* My knees trembled from being nervous to do as the voice commanded. A powerful desire came over me to speak boldly, and the fear was gone.

"Mr. Pete, do you remember the day you shared your life story with me? I didn't tell you, but my world was spiraling out of control. I did not commit any crimes, but I had the urge to hurt someone all the same." I had his attention now. He faced me with a blank expression. The words did not stop, so I kept going. "You knew what I was going through because you had been in the same situation. You gave me a pass; a way to move forward and not go backward. You saw the determination I needed to push me to where I am today." I used my hands to express myself. His eyes followed my movements. I saw his Adam's apple maneuver up and down as he swallowed hard. "Sadly, Dillon did not seek us for help, but his baby would surely experience discrimination because of his father's' mistakes." My mind went blank, so I left.

Mr. Pete stood up, rubbed his caramel bald spot with his right fingers. "Wait, Candee, on second thought, I agree, his family has not committed any crimes. Please prepare the *Thinking of You* meal box for them. I am not a perfect man either. Thank you for reminding me." He smiled, and I smiled back.

Chapter Seventeen: 360-Degrees

Shelly and I went to the hospital to see Dillon and his family. We found them in the Waiting Room. Ms. Holmes gave us both a hug and thanked us for coming. I handed her the box of food. She thanked Shelly and me with another hug. Dillon's girlfriend sat quietly on the black leather sofa beside a teenage girl. She wiped her eyes and rubbed her stomach. She whispered to her baby. I stepped closer to speak to her. "Hi, I am Candee; I was Dillon's supervisor at Pete's Grocery Store. How far along are you?" She glanced up to meet my eyes.

"Hi, I'm Jeanie Mae. I'm close to five months, it's a boy." Her lips trembled as she burst out an ear-splitting scream, "He won't wake up. Dillon! Ohh God...why?"

My heart broke for her because I sense how alone she was. I froze as a heavy-set woman dressed in white came over to console her. I motioned to Shelly; it was our reminder to go see Dillon.

"I know what you are thinking." She alluded. We walked up the hallway and headed to see Dillon. The smell was cold and stale it must be to kill germs. We found out from the nurse Dillon was in an induced coma from the gunshot wound to his head. His prognosis was grim. It would take a miracle if he could make it through the night. We stood at the window to see a glimpse of his face. His head covered in white bandages. His body connected to many different wires. I grabbed Shelly's hand, and we prayed.

***

Since my money stretched beyond unimaginable, I found a home daycare near the apartment. I hoped it would save me some money and time. Jemma had a friend with an aunt who had a home daycare two blocks away. Mrs. Lena babysat four children all under the age of 4 years old and had been a caregiver for over 25 years. The air was brisk from moisture mixed with icicles. I prayed the snow and ice were not on the way. The worst thing about living in NC was the unpredictable weather. One minute the sun was out and within minutes, the temperature would drop. We scurried to the cold car; regretting I did not have a chance to heat it up. Joshua whined, as I put him in the car seat.

"What's wrong sweet boy?" His eyes were teary, and his nose was running with clear mucus. "Oh, I hope you not getting sick." I found a napkin tucked in the back seat to wipe his face. He stopped whining and gazed out the side window.

I was proud to hear he had a good day without any biting. Momma told me when I was about his age I was a biter too. She assured me most children went through a phase to communicate when they were upset. Therefore, I talked to Joshua in words and not baby talk to encourage him to talk more. I was working hard to use his nickname less so he could learn his birth name. As I buckle him in his car seat, I saw a mark on the left side of his neck. The scratch was not deep, but it sure was noticeable. The staff at the daycare did not recant about it.

"My sweet boy I missed you!" I gave him a big kiss on his left cheek. "How was your day? I heard from Mrs. Lena you played nicely today. Great job!" I gave him a high-five. He responded by throwing up both hands. I tapped them and asked, "How did you get this?" I pointed to his neck. "You got a boo-boo. I mean a scratch."

"Nee-nee bad..." His bottom lip poked out. I knew her name all too well. Nicole was Mrs. Lena's four-year-old granddaughter. She is known for fighting the younger children. I would make sure to address it tomorrow, but for now. We are on our way to Bible study I needed to be around some praying folks. With all this going on with me, I am wiped out I needed to hurry to my sanctuary, my church.

There was a deeper connection when I picked apart the verse in the scriptures. It made me think I knew a little bit about the Bible. Sister Robbie-Ann was teaching from the book of Ruth. I was unfamiliar with the story. I knew about David, Noah, Moses, and even a few stories about Jesus. It was a surprise, to hear the preacher talking about a woman from the Holy Bible. As I listened intently to the story, I hoped someday my Boaz would come to my rescue. He would be a strong man, with money and prestige. I would be a faithful wife and take care of his needs. Sister Robbie-Ann asked us to pray for guidance and read the Bible daily to become strong in the word of God. One of the elders led us in prayer, and the class dismissed. I walked up to Sister Robbie-Ann and asked if she had a minute for me to ask for an extra prayer. She obliged without hesitation. She did not ask the details and bowed her head, and I did the same.

After the prayer, she said, "Candee, God says He is here for you to lean on when you are burdened. He says come to Him anytime. He is waiting."

I was not sure what she meant, so I asked. "Is God physically with me all the time?"

Her face relaxed, and she said, "Yes, my dear. God lives in your heart. You can pray anytime and anywhere. He will hear you, and He will answer."

Hearing those words lifted my spirit. As I got up to leave, I was approached by a church member named Omar. "Why hello, Miss Candee, how are you doing tonight?"

Omar was an average height man with a neat haircut. His skin was what we called *high yellow*; which is a pastel-skin color.

His eyes were sexy as hell. *Forgive me, God.* Hazel colored they looked like cat eyes. He had a thin goatee which gave him an attractive appearance. He normally sat in the back and did little to no talking. I was surprised to see him talking to me.

"Good evening, Omar, I am doing well. How about you?"

"Why yes ma'am, I am doing as good as can be." He had a thick country accent. "Did you enjoy the lesson tonight?" he asked as his eyes focused on my mouth.

"Sure, it was appealing. I plan to do more research on the story."

He hesitated, and I took it as my exit cue. "I hope we get to know each other outside the church walls," he winked, shifting his folded arms to his sides.

"You mean like a date? Or hanging out?" I asked him, not sure what to think.

"A date would be kind of nice. I got no problem with hanging out either. A fine lady like yourself would be nice to be round."

So far, I was not attracted to his conversation, but hoping he needed to warm up. It had been a long time since I had been with anyone. I guess it was time to move on. I answered him without hesitation. "Sure we could take it slow as getting to know each other. But I guess we could exchange telephone numbers and make plans later."

"I agree, yes ma'am." Calling me ma'am was a turn off, but I ignored it for now. He walked over to the desk in the corner and found a pen. He came back to me and gestured, "Write it on my hand?"

I was amused. "That's, fine. I can use this." I scribbled my number on an old grocery receipt.

"Can I walk you to your car?" he asked as I put my coat on.

"Sure, I have to go by the nursery to get my son." We made small talk as we walked to the nursery. He opened each door along the way. *I like this guy right away.* I sensed he was older than I am. Not a problem with me, how much older was the question.

By week five, Omar Doolittle and I were entertaining each other at least four days a week. I discovered he was 26 years old, divorced four years, and no children. Our age differences did not deter him; it seemed to make him pursue me more. We talked on the phone at least four times a day. At first, it was annoying to have him calling me before 7:00 a.m. However, his sweet country voice won me over, and now I was eager to get his calls. He worked the day shift at the Marriott Hotel downtown in the Maintenance department. He enlisted in the Army for eight years and discharged for health reasons. When I probed him about his military experience, he darted away from the conversation as if he was running from a ghost. He avoided talking about his years in the military. He shared each time he deployed his marriage grew farther apart. We spent most of our time getting to know each other by participating in activities at the church and going out to eat and to the movies. His annoying habit so far was he smoked cigars. He was respectful not to light up around Joshua, though. When we were together, he smoked outdoors. He seemed to have no problem being around Joshua because he ran around chasing him as soon as Joshua says, "Catch me Omm." He was not rich as Boaz was, but he made me optimistic. We hadn't had sex yet, but we had kissed and held hands, and it was nice. He made a joke about how long he had to wait to get between my thighs. I laughed it off and told him, I needed more time to get to know him better. "Ask me about sex in 3 months." His facial expression revealed he did not agree with me.

One Saturday, I went by Mrs. McDoogle's house to check in with her because I had not heard from her in a few weeks. When I was younger, her neighborhood seemed so vast, but today it appeared so small. I saw her brown car parked in the driveway and several old newspapers scattered about. Mrs. McDoogle loved to read the newspaper and keep up with what was going on. I knew this scene was noticeably unusual about her. Instead of removing Joshua from the car, I let him know I would be right back. He seemed content playing with Doggie. I rang the doorbell, and it was not working. I peeked through the front windows it appeared eerily dark inside the house. No sounds inside. The mailbox stuffed as though it had not been checked all week. I knew it was illegal for anyone to touch another person's mail, but I was forced to look. Especially when I saw a letter sticking out from Jermaine. I had to open it. I left the rest of the mail in the box.

I was at the car when the neighbor across the street, Mrs. Katie came outside and waved at me. "Good afternoon, to you Candee?"

I give her a half smile as I tucked the letter in my back pocket. "Yes, Mrs. Katie, how you been doing?"

She walked methodically with a cane. "Sweetie, know when you get to be 72; the body don't work the same. No, mind me, the good Lord keeping me here for some reason. You over there to check on the house for Patricia?"

Check on house statement caught me off guard, so I responded with the truth. "I have not heard from her in a couple of weeks. Joshua and I dropped by to see how she was doing, but I see the mail and newspapers are piling up. What is going on?"

"Honey, I heard from her twin sister Patrice, Patricia, was over there with no heat running." She stepped one foot at a time. "Patrice says she forgot to pay it or did not have the money for the oil and did the best she could. She got pneumonia and been in the hospital for two weeks now. Patrice said she may have had a stroke. I go over to grab the mail if it's full and hold it until Patrice drops by."

"My goodness, this is terrible to hear." I am sorry for Mrs. McDoogle. "The box is full. I can get the mail and throw away the newspapers." My heart was heavy about the situation. I was itching to read what Jermaine had to say in this letter.

I drove away a total wreck. Not so much about Mrs. McDoogle, but more so about what the letter might reveal. My affections towards Mrs. McDoogle had been neutral. She and I have not had the greatest nor worst relationship with each other. I think we became amicable for Joshua's sake. I knew from our short conversations she was not supportive of Jermaine leaving out of town, but did not stand in his way. I turned right at the traffic light and pulled into the Laundromat parking lot. My hands were sweating. I pulled out the envelope and read the return address was from Hamburg, Germany. "He jetted out of the country, not town!" I blurted out before I catch on how loud and quick I was. I swallowed my pride and opened the letter.

By now, Joshua's attention span was waning. He whined sitting in his car seat too long; especially at a standstill. "Hold on, big boy," I asked, keeping my eyes on opening the envelope. The first thing I saw was a money order in my name for $200.00. I am not a thief. I smiled and said, "Thanks." I was grateful for the money. Jermaine's handwriting was lazy and choppy. He cut off long words and avoided the use of a period or capitalization.

His mood sounded concern for why his mother's phone was not working. He mentioned he missed her and his son. He asked if we had been by to pick up the $50.00 he sent a couple of weeks ago. *Yes, I did get it.* He went on to ask her to call him at a 14-digit number (0114940-555-1110) as soon a she got the letter. He informed her he met several players whom attended church and had been invited him to attend. He was looking forward to it. He told her his football team was doing well (10-3) so far in the league division. He did not mention anything else about his son or me.

I contemplated if I should call Jermaine about his mom or call him for Joshua. I was not prepared to go to the hospital alone. I stopped wrestling with what ifs and went with my heart and head on home. Right away, I spotted Omar's red Ford Thunderbird car parked near my front door. I did not see him sitting in the front seat when I parked beside the car. When I went around to the passenger backdoor to get Joshua, he was lying back in his front seat apparently asleep. I tapped on the window, and he bolted looking dazed. His eyes shifted left to right, and he focused on me. *What a grumpy bear*, I mumbled to myself.

He emerged from his car growling obscenities as I stepped toward my front door with Joshua walking close behind. I heard Joshua trying to get his attention. "Omm, catch." I was snappy with him because he was unannounced. I went inside, and as soon as I turned around, he went ballistic.

"Where the hell ya, been huh? I was here waiting on ya for hours! You cheating on me?"

His demeanor was scary. His eyes were dark and wide. His face was sweaty. Before I could answer or yell back, he kept going with his right finger in my face. I stepped back, ready to pick up the remote control to defend myself.

I heard Joshua whimpering and mommy instinct kicked in like a wild bear. "Get the hell out of my house! I did not ask you to wait on me! Are you crazy?"

He stood there like a little boy scolded by his wicked

stepmother. His head dropped, and he shook it back and forth. I was
so furious, I declared. "I don't want to see you anymore!" I held
Joshua close to my chest. Our heartbeats were pounding against each
other. Our bodies were shaking.

He stuttered, "I-I-I, so-r-r-y. I need… you…and, and lil man."

I shook my head. "No. Please leave, or I will call the Police." I
was too afraid to move towards the phone, but he did not know it. He
turned around and before walking out the door, he knocked over the
lamp sitting on the table near the door. The lamp hit the wooden floor
causing the bulb to shatter into hundreds of pieces. As soon as he
disappeared, I chained the door and bolt locked it. I wanted to crawl
in the closet but had to hold it together for my baby. I questioned God
about why this happened. I prayed for Omar to be a decent man. I
found him in church! His personality had changed into something
dark and terrifying. The comments from dad echoed when I told him
whom I was dating. He referred, "Watch them Doolittle men they got
some mental problems, so tread water around him." I theorized dad
had a reason to act overly protective. My heartbeat paced and soon
return to normal. I kissed Joshua all over his face. I would die for him.

It was lunchtime, so I put together a peanut butter and jelly
sandwich. Cut it up into foursquare pieces and sliced up a red apple. I
knew he would ask for juice if I did not give him milk first. Therefore,
I poured milk into his cup and gestured for him to get in the chair. No
complaints, so he must have been hungry. He grabbed a slice of apple
and chewed.

"Slow down, Joshua."

He obeys. I grabbed the dustpan and broom and cleaned up

the asshole's mess. The lamp was cheap, but it looked fine. I would replace the bulb later.

I found the heavy telephone book to find the number to High Point Memorial Hospital. I stood up to get the telephone off the kitchen wall and dialed the number. The receptionist transferred me to Mrs. McDoogle's room, and a woman answered.

"Hi, this is Candee Black. Is this a family member for Mrs. Patricia?"

"Yes, it is. This is Patrice, her twin sister. You Charlene's and Joseph's daughter, right?"

"Yes, ma'am. I am calling to check on Mrs. Patricia. I had no idea she been sick."

Patrice paused and asked me to hold on while she coughed. After a few seconds, she returned. "My dear sister is not doing well. The family is here waiting on the good Lord to take her home. The sickness debilitated her body. They can do nothing else to heal her. She already had a weak heart."

"My goodness, I am so sorry. I didn't realize she was in trouble. Has anyone contacted Jermaine?"

Patrice expressed his sister Noreen was not close to him; something about sibling rivalry. She had no way of contacting him because Patricia was mute about where he was. She assumed he must be in prison or worse dead somewhere. I did not know his family too well, so I kept the telephone number a secret. I hung up with an ache in my heart for Jermaine to know about his mother before she passed.

My breathing restrained, overwhelmed with dread to tell Jermaine his mother was gravely ill. I said another silent prayer before dialing the operator to help me with the long distance number. It would cost me extra on my monthly telephone bill, but it was urgent. The rings sounded so far away as I waited for the call to connect.

"Hallo?"

I could not tell if it was Jermaine's voice. It had been a year since we last spoke. "Hello, I need to speak to Jermaine McDoogle please."

"Sicher." He spoke German, and I had no idea what he said. Therefore, I waited patiently for his next move. I heard in the background; he was yelling for Jermaine. I heard laughing, and someone giggled, "Eine Dame." Some more talk and laughing.

"Hallo." It was Jermaine's voice. I froze imagining if he spoke English anymore. "Hallo, Hallo?"

"Jermaine, hey. It's Candee."

He broke the silence first, "Candee, What a surprise. Is everything all right? Is Joshua okay? I asked Mom to make sure you had this number. I... lately I've had you both on my mind."

I interjected, "We are both well. Life is crazy, but we are surviving. He is growing so fast! Did you get the last picture I gave your mom?" I envisioned his handsome smile through the telephone.

"My goodness, he's growing so tall. I bet him talking like he grown too." He chuckled hard. "Thank you for taking good care of him."

It dawned on me this call was not free, so I went right into what I need to say. "Jermaine, I got some dreadful news. It's your mom. She has been in the hospital with pneumonia. I bite my bottom

243

lip after blurting it out so fast, but time was not on our side.

I had seen Jermaine shed a few tears before, but he moaned like a wounded animal. No words as he sobbed deeply. I heard someone talking low to him as he sniffled. "Thank you for calling me. I will prepare to come home as soon as possible." Before hanging up, I asked him to write down my telephone number. "I will call you when I get in town," he sniffed, and we hung up. I slumped over in the chair and wept in front of Joshua. Thank God, he was fast asleep and leaning to one side in his highchair.

Before I get to my office at work, Shelly greeted me with a kooky looking grin. "Good morning, I bet you had a great weekend. The evidence showed up this morning. Someone is in love..."

I raised an eyebrow. "What are you talking about? My weekend... Shelly don't make me go there." I continued walking towards my office and saw a huge bouquet of red roses, so many I stopped counting. The card read, **I can't go a day without you. Sorry. 4ever yours, Omar.**

Roses? No man had ever given me flowers before. This gesture gave him a gold star, at least for trying to win me back. Shelly came over and helped me get into my office. Now we both were smiling.

I allowed Omar to crawl back into my world. We talked on the telephone here and there. He asked to see me, but I made excuses why it wasn't the right time. He begged, begged, and flirted in church. It made me awkward in a way, I wanted to see him, but he had to earn his way back. Over the next two weeks, Omar won me back into his world and it was nice. He was attentive, and his moods were cheerful – on some days too cheery. After playing Tarzan and Jane close to my

90-day deadline, we had sex. He performed the kinkiest sex I had ever had! Omar was into sex toys. He brought out four different toys the first time we had sex on his living room love seat, floor, and kitchen table. It was a thrill ride, but I did not have any orgasms.

Unless he was a great actor, he didn't have one either. His sexual appetite was foreign to me. He seems to enjoy the actual act of having sex more than the intimacy part of it. I was not in love or even in like with him. I disregarded any hints from him associated with the relationship. He was on borrowed time. After sex, we ate nachos and cheese dip right in his bed. He licked his fingers and blurted, "Did you like the extra dick? Not like I needed any help." He winked with a smile. His naughty side amused me. I confirmed his added gestures.

"I knew you were up to no good; when an object went up my booty hole. You a dang freak-boy!" We laughed uncontrollably.

The mood change on his part because his facial expression became serious. "So, you know beautiful... when we together God put us here."

Condemnation transferred to me when he talked about God. I got off the bed to wash my hands in the bathroom sink. He did not stop talking. "I swear by love at first sight. What about you?"

I was dumbfounded, but spit out words to shut him up. "Love at first sight? I guess it could happen. If both people are looking for it." I got dressed to leave. I found a piece of Wrigley's chewing gum in my front pocket jeans. I loved the sweet fruity taste. I chewed and smacked while putting on my low black heels. "It's getting late. I need to get out of here."

He wasn't excited to hear my urgency. "I wanted to tell you I'm for sure in love with you. I think it's about time we spend more time together. You know, to make this official, like we a couple."

I choked on my gum as I swallowed the saliva. "Omar...let's take it slow and easy. Remember, we in the dating phase." He walked me outside to my car, grabbed my butt, and kissed me hard. I pulled back, slide in slow, and kissed him again hoping he would catch the hint. This time the kiss was better because his lips were soft even though his breath smelled tart.

Jermaine scheduled to arrive in a couple of days at Greensboro airport at 2:30 p.m. He asked me to pick him up and to bring Joshua. I was excited and nervous. I missed him. I hadn't mentioned to Omar I was seeing Jermaine. I know he had a jealous side. We avoided talking about the day he lost his mind on me and tried to keep the mood cheerful. He told me he was going to a job training for the next three days. He made it known he would call after 9:00 p.m. to check on us.

I try to stay focused during Bible study. I normally wrote questions during the lesson. I was distracted by all I wanted to say to Jermaine. Journaling become beneficial for me. Even though my therapy sessions ended a while ago, the best advice given was to express myself by writing. I wrote a letter to Jermaine. One page turned into five pages by the time it was time to leave church. On the way home, my mind seemed clearer. All was peaceful until I heard Joshua say, "Pee-pee mommy."

On the one hand, I was beaming inside he was saying he needed to go, but on the other hand, not good timing. I looked in the rearview mirror. "Joshua, mommy has to stop at a store so hold on."

He continued to look out the back window. I saw a McDonald's up ahead and stopped. We were in and out within ten minutes and back on the road again. My gas hand hit the **E** sooner than I anticipated, so I stopped again before my exit and got gas. I peeked at Joshua and his eyes glazed over; he could barely hold his head up.

As soon as I tucked him into the bed, the telephone rang. The clock on the kitchen wall read 9:40 p.m. The answering machine blinking too, someone had left a message. I answered the telephone on the fourth ring.

"It's about time I got you. I was getting antsy about you and Joshua." It was Omar.

"Naw we good. I had to make a few stops from church, and it threw my time off," I said yawned softly.

"It's not okay to stop at night. You a purdy gal, Candee. People crazy at night time. Had me worried." He sounds overly protective, but it warmed my heart.

"Please don't worry. God has it under control. You know it." Saying it seemed to mellow his mood out and we talked for about thirty minutes, about nothing of substance. We said goodnight, and he reiterated he'd call tomorrow. I reminded him on top of work I had school until 9 p.m.

"I will give you a wakeup call and check back in around 9:30 p.m."

I shook my head in disbelief at how desperate he was. I retrieved the message from the machine. "Candee, its Jermaine. I called the hospital and checked in on mom. She is hanging on for me. I know it. My flight plans have changed. I need you to be there at 11:30

a.m. on Wednesday, and not 2:30 p.m. I was able to change flights for an earlier departure. I hope you can accommodate this change. See you soon." My heart melted at the sound of his voice.

As soon as the alarm clock went off, I called Shelly to let her know I needed to take a sick day. Shelly was like an older version of me, and we got along like sisters. She reassured me not to worry about the job and to get well soon. I called Mrs. Lena and let her know Joshua would be absent as well. She sounded grateful to hear she would have one less child to deal with. The telephone rang. I guessed it was Omar. "Hello."

"Good morning, beautiful." I guessed right.

"Good morning, Omar."

"How my two babies doing?" He sounded like Jermaine. He was trying too hard. I gave him some of my time but did not inform him I was not working today. He seemed satisfied with our chattiness and ended with, "I talk to you tonight baby. I love you."

I was prepared to say good-bye sweetie or even baby, but not those three words. I stutter a reply, but a small voice squealed, "Mommy...I go poop." Saved by my sweet boy. "We talk tonight, bye." I hung up the telephone so fast I did not hear his response.

I spent the rest of the morning cleaning up the apartment. I even washed the bed sheets on my bed in case I might get lucky. For a split-second, I questioned if we were physically attracted to each other. What if the attraction doesn't flicker any sparks?

I guess we would soon find out. I sprayed air freshener and mopped the floors. I loved the smell of Bleach, especially in the bathroom. It gave me a sense all was clean. Joshua watched TV cartoons. I found Tom & Jerry, and he plopped on the floor, laid on his favorite blue fleece blanket. My little man was growing up so fast. Some moments, I desired to freeze time and put in a bottle.

The traffic on the way to the airport was thick. The rain had fallen harder than it had as we left home. I fear driving in the rain. I checked the time on my white plastic wristwatch; it was 10:20 a.m. I told myself I needed to take my time and drive in the right lane. This hard rain reminded me I needed to change the wiper blades soon. I could barely see the street. I was afraid to pull over and wait it out. I prayed and kept driving. Within a few minutes, the sun came out, and the rain-softened. "Thank you, Jesus," I whispered.

So many signs to read at the airport. I looked for the Delta Airlines terminal glancing from right to left at the tall signs. I got in the left lane to find a place to park. Airport parking lots was another stressor. I hoped to remember where I parked the car. Next time, when he came to town, he better rent a car or do whatever because this was stressing me out. I took Joshua by the hand and looked for a way to cross over to the terminals. The time was now 11:30 a.m. I picked up the pace as we got on the escalator to go up. I looked at the arrival flights and saw his flight had landed fifteen minutes ago! My heart thumped as though it was on acid. I was getting anxious about where he might be. I approached a man passing by briskly with a suitcase, "Excuse me, sir, can you tell me where people go after the plane lands?"

He glared at me and moved his shoulders nonchalantly, "They might go to baggage claims, – and it's down this escalator."

I smiled, "Thank you."

The escalators normally made me nervous. I feared my feet would be sucked into the steps. Joshua, on the other hand, not phased as he stood beside me. His eyes fascinated by the noises and crowds of people walking steadily by us. I stepped off first, and he followed as I scanned the room trying to find Jermaine. I second guessed if I would see him if he had cut his Afro.

Joshua grabbed my legs. "Up Mommy."

"Sweetheart, I know you not used to this much walking." I bent to pick him up, and a hand touched my back.

"Candee." I did a full turn to face the voice. It was Jermaine. He was as handsome as ever. His afro was gone, and he had a clean low-cut with a part on the right side. He was wearing a cream turtleneck shirt covered by a tweed jacket and dark blue jeans. I got a quick whiff from his musk-scented cologne. As he picked Joshua up and gave him a short squeeze. Joshua stared at him and looked at me.

"It's your daddy," I mouthed with such a relief in my soul.

He kissed me on the nose and whispered, "Candee-girl, I've missed you both." His arms were strong and warm. He smelled so nice.

Our conversations were full as we caught up with each other, and I filled him in on what was going on, but I decline to mention about a boyfriend. He told me he had an opportunity to play overseas when an old friend of his contacted him to replace an injured linebacker. He was afraid to tell anyone about the news because it was a 50/50 chance he might be cut during try-outs. He was not sure if he was going to make the first cuts, but he had played with the Hamburg Huskies for over 9 months now. His face lit up as his voice heightened talking about playing ball. They were on a one-month break before the first practice. He made a nice salary and let me know he would send money each month. As we slowed our talking, he shifted gears and talked about his mother.

"I feel so ... guilty. I hate the fact she did not tell me she needed help. I would have dropped everything and got here." He covered his face with both hands and wiped his eyes with his fingers. My heart broke for him. She meant a lot to him. He continued to tell me about the last time they had talked, and he forgot to say, "I love you." He expressed he may never get over this mistake.

I drove to the hospital and was apprehensive about taking Joshua with us. We got to the fifth floor, and I found the Waiting Room and went there. Jermaine went on to his mother's room. In the Waiting Room, I met his family from Alabama and Florida. I was unaware Jermaine had a large extended family. There were at least twelve people in the room related to him. They greeted us with smiles and hugs. Several commented how much Joshua looked like Jermaine when he was his age. I sat beside his great-aunt Myra. She remarked the family had been there around the clock. "Myra, can you watch Joshua for me? I want to see Mrs. Patricia."

She motioned with her left hand . "Sure, honey you go on in."

I didn't consider myself a strong person when it came to witnessing someone dying or someone in mourning.
I approached the low-lit room as if I was walking on eggshells. I assumed when someone is dying the movements of the living should be in reverence to the one passing. For a few seconds, my mind drifts to the mountain scene for my birthday. I was trying to block this

scene out. My heart raced as the mood in the room went stagnant. All eyes were on Jermaine kneeling beside the hospital bed. He appeared to be praying and sobbing at the same time. I stood in a corner near the window hoping to blend in and not interrupt. I need to pray too, but not sure for what.

I watched Mrs. Patricia's chest rise and fall like a roller coaster. I wanted to let her know I had no problems with her. I see his sister, Noreen kneeling beside the left side of the bed as though she was praying as well. I could not move; I knew they would stare at me. I bowed my head and asked God to forgive my wrong motives towards her. When I opened my eyes, Jermaine was holding his mother's' right hand. A middle-aged Caucasian nurse came in and took Mrs. Patricia's vitals. She scribbled on a clipboard and whispered to the family her heart had stopped beating. The room was motionless. Noreen cried quietly, and the others sniffed and softly moaned. Jermaine sobbed deeply and did not let go of her hand.

When we left the hospital, we both were numb. He was mute as I drove us home. The radio was my company when I drove. Out of respect, I did not turn it on. I rolled down the driver side window to get a whiff of the clean smell of the rain. This helped me concentrate on the road. Jermaine leaned back in the passenger seat with his eyes closed. He looked somnolent. I reached back and handed Joshua two cheese crackers. It was past lunchtime, so I knew he was ready to eat.

As soon as we settled at home, I told Jermaine I was going to cook meatloaf, cream potatoes, and green beans. He grinned, "Yummy sounds good." He was sitting in the living room, seemingly dazed.

"You need to go rest. I know you drained from the long trip.

You are welcome to rest in the bed."

He got up and walked to my bedroom. Joshua had already knocked out in the car. I put him in his bed for a nap. It was a relaxing moment. The stillness made me uncomfortable. I turned on the small electric radio and cranked up the volume for my ears. The Jazz music mellowed the tension in my body. I needed to warm the oven for the canned biscuits. I could not make homemade biscuits like momma. She did not teach me how to cook anything. I had to learn on my own. I was not sure why, but I figured she did not have time. I went into wake Jermaine to eat dinner and saw he was wide-awake sitting on the edge of the bed.

"You hungry? Dinner is ready," I announced softly.

"I am hungry. It smells good." I stared at him reflecting how much I had missed his sexy voice. "Come here," sounding seductive, and motioning me with his head. I glided over to him, and before I get to him, he stood, pulled me close, and kissed me intensely.

I see Omar's face for a split second, but I could not stop wanting Jermaine inside of me. He kissed me as though he wanted to eat me for dinner. Before I knew it, our clothes were off, and we were humping like dogs in heat. He flipped me over on all fours, got behind me, and plunged to depths of my uterus. His hands were rubbing my boobs, and he was kissing my neck. We both moaned and our bodies paced in sweet harmony.

He bucks his body slapping into me erratically. I sensed his body going limp, and to my surprise, he turned me over on my back. His hands between my legs and his tongue licked my body. Within a few minutes, my orgasm was intense I howled letting go of the tension in my body. I cried sweet tears and covered my mouth with my pillow.

While we laid together facing each other trying to recover from the sexual encounter; he said he needs to confess information he had kept from me. My mood instantly changed, dreading what I would hear. "What is it?" I muttered, trying to look brave. Although truthfully, I prefer to hide under a turtle shell.

He turned away and peers up at the ceiling placing his right arm behind his head. "When you told me you were pregnant, I tried to run from you. I wanted to ignore the situation. During the same month, I got the letter from Carolina Tar Heels; I received a full athletic scholarship."

Remorse dominated me. He paused and faced me, licking those amazing lips. He stared right into my eyes. "I wanted to go but was guilt-ridden knowing we made this baby together. I became distant and angry with myself, not at you."

He blinked rapidly and continued. "While I wallowed in my pain, I passed the anger onto you anyhow. I made the decision to refuse the offer. My mother rolled her eyes at me for months."

I wanted to hold him, but instead, I commented, "We both were kids having a kid. I guess we were scared."

He cradled me in his muscular arms. He kissed me and slowly the shame melted away. Afterward, our pillow talk was light-hearted as we teased each other about our grown-up sex skills. We both laughed about it and admitted how much we had missed each other. "You on the birth control pills, right?" he asked.

" Yes sir, thank goodness!" I giggled.

After dinner, I sat in the living room and watched TV. Jermaine and Joshua spent time playing together on the floor with toy cars. Throughout the day, Jermaine read books, they build blocks, and he showed him how to use the potty standing up. Jermaine had not informed me how long he was staying in town. I needed to find out what his plans were before Omar showed up. "Jermaine, could you come here please?"

"Yeah, hold one second." He told Joshua he would be right back. He stood with his arms folded against the kitchen wall. "What's up?"

"I wanted to know what your plans are. When are you going back?" I implored not blinking.

"I must be back in Germany in two weeks to get ready for practice. Since I am in the first division, we play in early April. *He will not be here for my birthday.* He kept on talking while folding his arms.

"I will stay at the house and help clean out the place. I spoke with Auntie Patrice, and she disclosed Mom left the house to me and my sister Noreen." He didn't look phased about the news. He shifted his left leg to cross over the right. "I assume mom has a Will of some sort. I will look around for it in the house."

"Great, sounds like you got a plan of action." I remarked as I looked back at the TV.

"You got a man who you don't want me to meet?" he grins showing those beautiful white teeth. I acted coy and lied about having a friend. He responded as if he did not care. "Call it what you want. If he grinding you, he is not a friend."

He walked off, and I came back with, "Admit it, you banging

someone in Germany?" I smirked. He was silent this time. I knew I had my answer.

I went ahead and told him about Omar because I knew Omar was going to call. Jermaine's reaction was copacetic, and he was not going to interfere with my relationship. After he bathed Joshua and prepared him for bed, he stepped into the shower. Like an alarm clock, the phone rang at precisely 9:30 p.m. For spite, I let it go to the answering machine. Although ashamed for having sex with Jermaine, I answered on the third ring. "Hello."

"Hi beautiful, how was your day?"

"Good evening Omar, it was a tough day. Jermaine's mother passed away today."

His response was appropriate, "Sorry… to hear she is gone. Was she sick from a disease?"

"It was pneumonia. I heard she couldn't fight it any longer."

He expressed his condolences and asked if I was going to the funeral. I told him I wanted to go. "Do you need me to go with you?"

I knew him, trying to find out if I am going with Jermaine. "Let me see what the arrangements are before I decide anything," I responded mildly.

Omar continued to talk about his day, as my mind wanders farther away to the man in my shower. I fantasized about his soapy wet body. I had fallen in love with his body as a teenager. As a woman, my Jewel tingled fantasizing about his handy tool. I let out a long yawn, and Omar took the hint.

"Aight, baby, you sound weary, so I let you go. Tell lil man I be home soon. I love you both."

I did not love him. He was but a dick to kill the loneliness. Times like this, I barely liked him. Someday sooner than later, I had to tell him the truth. "Goodnight Omar, kiss, kiss." I threw kisses in the telephone, and we hung up in unison.

I peeked inside the bathroom. I needed a shower too. Jermaine couldn't see me through the navy blue shower curtain, and he acted as if he didn't hear me coming in. I undressed quietly and pulled the shower curtain to the left. My dream man smiled, takes my hand, and pulls me close to him. Although his manhood stood at attention, he uttered nothing. He handed me the loofah brush, and I applied the cucumber scented body wash. He offered to scrub my back, and I accepted. One hand scrubs my back while the other hand massaged my shoulders. I am euphoric with the private massagist.

I rinse the suds in the drain. He kissed my boobs, pulling on each nipple and palmed my ass with both hands. His seductive ways got me weak and begging for more. "Deeper, Jermaine...Ohh, baby right there, don't stop." Without warning, he bent me over and plows inside me. The pressure was unbearable in this position. I tried to relax hoping to ease the tension in my woman parts. The warm water splashed on my back and relaxed my muscles. Before I blinked, he was at the finish line. I stood up and kissed his neck, tasting the clean sweat. "Do you want to get yours in here?" he teased, licking his bottom lip. He was such a freak!

"I can wait until we get on dry land," I winked and soaped off his lustful juices.

The family made the funeral arrangements, and instead of holding the body for more than a week, they had the homecoming service on Monday at 1:00p.m. Family and friends could drop by the home from 11 a.m.-12 p.m. to drop off food and flowers. I took a half day off from work to attend the service. Attending another funeral in such a short time span was exhausting. Even though I had barely known Dillon, I shed tears as if he was a close family member. I knew my heart was going to hurt for Jermaine and his family. It was a shame all I ever heard about Mrs. Patricia, the gossiper in the neighborhood. I found out she volunteered at the homeless shelter, sung at the nursing homes, and knitted baby hats for the hospitals. I was remorseful; it took a death to get to know her.

For the next couple of days, I did not see Jermaine. We talked on the telephone each day to check in on each other. He focused on tending to his mother's affairs, so I tried not to bother him. Jermaine expressed he wanted to go see his father to tell him in person about his mother passing. He tried to call him at the Neuse Correctional Institution, in Goldsboro, but his father was on work duty off campus. He admitted he was nervous about seeing him after 12 years, but most importantly, he missed him. Momma and Richard, Cara, and Daddy informed they would be at his mother's homecoming. Vaughn apologized because she was going to be in Hawaii, but arranged to send flowers to the church. Mallory had been out of touch with the gang after high school graduation. Jemma lived in Charlotte and had to work. Lil FIFI , Tiny, and Brandon implied they would try to make it. Donovan no longer lived close by, and the gang had not seen him in years.

I invited Omar to go with me because he eluded the fact he had not seen me since he got back. My mind jacked up for Jermaine. I needed to tell Omar the truth. I informed Jermaine, about Omar

would attend with me. Jermaine and I agreed he should stay with his

family afterwards to get through the day.

After attending the gravesite, Omar, and I left to get lunch and

headed to his place. I had a few hours free. I want to give him a piece

of me for the last time. I had given up drinking alcohol when I joined

the church, but since dating him, I indulged in a glass or two of wine. I

drank a glass and a half of Merlot wine. He drank six cans of Colt 45

beers. As usual, foreplay lasted about five minutes, and the toys come

out to play for at least 45 minutes. He put on the condom. "Let's do

some role-playing." He brought out a pair of handcuffs and a scarf to

blindfold me. I giggled out of control and gushed, "Naw...who wearing

those?"

The buzz from the alcohol made it easy to be his hostage. I

was lying on my back as he licked my ears, neck, nipples, and navel.

His wet lips seduced me. "Yessss. Sooo good," I moaned, from tingling.

"Don't talk...," he growled in a rugged voice. He spreads my

legs, inserts his fingers, and an object smaller than his penis. I moan

because I want to climax, it's damn good. For some reason, he pulled

out the fingers, the object, and put my bound hands around his neck.

He pounced on top, thrusting his curved penis in me. My sex drive

heightened as I tried to connect with his rhythm. Not gonna happen,

as his body jerked like a wild animal in a cage. I could not keep going.

I laid there and waited until he finishes doing whatever he was doing.

"Aww... Yeaaa...Ohhh...Damnnn." He uttered. I did not think there

was a better time to leave Omar alone but knew I had to end it. I will

wait until our next telephone call. I had reservations about his mental status.

At the last minute, I avoided Bible study tonight. I wanted to put distance between Omar and me to get the courage to end the relationship. Jermaine had not contacted me either. I guess he needed his space too. When I got anxious, I tended to have OCD symptoms. I cleaned like crazy. Washing, mopping, dusting, and wiping anything in my path. I even repainted the kitchen walls during this burst of energy. Joshua, the poor baby, caught my madness and I had him rearranging his toys on the shelf. After finishing his shelf, he laid on the cream carpet looking dazed. "Someone is a sleepy head," I assessed. He closed his eyes, my cue to put him to bed for a nap.

While cleaning out the fridge, I heard a knock at the door. I looked out the peephole. It was a girl scout selling those addictive once a year cookies. I opened the door and saw an adult standing on the sidewalk holding a box. The blonde haired girl with silver-blue eyes smiled. "Hi, I'm from Troop 217. Will you support us by buying a box of cookies today?"

She sounded programmed, but I respected her because Crystal and I were Girl Scouts once upon a time. It seemed so long ago. "Sure, you got Shortbread?"

She smiled, "How many?"

"I need one box. Hold on let me get the money," I urged, stepping backward to locate my oversized purse to dig out $5.00. "Do you have change for a five?" I asked, hoping to get some ones for the Laundromat.

"Sorry, ma'am. You are my first customer." I was familiar with the line because it was told to a customer to get an extra sell. I grinned, "No problem give me another box of Shortbread." She walked to the adult and picked out two cookie boxes. The adult looks pleased, waving and smiling at me.

I needed to clean out my closet while Jermaine was in town. A while back, I came across a bag of clothes, a thick gray wool coat, and an old Nike shoebox. Before I tossed them, I would ask him if he wanted them. I started at the top of the white wire shelf and grabbed bags full of Christmas wrapping paper. I was in a toss out old crap mood. I grabbed the worn snowman paper and tossed it in the black trash bag. I pulled Jermaine's' stuff out and set it aside for later. I had too many pants to not fit me since pre-pregnancy. It was time to toss out all those size six jeans and shorts would surely show my ass.

I saw a white and red Nike shoebox in the back corner. I could use this box to hide my journal. It also reminded me – I needed to give Jermaine the letter I wrote in Bible study. I tried to touch the box, but it was too far back for my hands. "Another dang pair of shoes you obviously don't need, Jermaine," I grumbled. I looked through the hanging clothes and got a wire hanger to grab the box. It worked like a third arm. I yanked hard, and the box dropped to the floor. To my surprise, the contents spilled out – it wasn't shoes. I touched and picked up the brown paper lunch bag. Inside the bag were photos of females, posing explicitly. In a few pictures, they were in lingerie. My heart sank to the pit of my stomach. No doubt, this box belonged to Jermaine. No names were on the Polaroid pictures, but I recognize several girls from high school. I found a couple of my nude pictures too. I collapsed on the closet floor. "What the hell?" I gasped for air because I am suffocating inside this small space. I clutched the carpet

261

in my fist. Broken inside once again by the man who declared he loved me.

Within a few minutes, I gathered my composure to evaluate my next move to get over the pain. I learned in therapy when unpredictable life moments upset me, I should respond to them head-on. I conditioned my mind to hold in the pain, anger, and frustration. Nonetheless, for me to heal properly, I had to deal with it head-on. I thumbed through my journal in search of a clean sheet to get cracking. I wrote a poem about what I had experienced. Before being in love, I used to write poems about love. I guess deep inside my heart longed for someone special to want me as such. The words flowed from my mind through the pen onto the notebook paper. It was as though my head and heart were in one accord for once.

"Submerged"

With the weight of this world upon my shoulders,
I sink to the bottom of my problems.
I grow weaker in strength, and my Spirit suppressed.
Suffocation overtakes my breath,
I'm dying.
I'm falling…unable to grasp my dreams or visions of yesterday,
Sea of forgiveness becomes my Strength.
Where can I begin not from yesterday, but today?
A will not an excuse to understand the wrong choices,
Shallow is only to cover up the truth with the why and how.
I realize to surrender to the heaviness,
It burdens the heart, soul, and spirit.
To accept forgiveness the weights would fall into the sea,
And never to surface again.

I sat drained but pleased with the outcome. I knew the next

time I heard from Jermaine, I needed to clear my heart and mind. When Joshua woke, from his nap, instead of eating a healthy snack I opted for sweets. Sugar chases the blues away. I pulled out the famous Shortbread cookies. Joshua loved those cookies, as did I. We took a snack break and crunched on cookies with a glass of cold milk.

The next morning, I woke up with a pounding headache. I had too much to do, and I needed to get out bed, but I could not move. The sun was peeking through the right side of the burgundy thermaback window curtains. I saw momma's big boy sleeping on my other side. He refused to sleep in his own bed last night. I did not mind his company. "I need BC powders to knock this pain out quick," I whispered as I rose, pulling the left foot to the floor dragging the right. I forced air into my lungs to allow the blood to flow to my brain. There was some pain in my neck. I leaned my head to the left, stretching the muscle out. I leaned my neck to the right side. I did the same exercises when I was pregnant minus the saltine crackers. The pain in my head was throbbing, but I had to ignore it. I mapped out my agenda and got the idea it might not happen. I had slept through the alarm clock. I dragged myself to the bathroom to relieve my bladder, wash my face, and looked for the BC powders. I opened the medicine cabinet behind the bathroom mirror and found the blue box with two powders in it. I disapprove the taste, but the cocaine looking stuff worked like nothing else. I placed the powder on my tongue and gulped the water fast.

Out of nowhere, Joshua had scrambled out of bed and was standing next to me rubbing his eyes. "Good morning, sweet boy. You ready to sit on the potty?"

He shook his head. "No…cake…"

"Sorry, Pooh." I catch my mistake. "I mean Joshua, we got no time for pancakes." I sprang into Superwoman powers and got us both dressed within fifteen minutes. I grabbed a box of pop tarts for breakfast. As I helped Joshua put on his brown wool coat, I told him he could eat the pop tarts at Mrs. Lena house. His round mocha eyes were sleepy as he complied with me, hurrying to put the coat on him. I got him to the daycare and stopped at the Burger King to grab a cup of Java and a egg, cheese, and ham Croissan'wich. I ate as I drove to work. I do not look forward to doing payroll and schedules, but they had to be done before 10:00 a.m. I walked in the store and passed by an Easter display decorated with cakes and candies. One day, I might tell Mr. Pete sweets were not the true meaning of Easter for Christians. How did history go from the son of God crucified to colorful eggs and bunnies? Such blasphemy! He might fire me if I correct him. I had better wait until I secured another job to express my viewpoint.

I had been sitting in my chair for over an hour grinding the time cards when my headache returned. I know I should drink water and stretch my aching body. I took the last BC powders at home. I walked around to the medicine aisle and purchased a bottle of Tylenol tablets. I took two with a sip of my coffee and a cup of water. Within minutes, the pain was subsiding, and I got my groove back to complete the schedules. I was in the process of doing interviews for Dillon's position. There would be a flyer posted in front to inform potential candidates to apply at customer service. The telephone rang, and I habitually picked it up. I hesitated, considered if it was

Omar. There was no answering machine, so after six rings the ringing stopped.

I reviewed several applications to fill the open position. I tried to contact two applicants and left messages to contact me. As soon as I hung up with the last call, the phone rang. "Perfect timing," I murmured to myself. "Hello, Candee Black speaking."

The line was soundless. "Hello..." I have no use for prank calls. I tried not to be rude. "I am hanging up now." It was close to noontime; I would leave for lunch now.

"Hi Candee, you must be hiding in your office," Shelly winked as I stamped my timecard.

I smiled and threw up my right hand. "Yes girl, you know it's crunch time for me. You like a paycheck, right?"

Shelly giggled. "And you know my kids love to eat now and again."

She took a second look at me and asked, "Is everything alright, how is Joshua?"

I smiled and made eye contact to distract the agitation brewing inside of me. "Yes, you know he on cloud 99 because Jermaine is around, at least for now."

She sensed the topic was the darkness looming over me. I turned to open the doorknob, and she went on to say, "I been where you are with Jermaine. My baby's daddy left us for some chick in California with no warning. The next time my kids saw him they were nonchalant and soon detached from him altogether."

I respected her sharing the information. "It is sinful what the children go through when these men won't act right. My prayer is not to lose my son to these mean streets. It takes a strong man to help with this."

She agreed with a nod.

I got to my car, and right away, I plainly see a white flyer on the front windshield under the driver's wiper blade. "These dang club people recruiting," I mumbled aloud. I grabbed the paper and opened my car door to get in. I read the flyer; it was not from the club. It was a handwritten note from Omar. ***Candee- why you don't answer my calls or call me? You know this ain't right! I know you love me. I bet you back with the nigga who dumped you. He don't love you. I watched you the other day. I miss kissing your Purdy pink lips. I need to hold you. We should get married and leave this town. We gotta talk soon!!!! Tonight, after school CALL ME PLEASE!!! God sent you to me nobody taking you-Your man Omar B.***

My heart fluttered through my white blouse, my hands shook, and my eyes filled with tears. I needed to break it off with him, and now he was leaving delusional notes. God, what was I going to do? He scared me. My appetite was gone. I sat in the car wiping the tears and contemplating how I needed to handle Omar. I figured he was at work so I would call him there and break it off. Today was the day my problems with him would disappear. I was thirsty and drove through the drive-thru at Kentucky Fried Chicken and got a large Dr. Pepper. I loved caffeine, and it gave me the surge I needed to get through the rest of the workday. I prepared what I would say to Omar. No more playing games. He was clearly a looney bin, and I regretted meeting him.

I dialed Omar's work number and waited until he was

summoned. It took a while for him to pick up. I heard, "This Omar." His voice is raspy.

"Omar, its Candee. I need to let you know I do not want to continue this relationship."

He interrupted by fast-talking to get his point of view out. "Why you saying this, huh? I was saying the truth in the letter."

I interrupted him, "I do not have the same desires as you do. You got it twisted. I hoped we could end this amicably. Not after today, I want nothing else to do with you. Do not call, come by, do nothing!" My blood pressure had risen. I could sense my face heating up. He was silent for once. I hung up, bowed my head, and prayed he got the message loud and clear.

I was tempted to call Jermaine, but I restrained myself. I had thirty minutes left from lunch, so I diverted my attention by reading a chapter for the Social Studies test. I disliked the subject in middle and high school. I tried to think positive about the outcome because it was greater this time around. Back at work, I received four more applications. I would review them first thing tomorrow. I packed up my belongings, and the telephone rang. It was 3:20 in the afternoon and I did not want to be caught on a disgruntled customer call. I picked up the receiver. "Hello, this is Candee Black. How may I help you?"

"Hello, it's Jermaine. I hope you and Joshua are well."

I tapped my right index fingernail on the desk, a way to relieve stress. "Yes, we are fine. How are you?" I asked pretending to care.

"I'm making it one day at a time. Listen, I know you got school tonight. I can get Joshua, and he can spend the night with me if you good. I got two more days before heading out. Also, my sister, Noreen is taking me to the airport because the plane leaves at 11:45 p.m. She and I got some catching up to do, it's been too long for us." His voice trailed off saying.

My plan to spit nails in his face about those pictures was derailed. I tried not to sound disappointed. "Sure, no problem. I need to call Crystal and let her know she has the night off. What time are you bringing him back?"

"He can do a half day at daycare; let Mrs. Lena know he'll get there by lunchtime." I'm troubled about the stuff he left in the closet. I didn't want to wake up his dormant memory. I didn't mention it. I would hand them to him later. "You sound different. Is everything all right?" He asked, sounding concerned.

I wanted to spill my guts about the pictures, scary Omar, life in general, but my pride took center stage, and I lied. "Work today has my mind crossed up dealing with payroll, can be a headache."

He did not press further, and we ended the call.

I got through the test. I knew more than I gave myself credit. I made an 85, I celebrated by stopping at McDonald's and getting an ice cream cone. The weather was a wintry 35 degrees, but it did not deter my taste buds. There was a 55% chance of snow after midnight and 75% chance of freezing rain after 7:00 in the morning according to the radio news. NC shuts down when the snow and ice came to town. I for one did not drive out in the icy mess. I hope it would not happen.

I struggled to fall to sleep, so I got out my journal and wrote about my experience with Omar to clear my head. I went ahead and wrote another letter to Jermaine to say what I might not get to say before he left. I wiped tears, snot flowed, and I spat derogatory language fueled by vehemence. Overall, my head was clear, and soon after the sleepy spirit came.

When I woke up at 6:30 a.m., the temperature in the room was chillier than before I went to bed. My icy feet wanted to stay bundled beneath the covers, but the day is here. I crawled out of bed and headed to the toilet. I washed my face with hot water and then ice cubes. My morning ritual woke me up. I peeked in Joshua's room. I missed him. Upon making my first cup of coffee, I peeked out the kitchen window, the weatherman had been right. A thin layer of snow had covered my cement patio. I made a call to Jermaine to find out the expected plans for the day. He answered on the second ring. "This Jermaine."

"Good morning, how are you and lil man?" I asked.

"Good morning, I am up, but he is snoring and dreaming."

"I guess he has you fooled too. He hates the mornings." I snickered. "Have you checked the weather?"

"Yep, it is falling fast and thick over here. We are going to stay inside. Are you going to work later today? It's supposed to get above freezing after 1:00 p.m."

"Alright, I refuse to drive in the slick weather too, but I gotta call my supervisor about a ride there. Give Joshua a big morning squeeze from me. I catch up with you later."

When I spoke with Mr. Pete, he reminded me the Deli was getting new floors. He had assigned the Deli crew a different work assignment and assigned me to manage the Bakery shop. He would send Reuben, one of the morning stockers to come and pick me up. Mr. Pete already knew how terrified I was about driving in the inclement weather. I am grateful he planned to rescue me.

I turned on the Jazz music radio station to put me in a 'get going' mood. I had given up on listening to sappy love songs months ago. I wandered from the living room to the bedroom and the kitchen, before realizing I'd left my work badge in the car. I slipped on a pair of brown suede boots with low heels, wool red scarf, and wool gray coat. I methodically went out onto the snow-covered front porch looking for the first step. My boots covered up to my ankles with snow. I loved the smell of the first snow. Clean, crisp, and untouched. Anything not protected had snow and ice covering it. It was a tranquil moment, frozen in time. I trekked toward my car and got the key ready to open the door. I opened the driver's side and untangled the badge hanging from the rearview mirror. I picked up the balled-up note from Omar to toss it in the trash. My seventh sense alerted me about the car, but I had no time to investigate. At a scan, I saw nothing wrong. I walked back to wait on Reuben.

Reuben drove at a steady pace and was an elusive talker, but a safe driver. We witnessed several preventable accidents on the way. I stayed in prayer mode as he continued to talk about his dream to become a sought-after disc jockey. We made it without any accidents. I stepped lightly up the salt-covered sidewalk into the store. For a day with bad weather, the store was overflowing with customers. I clocked in and went straight to the Bakery Shop. I had no problem working there. The last time I did, it was interesting watching the bakers decorating wedding and birthday cakes. Time seemed to pass quicker too.

Mr. Pete offered to take me home. I kindly accepted his offer. We had a respectful relationship I did not take for granted. He inquired how I was doing in school.

"It is a bit draining. I regret dropping out of high school", I answered, shaking my head in disbelief.

"Candee, one thing I can say is don't waste too much time looking back. As you get older, the mind tends to reminisce about the younger years. I can vouch from my experiences. Don't punish yourself."

I knew he was speaking the truth. I needed to work on forgiving others and myself. I looked at him and out the passenger window and replied, "I know you are right saying this. Somedays I want to give up and bury my head. Please know I am grateful for this job."

He waved his right hand. "I know you are. I see the potential. You have to convince yourself and others will confirm it by your actions."

I smiled, more at ease.

The roads were treacherous even with brine applied to help keep the ice from bonding to the pavement. Mr. Pete reassured me he was a safe driver even though his wife would say otherwise. He drove me safely home without hitting any black ice spots or pumping his brakes.

Another lonely night at home, but I was exhausted mentally. I rushed in to run water for a hot bubble bath. I lit a few scented vanilla candles, turned on some jazz music, and stripped to take the plunge. I

271

simply loved hot water. It burned my skin. I watched my toes, feet; legs, butt, and stomach turn bright pink. This beauty treatment relaxed me in an instant. I put my eye mask on as I laid my head back on the white neck bath pillow. My body drifted, and I jerked from fear of falling asleep and drowning.

"What in the world?" I plummet from hearing glass breaking. My heart had leaped into my throat. I pleaded to God to protect me. I could not imagine someone robbing me; we had nothing of value – but our lives! I carefully eased out of the tub; tread warily to close the door and locked it. I turned on the light, grabbed a towel, dabbed, and dressed in my two-piece pajamas. I looked for a weapon and found a stainless steel fingernail file. My mouth was getting dry from breathing abnormally. I was so petrified from fear for who might be there uninvited. I took slow and low steps back to the door to listen for any more noises. There was stillness. Maybe I dreamed it. Now and then, I jerked in my sleep as if I was falling. It happens, but this time it seemed real.

I gently cracked the door, listened, and listened some more while standing still. My body was shuddering uncontrollably. I heard my mind telling me it was okay to come out. I whispered the Lord's Prayer and opened the door wide enough to walk out. Instantly the chilly air took over the apartment. I paced in slow motion toward the living room and kitchen area. I saw the front window blinds shifting back and forth. As I got closer, I see a large round rock with a bent red rose tied around it. The rock had landed on the floor in the broken glass from the window. Of course, glass was in a thousand jigger pieces. Right away, I knew this was the stupidity of dumbass Omar. I am nauseated at the pit of my stomach. *How could I be so ignorant to be involved with such a creep!*

When the Police arrived, my nerves were calm, and I made sure they took fingerprints. The tall black officer told me most of the stalking cases were dismissed because the perpetrator was rarely caught in the act. Since I had invited Omar to my house before, he could say I invited him over, and he left on his own. This meant his fingerprints could easily be anywhere in my house. The audacity of him getting away with it boiled my brains! I patched up the window with cardboard and packing tape and woke daddy up to tell him about the incident. He rushed over to take me to his house for the night. On the way to Dad's car, I went to my car to follow Dad. Right away, I discern the back tires were flat. I inspected them and could visibly see short and deep cut marks on each tire. *God, I cannot take any more of this nonsense.* We made it to Dad's house, and Ursula was asleep. I lay on the pulled out flat sofa bed, struggling to fall asleep. Tears flowed like a stormy night. I wanted to hurt Omar; I wanted him to leave me alone for good!

First thing I needed to do was contact Jermaine before he called to bring Joshua home. The temperature was going up to 55 degrees. Therefore, if any snow leftover, it would surely melt. I got Jermaine on the first ring and told him all about what I was going through with Omar. He fumed about finding him and kicking his low-down dirty behind. Even if I agreed with him I did not think Omar was worth going to jail for. Therefore, I talked Jermaine down. "What if he came to the apartment and tried to hurt you? My God, what if Joshua had been there. You think he is nutty, no I am a beast!" He blasted obscenities through the telephone. "Son-of-a-bitch! I will kick his crazy ass if he comes back!"

After a few minutes, he was calm long enough for me to find out when he was dropping Joshua at my Dad's house. "I plan to be here until the property owner fixes the window. What time can you come here?"

"Let me get him ready, and we can head out in the next hour." He expressed he would be relieved if I took out a Permanent Restraining Order on Omar. I could not agree more. When Jermaine arrived, he took me to the Magistrate office to file for the restraint. I was relieved when the restraining order was enforced. The Sheriff would serve Omar his papers soon.

Before I knew it, it was time for Jermaine to say goodbye. The time left we spent together today was not much quality time. I guessed I wanted more of him than I dared to admit. He walked Joshua and I to the front door and came inside for a few minutes. He stood there long enough to hug, kiss, and tickle his big boy. He gazed those piercing nut-brown colored eyes at me. "I will miss you both so much. I am working on getting the child support to you on a regular schedule. I plan to return on my breaks." He was not smiling; his demeanor crushed. I gave him a long hug and a kiss with no tongue. I was shamefaced about the letters I sent in his belongings, but I had to let him know what I knew. I walked over the blue duffle bag over in the corner in the kitchen. "Here are those left behind items I mentioned last week."

"Thanks. I had better go." His voice is monotone. "Noreen is waiting at the house for me." We waved goodbye, and he was gone.

While we were at the courthouse, Dad bought me two used tires and put them on. He hung around for about an hour to make sure we were going to be okay. I reassured him I knew how to call 911 if Omar returned.

Dad responded, "The crazy in me wants to go hunt him, but the dad in me says I can't be here for you if I am in jail." He embraced me not like before. I cannot remember the last time I got a real hug from dad. I was secured in his arms. He gave Joshua a high-five and a hug. "Have a good night you two."

Joshua looked sleepy. "Nite, nite," he muttered. My nerves heightened as we prepared for bed. I put Joshua in my bed, fearing the worst. I was full of fear and prayed for strength. I also prayed God would keep Omar away from us.

We had a good rest and seemed to be off to a great start. I had a shorter work schedule due to taking off early for an exam at school. It was a pre-exam to see if I was ready to take the final exam to achieve my GED Diploma. Even with the stressors, I was confident I could make a passing score. At work, the store was normally hectic at the first of the month, but today it had been steady. Mr. Pete came to my office to say he had a meeting across town and was on his way out. Aram Perez was the night manager for the store. Aram was a gentle Mexican man who was soft spoken but had a keen eye for details. He could take one glance at the aisles and know which items were out or needed replenishing. "Have a good night, Candee, and good luck on the exam," exclaimed Mr. Pete.

"Thank you much!" I chimed back.

I asked Shelly to ring me up a Pastrami on rye bread with

Provolone cheese, lettuce, tomatoes, and pickles.

She smirked. "Girl, you want me to ring you up a Hershey's chocolate bar? I know how much you like them."

I giggled. "I was trying to be good…now you got me craving it." I scanned the candy counter and found the best tasting chocolate in the world. I grabbed my brown bag and waltzed out the door. I knew where I wanted to go and study. There was a small park near the school. I had passed by it tons of times. It was time to take advantage of the scenery. Spring weather is divine and peaceful.

I found a cozy spot to park near a picnic bench. The weather was mild with no rain predicted. The trees come alive as each one wakens as created to do. It was the week of Easter, and my mind shifted to the program at church. The choir was singing a couple of new songs I had yet to learn. I had missed several rehearsals, but I was able to beg my way back. I pulled out my study sheets and my sandwich. My taste buds loved this moment. I needed my classical music to get my head right. The dial was set, and Bach was playing harmoniously. After studying for about an hour, my eyes were tired. I leaned the seat back to rest. I made sure the doors were locked. The sun was bright. I took my jacket and covered my head. Nothing wrong with a little shut-eye.

I made it to class five minutes before the teacher shut the door. I had been tardy over five times, and if I got two more, I would lose 10 points off my grade. I slid in my seat and saw the teacher had placed a recording sheet for the answers.

"Class, please clean off your desks except for the sheet for your answers." Ms. Dooley was a good teacher. Most nights she was patient with the older students because they had been out of school a long time. On the other hand, she was not as patient with the younger students; she said they should have fresh memories. She presented the exam booklets and passed them out with a pre-sharpened No. 2 pencil. "As soon as you get your booklet and pencil, you may begin. This exam allotted two hours. It is okay if you are finished before time is up. Please bring me your items, and you may leave the classroom."

I was the next to last student leaving the classroom. I had faith I passed. Although it challenged my knowledge in Math, English, and Social Studies, I did not cave in. My new survival rule was to walk to the parking lot with someone. I saw a couple of students walking along the hallway going towards the parking lot. I walked close behind them trying not to startle anyone. A black girl with a white toboggan hat turned around and locked her eyes on me. I smiled back to show I was no threat. She kept walking. The night wind swept across my face like icicles on trees. I wrapped my head with my red wool scarf and kept up the pace. As we got closer to the parking lot, two of the students veered off to the left. I parked further to the center of the lot. I could see my car now. Keys were in my right hand, another safety skill in case I needed to fight. It took me two seconds to notice my front windshield had six long stem red roses on the driver's side.

I overheard one of the girl students saying, "Ahhh, someone is in love... how sweet!" I wanted to tell her the story behind the flowers. I wanted to throw the roses on the ground and crush them, but I knew better not to show my ass. I picked up the thorns in my side and tossed them to the passenger side floor. There was no note with the flowers. I knew Omar did this. He sickened me. I drove to my exit, and before rolling through the red light, I tossed the flowers to the right side of the highway. A chill came over me. I panicked and pressed hard on the gas pedal to get home in a hurry. The fear of endangering Joshua and Crystal was rampant in my mind as I swayed in and out of the lanes.

"Dear Jesus, please don't let anything crazy happen to my baby and sister. Please…. please…please" I whispered the prayer until I pulled in my driveway. Before jumping out of the car, my eyes shifted from left to right checking the scenery. I didn't see anything out of the ordinary, so I opened my door. I practically ran to the front door knocking frantically.

"Who is it?" Crystal asked.

"It's me, open up please." I tried not to sound desperate, but it was hard.

When she opened the door, I walked through in a hurry to check the windows. All was clear, and there were no signs of disturbance. Crystal was talking, but my ears were not listening. She bumped into me on the way to check the back door.

"Did you hear me?" she asked, and I was clueless.

"No, what did you say?"

She shook her head at me and informed me, "Jermaine left a message and Joshua's teeth giving him a fit, so I gave him a teaspoon of children's elixir."

"Thanks, sis." I walked in Joshua's room, kissed him on the head, and pulled his blanket up to his neck. He sleeps wild and kicks his covers off at night. "Is Mom on the way to get you tonight?" I asked walking over to the answering machine.

"Not tonight, my boyfriend Johnathan is coming," she announced loud and proud.

It got my attention. "Excuse me, young lady. Your boyfriend?" I gave her the *big sis* stare.

"Yes, we been together now for five months. Two months secretly, because we were friends and emotions changed when we kissed for the first time." She sounded grown up. I saw her differently.

"Tell me more about him," I gently intoned. "Age, background, don't leave out any juicy details."

She shared freely about how smitten she was with Jonathan. He sounded like a decent young fella. I was jubilated for her. After she left, I pranced over to hit the play button on the answering machine. "Hello, Candee, and Joshua. I want to let you know I made it back safely. It is in the wee hours here, about 3:00 a.m. I miss you both already. One dreadful thing happened. Some of my luggage is gone, but not my suitcases. The duffle bag I discovered was missing; I guess in the sky", he joked. He said he would call back later in the week. I was relieved he was not calling about the letters, not yet at least.

Over the next week, there was no contact from Omar. I slowly convince myself we are safe in hopes he has forgotten us. On Saturday, the church had a family day, and the church choir was singing. There would also be a few live bands and plenty of food. My family would hear me singing for the first time in the choir. I missed singing. The church was packed. The organ played our signal to march in. Pastor Whitehead addressed the congregation, and the choir chimed in with *When the Saints Go Marching In.* There was an anointing in the song; it touched the church folks to jump out of their seats. Before you knew it, people were shouting, dancing, clapping, and lifting their hands in the air.

After singing four songs, the choir dismissed, and we joined our families in the pews. The bands and other choirs came out and took us to church! I heard a keyboard playing in the background as the next band was announced. I did not catch the name, but I was entranced by the music playing from the keyboard. The band hummed to the keyboard and a man sings *Jesus Lord to Me*. The words touched me to the core. The voice sounded familiar. My tears flow unstoppably. Soothing words touched my heart. I closed my eyes and allowed the tears to spill over.

Christian handed me tissues, and when I opened my eyes, I saw the man at the keyboard escorted off the stage. Was he blind? Could it be Arthur? I didn't see his face. It had been at least five years since I last saw him. I stood and excused myself. I galloped to get to the back of the stage. The hallway was thick with singers and musicians. I glided by, searching for the man wearing sunglasses. I saw him sitting in a chair close to the water fountain. At first, I stared at him from at least 20 feet away. *What if it isn't him? What if it is and he won't talk to me.* My mind was trying to convince me to turn around and forget this.

I got closer to get a better view. My heart flipped, confirming it's him. I stepped closer and whispered, "Art, it's Candee."

He turned his face toward mine. He was silent for a few seconds, and he smiled. "How have you been, my dear?" The ice was broken, and I grabbed a chair to sat beside him. He was deliciously attractive. Salt and pepper hair and beard. His physique was intact as if he lifted weights. He put out his left hand to shake mine. My eyes glared at the golden wedding band. We hadn't talked long when Mom approached me. I did not have a chance to get in his business.

"Candee, we ready to eat and your son is hungry." She spoke to him while at the same time, giving me the *Hurry yo ass up* stare. I hoped he would ask about my love life, but he did not. I discerned he was in tune with his life, and I should move on too.

I left Art yearning for his affection. I replayed images asking what ifs had we stayed together. Seeing him made me pray for another life. A life without doubts, fears, or misery. I fixed our plates and found the table where my family had apparently taken over. The food was delicious! Fried chicken, collard greens, broccoli and cheese, stir-fried rice, and sweet ice tea. Joshua was not fussing. He was digging into his plate too. I needed to take a potty break. I got around the corner and saw at least five ladies in the line.

"Great!" I seethed. As I waited patiently, I feared someone was staring at me. To the left of the wall was the men's restroom. It had two men waiting to go in. I noticed a baldhead man staring at me. My line creeped inside and I used the toilet. While walking out, the baldhead man confronted me.

"Baby I miss you. We need to talk." I blinked, focused, and blinked again. It was Omar. My eyes flapping as if they are ready for take-off! Air struggles to seep out my mouth because my lungs are constricted to let go.

I bolted past him not looking back. I got to the table and tried to act as though nothing had happened. I took my seat rocking back and forth, and Cara sensed my fear. "What's wrong? What happened in the bathroom?"

I gave her no eye contact trying not to show my fear.

She was younger than I was, but she acted mature.

"Do we need to call the Police?"

I sat motionless, afraid to do anything to make Omar upset. Cara did not wait for my response. "Don't move, stay here," she casually whispered. I watch her get up and go towards the front of the church.

She returned and paused, not wanting to panic. "Family, the police are on the way. Omar is here harassing Candee. Let's stay together. I will meet them out front. We know he is dangerous."

I was mortified from bringing him around my family. Within a few minutes, Cara returned with two tall white police officers. They asked where I last saw Omar. I pointed towards the restrooms. They walked over there to inspect the area.

Mom coached, "Let's leave while they apprehend the fool!"

No family member disagreed because we hauled asses. Out of nowhere, I heard Omar screaming, "I didn't do nothing! Take your hands off me, devils! She loves me! Go get her! Candee! I will kill for you! Let me go!" For the first time, I am empathetic for him.

Omar went to jail, and after two weeks, his family bailed him out. We had a court date in four weeks. After one week, he returned to my apartment complex crying, shouting God was coming back, and he was there to make sure we went with him. Again, the police arrested him and took him to jail, this time he was assessed for mental illness. They denied bail. The next day, I try to start the car, but it stalled and died. Dad had the car towed, and the mechanic discovered sugar in the gas tank. My car was ruined it would cost too much to repair. After hearing the damages, my knees buckled with no warning. I let out a loud noise it made Joshua bust out crying. We were both crying profusely. Dad hugged us tight. I collapsed in his arms.

I woke up to sirens and a bumpy ride. My vision was blurred. A woman wrapping a blue thing around my left arm. A sense of urgency overcome me. My mouth covered with an oxygen mask. She asked, "Ma'am, can you hear me?"

I wanted to speak, but I struggled to form words. I tried to raise my head, but it was banging with pain. "No, ma'am please stay calm. Do you know your name?" Another question I could not answer.

"Her name is Candee Black. I'm her father, Joseph. Is she going to be okay?" My dad's voice was trembling as he continued to answer her questions.

"Her vitals are higher than normal. She has not spoken yet. Please tell me what happened." The woman was a paramedic. I was in an ambulance. I was not sure why.

"She's been under a lot of stress. Lately, she has been through hell and back, and one more thing has pushed her to the limits. She cried and screamed as if she was out of control. She collapsed without any warning," Dad stated with urgency in his voice. He was sniffling. I had never seen him cry about anything or anyone.

I heard a small voice. "Mommy...I want mommy."

After they examined, poked, and violated me in the emergency room, the doctor informed me I'd had an anxiety attack.

283

He prescribed Prozac and Trazadone to help with the symptoms. On the way home, Joshua was fast asleep, Dad was lull, and the shot in my ass was throbbing. I broke the silent contest.

"Dad I 'm tormented about this. I should have..."

He interjected. "Sweetheart, it's going to be fine. Please do not apologize for him. I want you to heal and get well soon. I been thinking I would rest better if y'all came to live with Ursula and me. Sweetheart, until the drama cease with psycho boy, I will not rest. If not, I have to get a shot-gun with hollow bullets." He grunted.

As much as I liked my freedom, I would be safer being around dad. I went to court and saw Omar locked in chains. The courtroom scene, a twilight zone listening to his Lawyer describing his childhood abuse by his father. Omar received harsh beatings from age 3-15 years old. He also witnessed one of his Army friends fall to his death during a freak parachute accident. My heart was filled with empathy because he had been through a lot. The judge sentenced Omar to 45 days in jail. After his sentence, he would transfer to a veteran's hospital in Salem, VA to receive treatment for his Depression and PTSD diagnosis. I did not get any information about how long he would be there. I humbly prayed he would get the help he was desperately seeking.

Chapter Eighteen: Trading Blue Skies for Rain

Last month, for my 20th birthday, Mom bought me a stereo player and gave me $25.00. I spent time to myself instead of making a big deal of my birthday. I spent the day reading the Bible and writing out a five-year life plan. I ended up withdrawing from college because I had feared Omar. I planned to return in the fall to finish. Year 1, I would get my GED and face obstacles head-on. I planned to enroll in the nursing program right after graduation. Year 2-4, enroll in nursing school and stop procrastinating. Year 5, graduate from nursing school, seek employment, and hope to find love again. After staying with Dad for five months, I found a cute little duplex near the college. The neighborhood was full of families and the elderly. Dad once again helped me to get a car. I found a 1980 white Honda Civic at a *Buy-Here Pay-Here* car lot with a 90-day warranty. I had to pay $185.00 a month for nine months. I loved the car. It was great on gas, and the radio sounded amazing. The interior color was peanut butter with no tears or stains.

On Mother's Day, I planned to spend the afternoon at Grandma Elaine's house. Mom and my sisters were going to church and would go as well. I looked forward to being around family; it had been too long.

Grandma Elaine had the biggest smile on her face I hadn't seen in a long time. "Candee apple, give me some sugar!" She grabbed my face and kissed me as if I was a two-year-old. I didn't fuss; I cherished those moments.

"Grandma...I love you too." I kissed her back. Joshua was in preschool now and was in his own little world. He blended in playing and running with his cousins. It was relaxing not to worry much about him. It was time to hold hands, bow heads, and give thanks for the day. My uncle Paul led the prayer my Grandpa Calvin had led for most of my life.

One thing about eating at Grandma's house was you would not leave empty-handed because there was plenty of leftovers. I made to-go plates. As I wrapped my two plates, mother approached me.

"Candee, how are y'all doing in the new place?" I watched how she was also making plates.

"Ma, we are good. I love the new neighborhood. Thanks for asking."

She seems pleased with my answers. Her face glowed from the sunlight coming through the thin white linen curtains. "I may never tell you this, but I worry about you and Joshua. I thank the good Lord, Omar is out of your life."

I hugged her. "Ma, we are much better. Please don't worry."

When we got home, the phone rang as soon as I placed the plates in the fridge. I needed to get Joshua ready for bed; it was getting late. I let the answering machine pick it up.

"Hi, Candee, it's Jermaine. I need to talk to you. Please call me soon."

I ran over to pick it up but froze in my tracks. *Did he get the letters?* Each time he called, I held my stomach. I contemplated when to call him back. I knew I could not delay it for long. I read Joshua a bedtime story, and he fell asleep before I was finished. I called Jermaine back.

"Hello, Jermaine. I hope you are well."

"Yes, I am doing well. I hope you and Joshua the same. You settled in the new place?" he asked, sounding as though he was pushing the conversation along to a pivotal point.

"Yes, we love it here," I reassured him.

"Listen, I have to say what's been consuming my thoughts and recently weighing on my heart." He went silent.

"Sure, I'm listening," I commented, thinking the worse.

"I got this buddy of mine, Markus, who has taken me under his wings. He is a Christian. I mean a serious one." He chuckled lightly. "We go to church, and recently I confessed to him my sins. He led me to the sinners' prayer, and I trusted God. I am forgiven."

I needed to congratulate him. "Jermaine, I am happy for you."

He did not break the sincerity in his voice. He confessed he had cheated on me with some girls, plus Francine during high school. He confessed he was addicted to sex because it made him invincible. He disclosed about the photos and the abortion from Francine. He went on about how he had no positive male role models and did what he had learned. "My dad and I talked about some of this when I visited him in prison. I told him I remembered being around the gambling, drinking, and the whoring. For the first time, I watched my dad cry because of his sinful ways as a father." His voice muffled as he continued. "I'm sorry…deeply sorry for doing you wrong. Please, please forgive me."

My mind went blank. I was no longer listening. He had uttered those two words I had waited five years to hear. Now, I was crying too because I sensed he was broken. "I forgive you, Jermaine," I replied as my tears slowly escaped my eyes, falling into my lap.

In bed, I tossed and turned reliving the apology from Jermaine. I contemplated about telling him about the photos. It dawned on me he COULD already know. What good would it do now; it was over between us. I needed to journal to clear my head and, more importantly, my heart.

***

It was time to inventory the store. Most work finished in the evening hours. I was fortunate to get the deli completed in six hours. I worked around employees who were working with the customers. While finishing counting the paper products, I realize I forgot to call Mallory. It had been a couple of years since I had last seen her. We bumped into each other at church on Easter. I wrote the count on a white sticky note and stuck in on the plastic bin full of plastic silverware. I dug into my oversized workbag looking for Mallory's number. It was not there. I found my brown pleather wallet and pulled out old receipts.

"What did I write it on?" I replayed a memory of the day in my mind. I found a crinkled up white napkin with a name and number written on it. I was relieved it was Mallory's information.

I had promised to call her. She invited me to call anytime. Here we go… I dialed the number, and on the second ring, a woman answered.

"Hello. Mallory speaking."

"Hi... Mallory, its Candee!"

"Girl, glad you called! I am sending out invitations this week."

My mind flashed back to the church conversation, and I had no idea what she was referring. I played it off and responded, "What's coming up?"

"Walt proposed on Valentine's Day, he is such a romantic man," she gushed. I was jealous.

"My parents are the ones rushing to the big day," she noted, not sounding thrilled.

"I bet that's exciting news. Congratulations!" I exclaimed. I heard her walking around on hard floors.

"We have planned to get married on September 28. I have less than three months to prepare for this. I need your address please."

I heard the excitement and pressure in her voice. We chit chatted for about ten more minutes, mostly catching her up on how my world was going. She seemed interested I told her what I wanted her to know. I knew she had been in touch with my sisters and possibly Jemma and Lil FIFI.

"It was good to hear from you, Candee."

"Likewise, Mallory I look forward to your big day." The old me wanted to call Vaughn and gossip about Mallory's news, but I refrained and finished my work.

After picking Joshua up from the sitter, we went to the public library to check out some books. He had shown an interest in books, at least looking at the pictures long enough to say what he saw. The library appeared empty at first. We came across a group of elderly folks sitting at the tables. My library card had some dues for late books. I knew I have to pay it before checking out new ones. We walked up to the front desk, and I approached the white woman with pink lipstick. "Hello, how may I help you?"

"Yes, here is my card. I need to pay some dues."

She smiled and looked up my information from the index box file. "I found you. There is a two-dollars and twenty cents for eight late books." I handed her a five-dollar bill, collected my change, and we walked to the children's book section.

I did not want to make a fuss out of which books to get. I fingered through the first bookshelf with big pictures. Joshua seemed eager to hold the book. I found him a small chair, sat him in it, and pulled him close to a small desk. "Apple," he vocalized, turning the thick pages. It was a little distraction for me to find some other reading books for him. I sensed we were not alone when I heard someone clearing his or her throat. I peeked to my right and saw the noise was coming from a tall, slender man with a thin beard. He smiled, waved, and walked towards us. I was a bit apprehensive from post-Omar trauma. I watched each step. I asked, "Do I know you?"

He burst out laughing but must have remembered where he was. He covers his mouth and says, "Girlfriend, you don't remember me? Dang..."

The voice sounded familiar, the high pitch, and the way he walked. The light bulb came on. "Donovan?"

His face lit-up, confirming I was correct. "None other, in the flesh..." Now the flashy clothes made sense because nobody had ever out dressed Donovan.

"How have you been? It seemed like forever since the last time I have seen you." I was elated to see him. He looked the same, full of energy. He seemed to be doing well. I introduced him to Joshua and invited him to sit with us. We tried hard to whisper, but it was hard because we were both full of conversations. I had not been around him in a couple of years, but he had not changed. Of course, talking about himself and how much money he was making as a real estate entrepreneur.

"Let me tell ya, honey... I do not deal with chump change. Not me, I make contracts over $300,000 no matter where it is located. Baby girl, my clientele is high end, and I keep it going in the direction to bring in the money, honey." He snapped his fingers as if he is putting out a fire. He twirled around showing off his amateur modeling skills.

"My, my, Mr. Donovan I knew you were going to make it big one day. You know I am elated for you. Did you hear Mallory is getting married in September?"

"You know, she has called me because she wants me to help design her reception hall. I received a certification in Interior Design, and my specialty is Special Events."

I was highly impressed by his accolades. He informed me he was meeting his boyfriend up the street at a café and needed to drop off some books. I could have talked to him through the night, but Joshua was tired of us yakking in his ears and expressed it by whining. "Go, mommy, I want to go." We hugged and vowed to see each other at the wedding.

When we arrived at home, dinner was from McDonald's. I cut up his hamburger and fries and poured a cup of whole milk. He was too short to sit with me at the table so I laid a towel on the floor and sat him on it. "Mommy has to get you a table and chair." I took a big chunk out of the Big Mac sandwich and sat down on the floor beside him. No, TV or radio while we ate our food. It was nice for a change. I was learning to trust the quietness around me. I had planned to call Lil FIFI after we ate, but I bathed Joshua first. He seemed to love bath time. I handed him the warm rag and modeled how to put soap on it. He grinned and said, "Me turn." He was growing up fast. I envisioned him going to kindergarten.

Soon he would be old enough to drive. He splashed water in my face and giggled. My trance was broken, and I splashed it back lightly avoiding his face. I loved my baby too much. I put off calling Lil FIFI and found my Bible to read scriptures in Proverbs. For some reason, I needed to read the promises of how God was going to protect my child, no matter what happened to me. It never failed how clearer my mind is after reading and praying. I went to bed an hour earlier than normal.

I got a letter in the mail the next day from the community college. My classes would be starting in less than a month. It was time to grind again. I was ready for the challenge. I found time during lunch break at work to call Jermaine. I had to call him collect, but he affirmed I could anytime. I went through the tedious steps to connect the telephone lines. I waited patiently until the operator answered. "Operator, how may I help you?"

I ask myself why these white women sound angry. "Yes, this is a collect call for Jermaine McDoogle."

"Hold the line please." Dead silence for 10 seconds.

"Guten nachmittag das ist, Jermaine."

"Hello, how are you?" I imagined his sexy smile through the phone.

"I am so glad to hear your voice it seems like forever since I last heard from you two. Where is the big boy?" I walked over to where Joshua was watching TV. He was in a trance watching Big Bird dancing on Sesame Street. I interrupt him. "Daddy on the telephone." I put the end of the phone near his mouth.

"Daddy wat you doin? Big bird dance." He was giggling and rubbing his head. "I be good." I heard him say. I heard Jermaine's voice but not what he says. Within a few seconds, "Bye Daddy love you!" Joshua handed me the phone and waltzed back to the TV.

"I guess lil man is finished talking. I am amazed at the words he speaks. I cannot wait to hear him talking when he goes to school. Time flies so fast. Wouldn't it be nice to keep him at toddler age." He sounded like me saying those words.

"I agree our baby is growing up fast! Now he goes like a big boy, and he wet his bed twice." I said beaming from ear to ear.

"Sounds good! You are an amazing mother to our son. I don't worry as much- because you are a courageous person. I cannot express how grateful I am to have you as the mother to my child." He was silent for a few seconds. "You should receive $100.00 every two weeks starting the 15th of next month. I sent you a money order for $200.00 several days ago." Hearing the news sent tingles up my spine. Money gave me freedom and a small piece of happiness.

"I appreciate the money. What is going on with you?"

"I am glad you asked. I got a few projects lined up. I have joined a men's quartet choir to sing at the nursing homes and hospitals. It is exciting and rewarding. You know I have not done much singing in years. I have applied at the post office for some part-time work."

Hearing his news was exciting. "This is great! I bet you are going to bless many people. You have a soothing voice."

"Thank you, Candee girl. I appreciate you. Tell me what's up with you," he asked sounding nosey in a clever way.

"Things are getting better school returns in three weeks. You know I am determined to get this over." I start to speak, but he spoke first.

"You got this. You know what it takes."

It was rewarding to hear him say this. "In other news, I went to court, and Omar was sentenced to jail for 45 days. After his sentence, the prison will escort him to a VA hospital to receive mental health treatment. The doom and gloom chapter shut for good. Yeah, by the way, Mallory is getting married next month to Walt." I stated.

"What? Man... I didn't see her as the marrying type. Money changes people," he boasted. I laughed too confirming he was right. We chatted for a few more minutes giving me peace we would be a contented long-distance family. At least in my heart, I longed for him to be peaceful no matter our outcome.

As soon as I hung up, I remembered I needed to call Lil FIFI to borrow a formal dress for the wedding. She agreed to bring me a blue sequin sheath dress and a black lace flare dress to choose. I was excited about dressing up for someone else's big day. Within the core of my being, I imagined it was my special day too.

The air outside was crisp and refreshing to wake up my underactive brain. I strolled with Joshua to the local park to play on the playground. I watched him trek over to the slide where two other children were playing. I kept my eyes on him. I am conscious he was learning how to share and take turns. I watched them from a distance. No problems as they proceed to climb up the ladder to slide. I took advantage of the free time and sat on the tin metal bench. The coldness sent chills up my body. I shook it off and focused on Joshua. His bright eyes widened as he came sliding to the bottom. His mouth opened as if he was gobbling up the soft cool breeze.

My attention scanned to the right side of the park as a seemingly homeless man rambled through the trash can. He was dressed in an oversized brown coat with missing buttons. His face covered with a thick neglected beard. He poured over the dumped treasures as if gold was buried. I shifted my gaze back to Joshua who had sauntered to the swing set. I know my child, his eyes zoned on me. His facial expression expressed he needed my help. "Mama, mommy....come help me!"

I stood up, headed towards him, and put him on the swing even though it was high off the ground. He was joyful. I did not make a big deal about it. "Push me, please," he asked politely.

"Okay, let's go slow. Kick your legs out when I push you up." He kicked as instructed.

"Now when you come towards me pull your legs back. The legs go back and forth to keep the swing swaying." He followed my instructions.

"Push… Mommy, I want to go up," he demanded.

"Oh …no. Not yet. You have to go easy the first time."

The sun was setting, and now the breeze was chilly. It was time to leave. I helped him slow down the swing to get off it. As we prepared to leave, we passed by the homeless man who was sitting near the picnic tables. His dry gingerbread face was stoic. His lips were cracked. His face long and downcast. I did not have any money on me, and he did not beg for any. I wanted to help, but did not know how. I got the urge to ask him if he had a place to sleep.

"Excuse me, sir, the weather would be colder tonight. Do you have a warm place to go to?"

His eyes locked on me. We passed slowly by him, and he cleared his throat.

"No ma'am."

I gave him a warm smile and asked him if he would go to a church shelter if I arranged to have him picked up. "Yes, thanks." I introduced who we were, and he informed his name was Sonny T. Bookman, from Lumberton. His demeanor appeared friendly and inviting. I used a payphone to call Deacon Mark and let him know about Mr. Bookman. Deacon Mark confirmed there was room at the shelter. I informed Mr. Bookman the church van would be coming around before 6:00 p.m. As soon as I informed him; his eyes shifted to the ground.

I ask him, "Do you have a watch or a way to tell time?"

He was silent but pulled a gold-faced watch from his tattered coat pocket. "This used to belong to my dad, it's close to five years old, and it still ticks. Can you see if it's the right time?" His voice trailed off as he handed me the watch.

"Mommy I gotta pee," I heard Joshua say. I compared the time and confirmed his watch was running 10 minutes fast. He thanked me, and I scurried towards the park's restrooms.

Chapter Nineteen: Halfway

Mallory's wedding was beautiful. She wore a long white lace gown with a chapel train carried by the maid of honor, her sister Elsa. She strutted proudly along the church aisle with her head held high. Two weeks before the big day, a rumor went around she was two months pregnant. The rush to say, "I do" revealed. Nonetheless, she was an elegant bride; her long pinned up tresses accentuated the light facial makeup. As the two of them recited their vows, I envisioned it was Jermaine and me. I said a silent prayer for my day to come true. They both wiped tears from their eyes. I shed some tears too. Jemma and Donovan's faces appeared a mess from the waterfalls. I passed the tissues. Walt was a handsome man with strong facial features. He had a chiseled chin like a professional model. For an older man, at least 12 years, he had no facial hair. His skin tone was mahogany brown and blemish free. I saw why she snagged him up the first time they met. He looked ravishing in his gray pinstriped tuxedo with peach bowtie and cummerbund. The wedding party was surprisingly small. There were two bridesmaids, Mallory's distant cousins. Walt's best man was his younger brother Lawrence, who was also easy on the eyes. *I am curious if he is single and looking.* There were two average looking groomsmen, who are friends of Walt's.

The reception party held at the Community Building, the old gang showed up, and the party cranks up! Jemma, Lil FIFI, Donovan, and Cara, and I sat at a table. Each table had a vase with twelve peach roses surrounded by green foliage and a white bow tie around it. The food served was beef tips smothered in pilaf rice alongside buttered asparagus, roll, sweet tea, and ice water. Some sipped champagne and some chugged glasses of beer as fast as the servers placed them on the table. I, on the other hand, sipped a couple glasses of Zinfandel pink wine. The more I laughed, the worse my head pounded.

Mr. Roland Miller, Mallory's dad, held back tears as he introduced the newlywed couple for their first dance. The song was "You're Number One (In My Book) by Gladys Knight and The Pips. They smiled at each other as if nothing else in the world mattered. During the dance, Mallory's baby bump was slightly noticeable to me, but I kept it to myself. I used to love to gossip, but lately, I had been trying to avoid it.

I received raving reviews about the borrowed black lace dress I wore. It did accent my shapely curves. I could have partied through the night; I needed this outlet. The DJ announced it was time to form the Soul Train line dance. The dance moves appeared uncoordinated with tainted alcohol. I was born with rhythm, but tonight, two left feet were leading my steps. At that moment, who cared? I danced a hole in my black stocking. Elsa announced it was time for the wedding cake ceremony. The white cake had six tiers with white and peach flowers layered from top to bottom. It was so pretty, I bet the bride hesitated cutting it. They both fed each other a piece and Mallory took a piece of hers and mashed it in Walt's mouth. Laughter and clapping filled the room as family and friends received small cups of rice to toss.

We went outside and waited for the Groom and Bride. Within a few minutes, a medium framed black man dressed in a black tuxedo directed a gigantic white stallion hooked to a white carriage lined in burgundy to the front door. Not much later, Mr. and Mrs. Walter Leeks strolled through the open maple double doors. We cheered, tossed rice, and waved goodbye to the beaming newlyweds. They were on their way to settle in at her parents' house. They would fly out to Maui, Hawaii tomorrow. One thing about Mallory was she did things in style.

Before leaving the building, some of us met in the parking lot and talked about getting together at the new Jazz lounge downtown. We agreed to meet there next Sunday night because they also served appetizers before 9:00 p.m. Black folks love to eat, especially if it was free. I was looking forward to hanging out with my friends like old times. Moments such as this, I regret because Vaughn was not there to enjoy it with me.

At work, the new hire was two weeks in and called out sick. It was a good thing we had two extra cashiers on the first shift. I borrowed Sherita to get us through the day. I admired Sherita's work attitude. She plunged right in and did whatever it took to get the job done. She got my vote for employee of the year. Before Sherita came to the Deli, Shelly informed me her 8-year-old daughter was sick at school. She needed to leave right away. I took over the front to allow her to leave. Within twenty minutes, Sherita pranced over and gave me a wink.

"Candee, thanks for requesting me. I dread stocking canned goods."

I took about fifteen minutes to review how to process the checks and food stamps on the new cash register. "I think I am ready," she confirmed.

After work, I made it to choir rehearsal without Joshua. Last week, his Auntie Noreen called to ask if she could spend time with her nephew. Since Joshua had no idea who she was, we agreed to blend in short visits. Noreen planned to meet Crystal at the house and bring them dinner. It was a winning combination.

Choir rehearsal was going well. We had a Baptism coming up in another week. I plan to join the other members Pastor would baptize. A church member has a creek used for baptisms to confirm their conversions as a Christian. As soon as rehearsal was over, Sister Robbie-Ann approached me. She and I had a sisterhood relationship different from those in my inner circle. "Hello, my dear sister. How have you been doing?" she asked, giving me a warm hug.

"I will not complain, this time," I assured with a wide smile, embracing her back.

"I am pretty sure the choir director will speak to you about what's coming up next month; Single Parents Dedication."

"Yes, we were informed tonight. It sounds exciting."

She took a seat in an ancient wooden chair. Her right hand gestured for me to sit as well. Her voice tone turned somber. "Sister Candee, several women and men are going to be presenters, and the choir is going to sing. I want you to lead the choir. If you agree, you can choose the song. You have a beautiful voice."

I was speechless. Me leading the choir. My eyes fluttered, my throat was dry. I coughed lightly.

"Are you alright? Your face is turning red."

"I'm okay. It shocks me to hear this."

"Sister please bless the church with your gift; it glorifies God."

I thanked her and agreed to sing.

On the way home, I contemplated what to sing. I had much to be thankful for, but it was not about me. It was about the countless single parents in our community. The daily struggles dealing with absent parents, money issues, work, and the list goes on. I needed a song to uplift the people. Several songs come to mind as I concentrated on the road. Chilly rain tapped lightly on the windshield. I hit the defrost button to prevent the window from fogging up. The silence was hard for me, but I needed to learn how to do it.

A memory drifted back to the talent show I did when I was fourteen years old. Back in those days, I had the wrong motive for singing a church song. I tried to bribe God to bless me to win. Now, years later, along with maturity, I had a clear understanding of God. I was remorseful, so I repented. I loved singing. I settled in my heart and mind I had a great song for the right reasons.

Joshua was spending the night with his Auntie Noreen. He sounded like a grown man when I spoke to him before he went to bed. Noreen would drop him off at daycare tomorrow. I planned to meet my friends at the Jazz Lounge. I find out there was a new jazz band playing named, Vibes J7. I knew nothing about them, but I heard they played a variety of groovy tunes. The dress attire was dressy casual. This meant no blue jeans, tennis shoes, or T-shirts. I strummed through my closet and pulled out a pair of casual tan capris, and a coral cotton buttoned shirt. I grabbed the black zip-up cropped jacket hanging on the closet doorknob as well.

I needed to pick up Lil FIFI, who now preferred her given name, Felisha. Donovan was coming with his partner. At the last minute, Jemma canceled because her child was sick. I left out the door at 8:30 p.m. sharp; my mind was set on tasting some spicy jerk chicken. Felisha looked nice. She had the perfect shape for wearing a black spandex dress. No bulges on her body as she high stepped those sexy Tina Turner legs.

"Girl, you know I am ready to jam tonight. I hope this place is as hot as they say it is," Felisha bellowed as soon as she got in the car.

"I know what you mean. I heard their food would keep you coming back. Girlfriend, I hope to see some good-looking men here. I hate to dance with you!" I cracked up, laughing loudly.

The parking lot was close to full on both sides. I found a space at the back of the building to park. "Don't forget to bring your ID," she reminded me as we exited the car. I opened my black wallet to find my driver's license. The night air slapped me across the face. A quick image of meeting a man here, and he walked me back to my car. We had sex in the car. Guilt made me shut my eyes. I shook the devil off. Each time I read the Bible, I clearly believe condemnation is not from God. It was arduous work to keep a pure mind, but I was a work in progress.

The front line was moving steadily. As we waited, I applied a fresh layer of strawberry lip-gloss. I checked out the women standing in front of us; they were dressed as if this was a club scene. I flashed my ID when asked by the tall, dark, man with broad shoulders. His stoic, clean-shaven face glanced at me and looked at the picture with a flashlight. He smiled, showing six gold top teeth and answered, "Nice picture." I thanked him and waited on Felicia.

A Hispanic woman approached us and asked, "How many?"

"For a party of four Queens," Felisha dropped her shoulder to the right and winked. The hostess smiled and turned; we followed her to a round table with four chairs. She took our drink orders informed us the free food was gumbo soup, chicken wings, and jerk chicken. "We have a table set up to your left where you can get the hot food," she whispered.

"Thank you." Felisha and I responded at the same time. Before we got up to go and fix our plates, in walked Donovan without his partner. We greeted him with hugs and kisses. "Where is your boyfriend?" I asked curiously. "Honey, it's a long story." He snapped waving his right hand as to gesture he didn't want to discuss the matter. We all got up and strolled to get our food. There were several other people getting their food as well. A distinguished looking man reached for the jerk chicken the same time as I did.

"Pardon me," he spoke with a British accent.

"It's no problem," I replied, using the silver tongs to grab a couple pieces of jerk chicken. A whiff of his alluring cologne sprinted by my nostrils as he sidestepped to the hot wings. His Hershey chocolate skin appeared sweet enough to lick! Dang, he smelled tasty... even over the delicious spicy foods.

While his eyes focused on the task, I sized him up with one

glance from head to toe. He walked past me to the left side of the room. I tried to track him, but he was gone. I made it to the table and found Felisha's head in her plate. "Girl, I might have to lick my fingers this food is to die for!"

I giggled at her for talking silly and dug into my plate, but had to tell her about the mystery man. "Listen, girl, this gorgeous man bumped into me at the food table. I need to find him and get a number." I frowned hearing how desperate I sounded.

"Was he without a doubt fine?" she asked, head downward and smacking her lips. I looked around, hoping to catch a glimpse of him. Donovan was quiet, for once and chewed without conversing.

Soon afterward, the band played, and my mind wandered to the beat of the music. I enjoyed listening to jazz music because no other music resonated to me life ain't so bad. Donovan made small talk, but seemed to perk up after drinking two glasses of Lime Margaritas. He started dancing by himself and got the attention of another man who boogied along side of him. Within a few minutes, we were both wiggling our booties in our seats. Two men approached our table and asked the dumb question, "Do you ladies care to dance?"

It was obvious we did, but we answered anyway. "Sure!"

We got to the dance floor where several other couples were kicking up their heels. I loved to dance. It's a free expression of myself in my own way. As I grooved, it appeared the mystery man was checking me out. His eyes seem to track my moves, and I forgot all about the innocent man behind me. I put on a sexy dance for his chestnut alluring eyes. Wiggling my best asset seemed to put him in a trance. When the song ended, I turned and thanked my dance partner who at some point did not seem phased my back was turned.

"You sure are a great dancer, nice moves." He gushed with a wink.

I thanked him and exited the floor. Before I made it to my table, the mystery man stood next to the bar. He stretched out his hand and asked, "How do you do?"

My insides tickled with excitement. "Hello, I am fine, thank you."

"Mind if I sit a bit?" I saw our table was empty. I reflect for a few seconds where Felisha was. I wasn't worried about Donovan. My wandering put to rest as soon as we sat; I caught a glimpse of her getting down on the dance floor.

"I must say, I could not take my eyes off you. You are an intriguing beauty I must say." His words trickled from his mouth and put me in a hypnotic trance. I could listen to him talk for hours. "My dear, what may I call you?"

I dug his whole package; tall, dark, and delicious! His haircut was low, giving him a sophisticated look. His face had a thinly shaved beard, and rectangle glasses with black rims. He was wearing a white V-neck sweater with a black corduroy jacket, and gray dress pants. I told him my name.

"Nice to meet you Miss Candee Black. My name is Adlai Corban Edwards; I go by Ace."

Thank goodness, he had a nickname. We talked and sipped on a couple of alcoholic beverages before Felisha came back to the table looking slushy. Her face was drenched with sweat. She lay eyes on tall, dark, and delicious and gasped, "Oh, excuse me. Hello..."

"How do you do?" Ace answered.

Felisha does not fake the funk. "Let me tell ya the fool tried to out dance my ass. And instead of buying me a beer or a glass of juice, hell the dumbass offered me a cup of ice water." Without taking a pause, she continued, "I'm Felisha, nice to meet you, sweet chocolate."

He broke a smile and winked at me. She did not stay long and went to the restroom to freshen up.

We spent rest of the night talking and strutting on the dance floor a couple of times. He was a stimulating man. I found out he was born and raised in New England. He had a mixed ancestry from an African father and a Caribbean mother. He worked in architecture by trade, but a gifted artist at heart. He was there for the weekend visiting his younger brother, the bass player in the band. Ace lived in Manhattan, NY. We did not talk about our ages, or even past relationships. He let me know upfront he had been celibate for; 2 years. He would not give in until he found a wife. His directness tingled me in the right places. I did not want to lose interest because of his no sex life. His conversations fluid, drawing out words I seldom dreamed of saying for fear of judgment. He listened to the short version of my life. I was careful not to spill the dirty details. I wiggled my right leg in anticipation he would excuse himself after I disclosed being a single mother without a high school diploma. Instead, he ordered Cranberry Daiquiris for us.

"I say anytime is the right time to receive education," he added, looking at me as though he could see my heart beating for his attention. The atmosphere was alive as the band members finished their last set. "I would like for you to take my number. We could hang out and eat sushi." He smiled big as he handed me a business card.

I laughed and replied, "We could, someday."

After that night, I misplaced the telephone number and gave up looking for it. As usual, life got busy, and my mind occasionally brushed away the reminders of the British hunk. Over the next two weeks, while looking under my car seat for some loose coins, I found Ace's card. I wanted to call him, but I was too busy to think of entertaining. I was back in school. I seemed anxious but in a safe way. I knew the material, there should not be any surprises. It was my second chance to get my name on the certificate to frame on my wall.

Joshua has a consistent relationship with his Auntie Noreen, she was living in her mother's old house. The house rented out for the first year after Mrs. McDoogle passed away, and selling it was supposed to be the plan, but as time drifted on, Noreen and Jermaine did not want to sell. Noreen came to get Joshua twice a month, and I took full advantage of it which allowed me to have some alone time.

The *Single Parents' Dedication* was coming up soon, and I had prepared my speech and practiced the song in a faint voice tone. I did not want to strain my chords. I sipped some hot tea and honey to soothe my irritated throat. The phone rang.

"Hello," I said, whispering.

"Hi, how are things?" It was Jermaine.

"We are doing pretty good here. Joshua with Noreen, this is their weekend," I replied.

"Your voice sounds nasally," he asked, sounding concerned.

"Naw, I have to sing tomorrow at church. My throat is a little itchy, hope it goes away soon."

"Try some hot lemon juice and honey it's good for soothing your throat." I confirmed, "Yep, doing that now." "That's good. I also wanted to let you know I have planned to come and visit during the Christmas holidays. I already worked it out with Sis."

I listened intently as he talked. "I hope to wake up Christmas morning with you both."

Now it was my turn to speak. "Sure, it's cool. I may have to work a few hours longer in the week because of the holidays."

"Alright, no problem we will work it out. I will call my son and see what he is up to. See you soon I hope all goes well at church."

"Thank you, see you soon."

The church crowd was thick, and my nerves were churning in my stomach. I tremble when speaking in front of a crowd. I prayed asking for strength not to faint. I took a seat beside Noreen and Joshua on the front pew. He looked handsome wearing an OshKosh B' Gosh outfit that she bought him. The rest of my family sat in the third pew from the front. I got up to go hug them before the presentation began. My mother smiled at me, and Grandma Elaine touched my left hand and squeezed it tight. It was a sign things were going to be alright. Mrs. Robbie-Ann walked up to the podium and welcomed the congregation. She explained why it was important to the community to honor our single parents. Pastor Whitehead led the prayer and announced my name. Heart beating steady. No locomotive this time.

"Hello, family and friends. Today is a special day because we are here to celebrate life and the importance of family. Most of you have known me most my life, and you may think you know my story.

Well, in case you do not, this is my truth. I became a teenage mother at the age of 16. I dropped out of high school and told myself I was ready for adulthood because I was a parent." I paused, staring into the distant eyes locked on me. Joshua grabbed my attention as he squirmed on Noreen's lap. "Mommy..." He whined, and she shushed him gently. I pushed through my nerves as my heart gained speed, but I continued speaking. "I stumbled many times as I struggled to provide a living for my child and me. I was defeated, frustrated, and angry with myself for making a trail of mistakes."

My throat tickled, I swallowed hard. A glass of water was inside the podium. I guessed it was for me. I took a sip and cleared my throat. "I grew bitter towards the baby's father because I needed him to do more. I could stand here and paint a roses and violets picture for you, but it would be a lie. I am here to say, I gave up plenty of times. I later found my strength in wanting to improve my life to support my child. I worked full-time, and am now working on my GED again..." I giggled slightly. "I tell you my story to embrace yours. We have common experiences– our struggles and our babies. Today we celebrate each other's hard work, frustrations, and accomplishments! We may cry tears when it gets hard. We may lose sleep from worrying, but one thing we will not settle for is "failure".

Tears of joy flowed. I found tissues inside the podium and wiped them away. I let out air through my mouth. I cued the organist Sister Pam, and she hit those keys to the tune of *"Oh Happy Day."* I swayed, and the choir chimed in harmoniously. We sang our hearts out. Within a few seconds, the folks were standing, clapping, and dancing around the pews. I believe the Holy Ghost visited us today. It was a joyful moment I would never forget. Momma hugged me as soon as I made it back to my seat. "Candee, your speech and song made me so proud of you. Forgive me for never telling you this; you are a great mother, and I am so happy for you. I love you, my first born." I hugged her back. I did not want to let go. As the service ended, I caught a glimpse of my dad standing near the back door. He winked at me and mouthed, "I'm proud of you."

The holidays brought cheerful people into the store. Most people were in pleasant moods and were cheerful givers. The store took up non-perishable foods and donated to the homeless shelter, and Mr. Pete gave away free hams and turkeys through a raffle drawing. I loved celebrating but was not thrilled about working harder. My feet were burning inside my worn-out pair of shoes. It was a sign I needed to buy a new pair sooner than I could afford to. I thumbed through my wallet calendar to check when the next child support payment was coming. It should arrive next week, God willing. I need to get a new pair along with my last-minute Christmas shopping. I made up my mind to get a few things for Joshua. His first three years, I went overboard and showered him with toys he paid no attention to the next day. I learned a big lesson it was a waste of money and gift-wrapping!

This holiday year, Mr. Pete had Christmas music for diverse types of religions. He had a warm heart during the holiday season. He enjoyed giving back to the community since his store was the first African-American owned grocery store in town. He hadn't forgotten the treatment of trying to succeed in a world full of resistance because of the color of your skin. We had bright lights strung in the front window, and white snow sprayed around it. There was also a decorated 8 ft. Douglas Fir tree standing in the wide front window. About a few years ago, I gave the store an idea for those who did celebrate Christmas, Hanukah, and Kwanzaa to bring decorations to work to display in the break room. Some staff members had no idea how others celebrated their own respected celebrations. It was important to be open to innovative ways of celebrating. Each year, the number of participants grew at a steady rate and the anticipation to see the different decorations was phenomenal.

In our home, Joshua and I decorated our little Charlie Brown fake tree, and he was proud of his painted Styrofoam ornaments. It stood about 4 ft. with each iron tree limb poking out. We did our best to fill in the holes. "You did a great job, sweetie. Daddy will be here soon to see your decorations."

He was focused on hanging the last ornament at the bottom of the tree. "Look Mommy! All done."

I took out my disposable camera to capture the special moment. "Joshua, stand in front of the tree and smile for me." Before going to bed, I made popcorn and hot chocolate. We watched Frosty the Snowman and Rudolph the Red-nosed Reindeer on the TV. I cherished such moments, realizing he would grow out of this stage sooner than I wanted him to.

The winter weather expected to bring a couple feet of snow by Christmas Eve. We got excited about snow because most winters we got a tease. Most of the winter months we got either ice, sleet, or a wintry mix. However, the weatherman was predicting 80% snow by Christmas Eve morning. Noreen confirmed yesterday she would be picking Jermaine up at the airport by 4:00 p.m., two days before Christmas Eve. Thinking about seeing him again gave me goosebumps. It was highly probable we would have sex. I admitted I was weak in resisting the urge to pounce on him as if he was my last supper. I figured I would forever be attracted to him.

The next day, I went shopping for last minute gifts for Noreen, Mrs. Lena, Ursula, and Sherita because I was her Secret Santa at work. I found some good bargains at Kmart and had no need to shop any other place. This year, Mr. Pete gave me a $250.00 Christmas bonus, and the money was such a blessing. I bought Momma Chanel perfume, Daddy a set of tools, and my sisters each got a pair of inexpensive silver earrings. I bought Jermaine some Cool Water Cologne. I almost got him a sweater but did not want to go overboard. *Although, he might not buy me anything.*

I wrapped each gift and placed them under the tree, which appeared to be leaning more to the right side. Fake trees were more work than live trees. Since Joshua was allergic to the pine trees, I did not want to chance it with any other tree.

"Joshua, did you clean up your room this morning?" I heard him throwing some things in the toy box. I walked to his room, and sure enough, he was busy picking up his toys. I had to say he was a good boy, most days he was no trouble. "Mommy, I'm done. Can I watch Sesame Street?"

"Sure sweetie. Thank you for doing your room. A big boy cleans his own mess. Mommy is proud of you. I love you."

He grinned. "I love you, Mommy." He took his right hand, covered his mouth, and blew me a kiss. I pretended to catch the kiss in my hands and put my hand to my right cheek.

To my surprise, NC might have a white Christmas in 1981. The weather forecast says Jamestown might see close to 1-5 inches before the snow ended. The thick snowflakes were falling in slow motion, barely covering the ground. The situation would change after midnight into heavy snow until late Christmas Day. I could not remember the last time it snowed for the holidays. It did make the meaning more sentimental as portrayed in the movies and famous songs. I had promised Joshua the next time it snowed we were going to make a snow angel. Therefore, it was no surprise when I heard him say, "Mommy we get to make a snow angel, yeah!" He tickles my heartstrings when he is excited.

Jermaine and Noreen arrived during the night with gifts in tow. Jermaine placed several bags under the tree. Joshua bounced up and down expressing how thrilled he was to see him.

"Come here big boy you are growing taller by the minute. You are going to outgrow me." Jermaine picked him up and spun him around like an airplane.

"Wee, daddy, wee…" Joshua squealed. He was ecstatic. I made a hearty, spicy spaghetti dinner with a Caesar salad, hot rolls, sweet tea, and a Mrs. Paul's apple pie. There was light chatter amongst us as we smacked our lips. I patted myself on the back.

We watched the best Christmas movie ever made *Little Drummer Boy*. I made Joshua a small bowl of popcorn because the rest of us were too full. I curled up on the loveseat with my white cotton blanket while Joshua and Jermaine snuggle under a flannel plaid blanket. Noreen left before the movie started because she did not want to be stuck here overnight. She had a boyfriend who was on his way to her house. I was glad to know it because this was their first Christmas without their mother. Even though she did not celebrate holidays, her presence missed.

I dozed off to sleep in the middle of the movie as Jermaine told me when he woke me up. "Hey, come on, let's get to bed." I stretched and dragged my drowsy body to the bed. I heard him walking close behind.

"Joshua in bed?" I asked, yawning.

"Of course, he been knocked out for close to ten minutes," he moaned.

I turned slowly to face him, "He was pooped." I made it the bed and stripped naked for no reason. I pulled the covers back, falling headfirst. I think he covered me up.

As I dozed, his hands rubbing me gently and slowly. I pretended to be sleep. I was horny. I wanted to play hard to get. He did not stop. Now his hands are on my ass, my boobs, caressing each one. It tingled as Jewel danced with joy. I told my heart, "No." However, my brain said, "Keep going we need sex!"

I discern his tongue licking my neck, and I could not fight the urge anymore. I turned around and kissed him hard, tongues, and saliva mixing. I caress his hard rod, and he moaned. Out of character for him, he leaped from the bed. My horny meter went flat and broke the mood. I called his name, and he did not respond. "What....is your problem," I grumbled.

I heard the shower running. I tapped on the door lightly. No answer. I knocked again.

"Yeah!" he shouted back.

"What's wrong? You okay?" I asked to pacify his rejection. No answer. I took the hint he didn't want to have sex with me. I returned to my bed. My ego wounded. My heart shattered.

He returned and sat on the right side of the bed. He turned the lamp on the nightstand. A sign, he wanted to be serious. He had put his bottom pajamas on. I could not help but think of jumping on top of him, but I resisted the urge. I huffed to let him know I was dissatisfied. His eyes locked on me. "Candee, I apologize for what happened. I should explain." He sounded sincere; he had my attention. "It has nothing to do with you. I hope you believe me. I have been celibate since the last time we were together, over a year. I plan to remain this way for as long as God gives me strength. I have been avoiding females, fighting my flesh not to give in."

He stopped and wiped his forehead with the back of his right hand. He stood up and paced back and forth. As he continued talking, I observed a tattoo covering most of his back.

"I will always have love for you. I never meant to hurt you, but I did. I do not need to continue this type of relationship with you knowing I have caused you a boatload of heartache. I need to know if you can respect what I am saying." I was numb from hearing those words. The fairytale dream is fading before my eyes. I want to act childish, crawl under my pillow, and cry myself to sleep. Instead, I cleared my throat and allowed the warm tears to fall right in front of him. No shame. I would not hold back. I covered my face with the white sheet and wept irrepressibly. He responded, to my surprise. He cradled my head close to his warm, clean, hairless chest. The best

316

thing was letting him hold me until I fell asleep.

I woke up before anyone else. The clock read 6:32 a.m. I had the jitters around Christmas. There was much to do such as cook breakfast, open gifts, and go to Mom's and Dad's houses. I peeked out the front window and saw the yard, sidewalk, and parking lot covered with snow and ice. I turned on the TV to see the weather. It reported our area had multiple closing. I pleaded we would not lose power. It was a bit chilly I bumped up the thermostat from 72 to 77. I went to the kitchen to make breakfast. I needed my first cup of java to get me going. I heard some footsteps coming closer. It was Jermaine, carrying Joshua.

"Good morning, Merry Christmas!" I shouted.

"Merry Christmas, Mommy." Joshua leaned towards me to give me a hug. I adored my sweet boy.

"Merry Christmas, Candee." I wink at Jermaine, letting him know we were good.

After breakfast, we took our son into the living area and read him the Christmas story from the Children's Bible. I knew he loved picture books. If he liked the book, he had no problem listening until the end. Jermaine animated while reading him the story about the baby Jesus, making the story fun and exciting. Joshua imitated the animal noises as Jermaine introduced them sitting around the manger. After the story, we exchanged gifts, and the mess ensued... I opened the gift from Jermaine, which was a beautiful silver bracelet with Joshua's name and my name in a heart. I loved it! He thanked me for my gift as well. Joshua was busy pushing his big tractor truck around the wooden floors. We cleaned up the many torn up gift-wrappings and decided to call and wake up other family members.

The roads were unsafe to drive on. Joshua mentioned the snow angel to me, and I knew we needed to get it done. To be truthful, I don't care to touch the pretty wet ice. I don't mind watching it fall and then take away the memory. Jermaine was eager to join us. We wrapped up and headed out the back door. The snow was untouched until we found a spot and counted to three, fell backward, and flapped our arms as if takeoff was imminent. We laughed like never before as spatters of snow covered our faces. "I cold Mommy." Those words warmed my heart.

We went inside and dumped the wet clothes in the bathtub. I would hang them up later to dry inside. I made hot chocolate as they cuddled on the couch. It was awkward not having sexual pleasure with Jermaine. I read a book or two to past the time away. Joshua was content laying on his lap while watching cartoons on TV. I need to journal the madness in my head before reading. I named this poem, *Higher Ground.* I laid my journal on the bed and went to the bathroom. When I returned, I saw Jermaine reading the poem. He was startled when he saw me.

"Candee girl... what are you writing about?"

I wasted no time telling him. "I write poems and journal my thoughts. I may have forgotten to mention during the dark times I went to therapy and journaling became a coping skill for me."

His facial expression showed he was surprised to hear me admitting the disturbing news.

"Yes, I went to therapy because, at one point in my life, I was falling apart. I had many dreams – to get married, buy a house, raise our son together, get a pet and die of old age." I paused as I saw his eyes filling up with tears. When he was uncomfortable, his bottom lip quivered, and his eyes darted left to right to avoid mine. "I was in agonizing pain. I was angry at you about my life because I needed someone to blame for it." Seeing his tears weakened me to the pit of my stomach.

"I am sorry to hear you were depressed because of me." He bowed his head and wept.

I got up, hugged him, and whispered, "God saved me. I am much better now. I have forgiven you and myself."

Later, I asked him about the tattoo. "Getting this made me scream like I was getting a butt whooping." He chuckled hard, holding in his chiseled abs. "I got the Phoenix about seven months ago. It defines who I am today. I've been through some bad moments and committed plenty of sins. This tattoo expresses a change in my life for a better me. I got a long way to go, but with God, I can do this."

I could have been envious he should have changed when we were together. Instead, I am elated for his transformation because he seemed mature about being a good father to our son. He seemed to have patience and respect for me. Jermaine freely disclosed about how he has embraced his birthday. He stated his God-given birthday was October 1, 1960. He shared the church he attends celebrates birthdays once a month. He plans to join in the celebration this year. He still did not buy into the concept of receiving gifts for his birthday. However, he had no problem giving gifts to Joshua and me. And frankly, I have no issue receiving them. I am delighted about his decision. Even though when we were together; I had not given him any birthday gifts to express how much I loved and cared for him.

The following afternoon, most of the snow and ice had melted under the sunshine, and the temperature was close to 50 degrees. The weather was unpredictable; snow today, heat wave tomorrow. Noreen came by and picked Jermaine and Joshua up to spend time with his family. I was okay because it gave me some quality time to myself. I left to visit Mom and my sisters.

When I arrived, I discovered Richard had proposed to Momma, and she accepted. The engagement ring was a small diamond with two silver hearts on each side. Momma was beaming when telling me how surprised she was to open the big box hiding the ring.

"We have been talking marriage for a couple of months, but no plans mentioned this soon."

"I guess he is securing his spot," I said, and we both laughed. I spent time telling them about how well our Christmas went. I discovered Cara had a new boyfriend and they were at the movies. Crystal had to return to work today. Christian was baking a chocolate cake for a friend's birthday party later. Richard was working on putting together a model racecar with his son RJ. I congratulated him on the proposal. "Richard, when is the big day? I know Mom is ready to jump the broom."

He smiled. "I can do it right now if she wants to get it over with. However, I think we may have a June wedding next year."

I heard Mom footsteps getting closer. "I hear y'all talking about me."

"Naw Momma, it's a good talk. June is a popular month for a

wedding. Let me know if you need my help," I urged. I made small talk with Christian who was concentrating on spreading the chocolate batter in the two cake pans. "What kind of icing you putting on it?" I asked, watching her.

"I got some Chocolate icing, and I am going to make some colorful designs on top," she says as she placed each pan in the oven. "What have you been up to, how is my nephew?"

"His daddy is in town for a couple more days, and right now he is visiting Jermaine's family," I told her as I took a finger and licked the creamy chocolate batter from the bowl.

"Girl, you know better," she spat at me.

"I know… it's tempting. I love chocolate!" I giggled. I gave out hugs and kisses before leaving to return home.

The day arrived when Jermaine was leaving for Germany and truthfully, I was at peace about it. I had come to terms with our relationship being what it was, and nothing could change it. Life had a bitter way of expressing love even when the outcome was not in my favor. When he came by to drop Joshua off, I made sure to put on a brave face to show him I was a strong woman. I believed he was changing for the better. It bothered me I guess, the thought of another woman reaping the benefits. God would have to help me to see the bigger picture. I believe his journey is for him and mine is for me. He gave no long speech when he came inside to lay Joshua on the sofa because he was asleep.

"I will dress him for bed," I stated as he gave him a kiss on both cheeks and forehead.

"I love you, son, so much. Soon he will be big enough to fly back with me," Jermaine beamed.

"I know... he would love flying," I commented.

We stood gazing at each other as if we are strangers. Not sure if we should touch each other for fear of lustful desires. He broke the silence. "I had better go now; you know how crazy the airport can get. I had a wonderful time. I... want you to have a blessed life, Candee girl. May God grant you both a blessed New Year." He smiled and kissed me on the left cheek. I breathed in his scent to keep a memory of him.

"Safe travels to you. I want the same for you too." I hugged him as he left.

****

I made plans to spend New Year's Eve at the Bottoms Up Lounge Bar & Grill with the gang. Vaughn and Arnold, Mallory and Walt, Donovan and his dude, Felisha, no Gina, but Brandon, and Crystal were planning to come. I found out at the last minute it was *Free Expressions Night.* I planned to read my poem, which I was keeping a secret until they called my name. Cara arrived on time to babysit this allowed me to spend a little extra time getting dressed. I decided to wear a Yves Saint Laurent (YSL) polyester long sleeve black jumper. I found it at the Goodwill with a brand new tag on it. It was too cute to leave hanging in the closet. I felt confident my curves would be hard to miss in this outfit. The back opened in the middle with one snap at the neck. The front had a long oval opening between the breast and under the breast were three small teardrops shaped holes. The push-up bra made my boobs appear smooth and firm. The pant legs flared out at the bottom which were too long for me. I had to wear a pair of 5-inch stilettos and prayed not to fall over. My make-up was light but fresh so I covered my lips with cinnamon lipstick. I lightly sprayed my body with a knock-off version of White Linen perfume. A last check in the mirror proved I was missing my earrings. I threw on a pair of fake silver hoops, fluffed my back curls, and smiled pretty.

While driving, I became a little nervous. My stomach was full of butterflies. I chewed on Wrigley's Juicy Fruit gum to help calm my nerves. I savored the sweet taste. Sugar was my drug fix. I scurried out the door in haste to beat the crowd.

I reserved a table to accommodate them. I was the first one to arrive. Our table was close to the front, and I could easily see them coming inside. They arrived soon after the laughter was heard across the room. Vaughn and Arnold came in holding hands, and both seemed cheerful. This is the first time I have met Arnold who is very handsome. His physic is at least 6 ft. tall, slender with hazelnut skin tone. They both are dressed in Armani denim outfits. We greet each other with hugs and kisses. Arnold compliments how nice I look. The music was upbeat, and the crowds were coming in thick. I spot Donovan and his partner, Scottie coming through the crowd. I did a double take by the pink glitter blinding me from Scottie's vest. His hair was in loose curls. Donovan hugs me with an apology. "Sweetheart, we took a wrong turn on Gordon Street." I hugged them both. Before I sat back down in walked Crystal, Mallory, and Walt. I thanked everyone for coming.

It was time to start the readings I was second to read. I needed water to clear my throat. I drank the no ice water and politely

323

burped into my hands. I zoned in and out fighting to focus on reader number one. Soon after, the MC was announcing my name. I got up, and my friends were speechless. I did not look back. I concentrated on not tripping as I stepped onto the stage. "Hello, friends, the name of my reading is *"Higher Ground."* I wrote this poem during a moment in my life which revealed I was stronger than I knew I was. I hope it inspires someone else if it resonates inside of you." I spoke each line as if my life depended on it. My voice tone mellow, shoulders relaxed, and spine aligned. This is my time to give back. No more talent shows.

The applauses validated my self-worthiness, which I knew I had hidden. The lights were bright as I took a short bow. My friends seemed overcome with emotions. People were dabbing their eyes with the white cotton napkins. As I got closer to my table, a familiar face was standing right in front of me smiling. "What's up, pretty lady. I have been waiting by the phone." I am humbly surprised to see him again.

Ace stood before me. I was speechless. I smiled back at him. He was interested, I speculated if he was seriously celibate. "I come a long way to ask you if we could go sky-diving, drink lattes, or catch a movie sometime." He was such a sweet tease. "You got some mad writing skills. Sounds like a writer on the rise to me." He winked.

"Thank you for the compliment. Latte and movies, I would like to some time. And sky-diving, sorry I'm no daredevil..." I giggled, and he took my right hand in his and kissed it. He escorted me to my party of friends. The night was right for anything.

Candee's Ending Thoughts

When we define love by rules, boundaries, and lies, it is no longer love. It becomes a force of convenience for the parties involved. Most would agree it takes a strong person to love someone who does not love back. The strength to give love even when none returned; is a beast to reckon with. It seems some women endure the tidal waves from trying to love someone who does not want their love. I am not saying men do not go through the same things, but since I am a woman I can be biased about this observation.

I learned from each experience how valuable my heart is and how it yearned to be nurtured. Some situations refuse to change, even with time. It took many tries to accomplish one goal, even though the water kept rising. You know I cannot swim, not even a little. I plunged deep, drowning in hopelessness, fearfulness, and plain messiness! I sprinted through life jumping hurdles, ducking darts, and failing miserably at being a teenager.

I wanted to grow up fast! On the other hand; I did not. Maybe, I was searching for answers to fill the gaps when I skipped over playing with jump ropes, old maid cards, and hula hoops. I went full throttle boy crazy! I could not blame the boys for my promiscuity or the grown men who solidified my company. I would say I was easy, desperate, and downright naive when it came to building relationships. I pretended to know what I was doing. What I understand is love does not require anything! Either you love someone for who they are, or you do not love them at ALL. If you require a list of dos and don'ts, you will be sadly disappointed in the results. Have you ever been in love? Was your first, the first for many things? I fell hard for my first. Jermaine meant so much to me even when it hurt. I did not have a clue about being in love at fifteen years old. I was reeled in by my heels. In such a way, I oozed with butterflies when I was with him.

The other side when things went bad for us it went out of control. I believe Jermaine loved me as much as he knew how. His world was upside down when he was a young boy. He grew up without a father figure, but his mother did her best to raise him.

I seem to learn life's lessons the hard way. When I was young, my parents called me 'hard-headed' because telling me "No" did not stop me from being rebellious. Nope, I needed to get beat to the ground before I accepted the truth. I questioned myself why I put up with someone else's bull shizzle! I believe it was a learning experience and I needed to learn how to accept my own faults and to discern what true love is.

Speaking of true love, finding the heart of God through Jesus Christ made the difference for me. I say most people desire something they can believe in which is stronger than they are. For me, I needed God when it comes to faith and belief. I knew I needed someone stronger than me to carry me when the weight of the world tried to bury me beneath the dirt. For me, I was seeking one who is greater than I was. My relationship with Him helped me see myself in a different way. Because of His love for me, I could receive love and give the same love to another.

In getting to know a new love, as in Ace, yes, he was charming and deviously handsome in his own finicky ways. I was attracted to his smile and his conversations which mesmerized me. When he spoke, I paid close attention to details. Because behind his serious demeanor, there was a quirky side; it seemed to peek out once and awhile. We were beginning a new journey as friends, but we hinted to each other it would be nice to keep going out of curiosity. I embrace cautiously into this new relationship. Of course, I am hoping for a long-term commitment along the way. However, I no longer rush my heart to burst into something it's not prepared to do. I have learned to tap the pause button and enjoy the journey before running to the next warm male body.

Indeed, I find my days packed with To-Do-Lists and my nights pushing to get ready for the next day. I worry less about the future and concentrate on today. No more daydreaming or sitting idle wishing things would get better those simple days are gone! It is time to be actively pursuing the dreams, the hopes, and the life I deserved. Someone once affirmed, your past does not define who you are meant to be- it prepares you to be who you are destined to be.

I am ready!

The End, for now....

Higher Ground
Rushing water land at my feet,
My ankles disappears deep in the sand
My mouth wants to scream out a cry,
Only streams of tears escape.
A voice tells me to accept this defeat,
Take a deep breath and let go.
The murky water wraps around my waist,
My past mistakes surface,
Above my chest what can I do?
Light shines and my destiny begins.
Love comes like the wind passing by.
My hand reaches out to meet His,
I know it is He for His love covers me.
My fears are gone my eyes are open,
I can see the green view not far away.
My feet can breathe the clean air,
A heart dances with joy for the one who never gives up.

About the Author

Cierra Bluu is an upcoming New Adult Book Author presented by, 7 Butterflies Publishing Group. *Paintball Love* is the first Novella. Cierra is interested in writing true life experiences woven into humorous and heartwarming stories to encourage, empower, and enlighten her readers. When she is not grinding out her next story; she enjoys spending time relaxing and watching sappy movies.

Look out for the second book,
I Been With a Lot of Men – But I Ain't No Ho coming out in 2019

Follow Cierra Bluu: www.cierrabluubooks.com
cierrabuubooks@gmail.com

Made in the USA
Columbia, SC
20 August 2018